AUTHENTIC HUMAN SEXUALITY

An Integrated
Christian Approach

JUDITH K. BALSWICK &
JACK O. BALSWICK

InterVarsity Press
Downers Grove, Illinois

InterVarsity Press
P.O. Box 1400, Downers Grove, IL 60515
World Wide Web: www. ivpress. com
E-mail: mail@ivpress. com

InterVarsity Press® is the book-publishing division of InterVarsity Christian Fellowship/USA®, a student movement active on campus at hundreds of universities, colleges and schools of nursing in the United States of America, and a member movement of the International Fellowship of Evangelical Students. For information about local and regional activities, write Public Relations Dept., InterVarsity Christian Fellowship/USA, 6400 Schroeder Rd., P.O. Box 7895, Madison, WI 53707-7895.

All Scripture quotations, unless otherwise indicated, are taken from the Holy Bible, New International Version®. NIV®. *Copyright ©1973, 1978, 1984 by International Bible Society. Used by permission of Zondervan Publishing House. All rights reserved.*

Cover illustration: Roberta Polfus
ISBN 0-8308-1595-3
Printed in the United States of America ∞

Library of Congress Cataloging-in-Publication Data
Balswick, Jack O.
    Authentic human sexuality : finding wholeness in a sexually
saturated society / Jack Balswick & Judith Balswick.
        p.   cm.
    Includes bibliographical references.
    ISBN 0-8308-1595-3 (cloth : alk. paper)
    1. Sex.   2. Sexual ethics.   3. Sex—Religious aspects—
Christianity.   I. Balswick, Judith K.   II. Title.
HQ21.B166   1999   *99-38845*
306.7—dc21   *CIP*

15   14   13   12   11   10   9   8   7   6   5   4   3   2   1

10   09   08   07   06   05   04   03   02   01   00   99

To our students,
who have taught us so much
and enriched our lives

Acknowledgments

This book represents a culmination of our teaching
in the course Gender and Sexuality
over the past fifteen years at Fuller Theological Seminary.

Several people must be acknowledged for the part they have played
in the final publication of this book. Dale Edwards provided
helpful insights into chapters four and five,
and Greg Carlsson read and made valuable suggestions for chapters
four, five and fourteen. Our research assistant Helen Kim
took great care to see that the text was consistently footnoted;
Sun Young used her creativity in designing our tables, and Jean Hedge
had the tedious task of typing the references.
We especially appreciate the initial encouragement of Rodney Clapp
as well as the ongoing work of Jim Hoover
and our copyeditor Stuart Hoffman. We are grateful
for their faithful overseeing of the final product.

We dedicate this book to Fuller students who have kept us "young at heart"
by engaging in honest and holy dialogue about this important topic.
We are indebted to our students not only for their service
as a sounding board for the ideas presented in this book
but for all we learned from them through questions,
class discussions and final class projects.

One of the most rewarding experiences of teaching
is the privilege of interacting with curious, bright students.
They affirm that the God-given gift of sexuality, lived out in authentic ways,
brings a life of fullness, harmony and wholeness.

Contents

Introduction

Few contemporary issues can generate as much heat and conflict as those having to do with human sexuality. Just when the Christian church is becoming more vocal in affirming a biblical standard of sexual relationships, reports show that 3 out of 4 single adults will engage in sexual intercourse before they reach age twenty, 1 in 2 will cohabit before marriage, and 25 percent of men and 15 percent of women will have already engaged in extramarital sex. Controversy continues over homosexuality, including debates over causation, legitimization and the ability to change orientation. Easy access to pornography on the Internet is a serious problem, accompanied by an ever-increasing bombardment of other pornographic materials and increased reports of sexual addiction even in the Christian community. Perhaps most disturbing of all are the high rates of uninvited and nonconsensual sex that are reported, especially by women, ranging from sexual harassment to sexual abuse, rape and other violent sex crimes.

At the heart of the issue is a contemporary struggle to define the meaning of human sexuality. Most needed, we believe, is a forthright and clearly articulated affirmation by the Christian community of the biblical meaning of sexuality. In this book we integrate evidence from biological, psychological and sociocultural factors with a biblical perspective in order to define and identify *authentic human sexuality.*

The book is divided into four parts. In part one, "The Origin & Formation of Sexuality," we look into the multitude of factors that contribute to human sexuality. Biological and sociocultural factors are introduced in chapter one, followed by a discussion in chapter two on the principles of authentic human sexuality. What it means to be created in the image of God as sexual beings is the foundation on which we build the true meaning and purpose of sexuality. In chapter three we take the biblical concepts of covenant, grace, empowerment and intimacy to develop a theology of authentic sexual relationships. Chapter four continues with a discussion of the specific bio-psycho-sociological forces that influence the formation of sexual orientation, including various explanations of homosexuality. Chapter five examines biblical references to homosexuality and describes various Christian ministry approaches to it.

Part two, "Authentic Sexuality," extends the theological model presented in chapter three and addresses a variety of relationships. Chapter six brings out the unique dynamics of sexual intimacy and singleness, while chapter seven pays particular attention to the emerging practice of premarital cohabitation, pointing out some concerns and cautions. Chapter eight presents a biblical foundation for maximizing marital sexual fulfillment, and chapter nine looks at some of the common causes of extramarital sex and the serious consequences it has on a relationship.

In part three, "Inauthentic Sexuality," we examine several inauthentic forms of human sexuality. Chapter ten sees sexual harassment as the uninvited eroticism of a relationship. Sexual abuse of children, the topic of chapter eleven, is discussed as a violation deep within the child's soul. Chapter twelve focuses on two forms of sexualized power—rape and other sexual violence—seeing them as destructive forces that emerge out of a violent world. Chapters thirteen and fourteen investigate two particularly self-defeating and devastating forms of inauthentic sexuality: pornography and sexual addiction.

The nature of our modern, electronic mass society determines that issues of authentic human sexuality transcend individual, familial and localized community boundaries. Part four ends the book with chapter fifteen, "The Sexually Authentic Society," which examines the importance of developing societal structures capable of promoting and sustaining authentic sexuality. A challenge is given to the Christian community to be intentional and proactive in bringing salt and light to a world that is in desperate need of theology that gives meaning and rightful understanding to human sexuality.

Part I
The Origin & Formation of Sexuality

1

Authentic Sexuality

Biological & Sociocultural Contributors

To be authentic is to be real, genuine, believable and trustworthy.
While it is appropriate to speak of normal, functional sexuality or
healthy sexuality, our focus in this book is on authentic sexuality. We
define and describe sexuality as something that is authentic, as
opposed to something inauthentic (a counterfeit version of the real
thing). Due to the complex factors contributing to and barriers hindering the development of sexuality, our task of defining authentic sexuality is far from simple. Human sexuality must be understood in light of
a variety of influences, including biological, sociological, psychological, theological, as well as gender, emotions, behaviors, attitudes and
values.

We begin with the presupposition that authentic sexuality is meant
to be a congruent, integral part of one's total being. Further, we believe
that God intends for our sexuality to be a real, genuine, believable and
trustworthy part of ourselves. In this way we embrace what God has
created and declare with God, "It is very good!"

Human sexuality is created as God's perfect design but is also
affected by the consequences of sin, fallen nature and deviation from

God's original design. This good "gift of sex" can be perverted and warped in many ways. Inauthentic sexuality, a consequence of our fallen condition, leaves us open to unreal, false, convoluted and unreliable expressions of sexual behavior. This happens through an interplay of societal attitudes and beliefs, sociocultural structures and biological and psychological factors. Authentic sexuality has to do with human beings seeking to live as sexual beings according to God's design and purpose.

This first chapter is devoted to identifying the various sociocultural and biological factors that contribute to the formation of sexuality. It will serve as a basis for chapter two, which addresses God's design and purpose for creating us as sexual beings and offers godly principles to guide our expression of sexuality. We openly acknowledge that human beings are complicated creatures whose bodies, personalities and social and cultural beliefs influence their sexuality. With this in mind we realize that people experience hurtful wounds and despair in this area of their lives, as well as pleasure, joy and fulfillment.

Significant relational aspects of human sexuality are found in biblical stories such as the Song of Songs and are developed in characters like Abraham, Sarah and Hagar; Jacob, Leah and Rachel; Rebekah and Isaac; and David and Bathsheba. Throughout the Old Testament the relationship between the children of Israel and Yahweh illustrates how movement toward or rejection of God's way leads to fulfillment or distortion in human relationships. In chapter three we complete this section by presenting a Christian theology of sexual relationships, which serves as a basis for various topics on sexuality presented in the remaining chapters.

Dimensions of Sexuality

The complexity of sexuality can be seen in figure 1.1, which illustrates the four criteria that contribute to defining the sexuality of an individual.

Natal sex has to do with the physical and biological features at birth that determine whether the baby is male or female. *Sexual identity* refers to a person's sexual self-concept, the view one has of oneself as a sexual person. *Gender role* refers to one's gender identity as defined by a particular culture. This includes such things as manner of talk, movement, expression, style of dress, as well as gender-based attitudes and

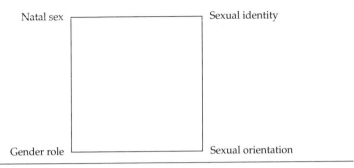

Figure 1.1.   **Four dimensions of sexuality**

interests, stereotypes and behavioral expectations. *Sexual orientation* refers to the direction of one's erotic attraction, which can be to the opposite sex (heterosexual), the same sex (homosexual) or both sexes (bisexual).

In the vast majority of cases there is consistency on all four dimensions of sexuality, resulting in a clear-cut definition of gender. However, for some there is inconsistency between the four dimensions; this lack of congruence causes confusion about gender. For example, some babies (hermaphrodites) are born with either full or partial male and female genitalia (see below). In such cases, medical experts assume the task of assigning the gender after careful exploration of known biological and hormonal factors at birth. Traditional wisdom assumes that children need to be assigned a gender identification in order for parents and others to relate to them in appropriate personal and sociocultural ways. Therefore medical professionals make a determination accompanied by appropriate surgical and hormonal procedures to provide congruence with the sex assignment. John Money, a leading sexologist, is a strong proponent of sex assignment soon after birth because it makes life easier for these children.

An alternative view has challenged this traditional practice. An increasing number of documented cases show that emergent sexual identities, sex roles or sexual orientations did not correspond to the assigned natal sex. Those who oppose sex assignment at birth believe it is important to wait until later life cycle factors such as puberty are taken into account. The argument has been spurred by the Jane/John case in Hawaii, in which a female assignment was made after an accidental severing of the penis soon after birth. Surgical and hormonal treatment accompanied the decision, yet Jane later experienced confusion, saying she felt more congruent as a male (John) in later development. So, Jane/John reversed the decision through a second sex change operation as an adult. John is adamant in his opinion that a family and society should tolerate a "neutral" sexual identity rather than misassign gender before all the facts are in.

This emerging view is based on *inversion theory,* the belief that people are sexually "wired" in a certain way and tampering with this complex process creates more problems than it solves. "Findings indicate that children have an innate sense of gender, and that the traditional practice of 'assigning' a male or female sex through surgery is damaging to the psyche of the child" (Diamond 1997:199). Diamond argues that there is a strong inherent interlinking between the four dimensions of sexuality in an individual, and this must be honored rather than altered. He believes that "society must come to accept people with ambiguous or hermaphroditic genitals, and such individuals must be allowed to choose their own sexual identity" (p. 199). So, according to this view, rather than forcing genital surgery at birth, parents and others should be able to relate to these children as "sexually special" until later developmental processes clarify gender more concretely. By implication, this view argues for the demedicalization of sexuality (such as assigning and then altering abnormal sexual characteristics) and the acceptance of what nature has created. From a religious perspective, hermaphrodites would need a supportive community while they seek to define themselves so they could eventually live life as the sexual beings God created them to be. It is a challenging problem, especially since gender role, sexual orientation and sexual identity are intervening influences through the life cycle, and it is unclear how this would affect a person without a gender designation during those development stages.

Biological Aspects of Sexuality

Human sexuality begins at conception. The sperm, carrying either a Y or an X sex chromosome, joins the ovum, which contains an X chromosome, to create a male (XY) or female (XX). If all of the biological details are in order, the child is born some nine months later, anatomically and genetically male or female. There are exceptions, however, as we've noted above.

Although not fully developed as sexual beings, all children experience sexual impulses from the moment of birth. Evidence shows that involuntary physical responses such as penile erection in males and vaginal lubrication in females can be observed during the first weeks after birth. In fact, the child's body is responsive to caressing, fondling, stroking and skin-to-skin touch. The obvious smiles and pleasurable sounds a baby makes in reply to such interaction indicate enjoyment. The mouth is a center of pleasure for infants as they receive nurture and comfort from their mother's breast. Then, as children develop motor skills they begin to explore their entire body, taking in the pleasurable feelings through self-touch, which is common during the early years of life. While these experiences of touch are different from adult erotic responses, children are born with a capacity for receiving pleasure as well as a potential for full sexual maturity.

Children who are born with a normal physiological package proceed through predictable physiological growth stages. At about age two, for instance, children show affection for others and an interest in gender differences and sexual body parts. Although much of this is curious exploration, young children seem to derive pleasure out of wrestling and tumbling together, hugging and even kissing each other. In a preschool setting, it is not unusual to observe children engaging in mutually satisfying touch. During these early years, it is unclear what meaning children attribute to such actions. Since sexual behavior is socially learned through the use of language, we can only assume that this early "sexual behavior" is primarily a physical response, a rehearsal of sorts. With the acquisition of language, children come to have a more complex understanding of the erotic meaning of these activities.

Freud assigned the term "latency" to children between the ages of seven and twelve, connoting the lack of sexual interest at this age. Recent evidence shows that "children's interest in and expression of sexuality remains lively throughout this period, even though it may not be overt. For many, 'sexual awakening' does not occur until the teens, but for others, it is a very real part of preadolescence" (Hyde 1994:314).

At the onset of puberty, more dramatic physiological changes occur due to a marked increase in hormone production. Hormones are body chemicals that are directly responsible for the body changes that occur at this time of life. The major male hormone, testosterone, contributes to the male reproductive process, while the main female hormones, estrogen and progesterone, are released by the ovaries. Hormones are primarily responsible for developing sexual characteristics such as breasts and the uterus, for promoting general body growth and for maintaining the female reproductive cycle. Among boys, testosterone brings about the development of genitals, the appearance of facial and body hair, increased height and a deepening of the voice. In a study of 13- to 16-year-old boys, Udry (1988) found testosterone levels to be related to the sexual activities of coitus and masturbation, and feeling sexually "turned on." But he also found that the decision to participate in sexual activities was affected by sociological factors such as living in an intact home, parent's educational level and church attendance.

As noted earlier, children usually emerge from puberty physiologically capable of reproduction. Nature is not always consistent, however, and we must also consider aberrations that interfere with the normal sexual developmental process. The presence of an extra Y or X chromosome seems to be responsible for some of the more striking forms of sexual abnormalities. For instance, males who are born with an XYY chromosomal makeup, when compared to normal XY males, have an "extra dose of maleness." These men tend to be taller, more muscular and more impulsive and have higher activity levels. Whereas some might be tempted to put a positive spin on these qualities, it should also be noted that a higher percentage of XYY than XY males have been convicted of committing violent and aggressive crimes.

On the other hand, males born with an XXY chromosomal makeup (Klinefelter's Syndrome) are shorter and less muscular; have smaller testicles and underdeveloped pubic, facial and body hair; and experience lower sexual arousal. They tend to be more timid and passive in general behavior. In most cases, the XXY male cannot produce sperm.

In females a chromosomal abnormality known as Turner's Syndrome results from the absence of an X chromosome (XO). Characteristics include abnormal ovarian development, failure to menstruate, infertility and the lack of secondary sexual characteristics, such as enlarged breasts. In addition, females with Turner's Syndrome have been found to be short in stature and predisposed to heart and kidney defects (Orten 1990). This brief summary of some of the effects of abnormal Y or X chromosomal makeup points to the significance of their contribution to one's sexuality.

Similarly, the presence of too much or too little of the wrong kind of hormones can also be a cause of abnormal sexual development. Two conditions that may result from hormonal abnormalities are hermaphroditism and pseudohermaphroditism. As described above, hermaphroditism is an extremely rare condition in which an individual is born with full or partial genital or reproductive organs of both sexes. Characteristics may include the presence of one ovary and one testicle, feminine breasts or a vaginal opening beneath the penis. Although the internal reproductive systems are usually mixed and incomplete, hermaphrodites are genetically female (XX) and capable of menstruating. They may be reared as either male or female, depending largely on their appearance.

Pseudohermaphroditism, more common than hermaphroditism, refers to individuals born with the gonads (internal reproductive glands) matching the sex chromosomes but genitals resembling the opposite sex. In females a condition known as androgenital syndrome can occur when the fetus is exposed to high levels of androgen, a "male" hormone. This causes the clitoris to enlarge and the labia to fuse together, producing a genital resembling the male scrotum. These particular individuals are referred to as female pseudohermaphrodites because they are genetically female (XX), yet are generally reared as males due to their outer appearance. During adolescence the female raised as a male may notice lack of facial hair growth, failure of the voice to deepen, and enlargement of the breasts.

A hormonal abnormality that can result in male pseudohermaphroditism is called testicular feminization syndrome (TFS). This condition is characterized by the lack of male genitals in individuals who are genetically male (XY). Although there are normal levels of androgen, the fetal tissues do not respond to the male hormones, and thus female external genitals are formed. While the newborn infant resembles a female externally, the testes are embedded in the abdomen.

Most parents are unaware of this hormonal abnormality until the child reaches adolescence and fails to menstruate. Surgery or hormone therapies are available to help correct some of the above abnormalities in sexual development.

Research on hormonal levels in both women and men indicates a relationship to sexual arousal and sexual passivity/aggressiveness. When we look at the accumulation of biological data, we can only conclude that a large proportion of what we call sexuality is based on biological factors.

Sociocultural Aspects of Sexuality

We use the concept "sociocultural" to encompass all life experiences—psychological, social and cultural—and their collective effect on the formation of human sexuality. The primary importance of sociocultural influence is in defining the meaning of sexuality to the individual. Human beings are unique among all living creatures because of the importance of language and ability to assign meaning to human behavior. A person doesn't learn the meaning of sexual behavior in a vacuum, but rather in a sociocultural context.

Sexuality is learned within a specific family, tribe, community and society. Since individuals are members of a number of social groupings, the messages about sexuality can vary widely. And in pluralistic industrial societies the messages can also be highly contradictory. Consistency in the meaning of sexuality within a certain social group or cultural system is hard to come by because it hinges on how meaning is transmitted, perceived and internalized. We must understand each of the three levels as they make a unique and joint contribution to the attitudes and meaning of sexuality. In the following three sections we shall consider the *cultural level*, which provides attitudes, values and beliefs about sexuality; the *social psychological level*, which results from the cultural scripting of sexuality; and the *sociological level*, which provides the context of sexuality.

Cultural level: Attitudes, values and beliefs. Prevailing cultural attitudes toward sex play a major role in the formation of sexuality within a person. In addition, prevailing cultural attitudes must be understood in light of past attitudes towards sexuality. The predominant cultural attitudes held in the United States, for example, have changed over several historical periods, but the "cultural memory" is still present today. The current cultural climate reflects the tension between *sexual repression*, a term used to describe sexual attitudes from past history, and *sexual liberation*, the trend in our modern world to eliminate the "hang-ups" developed during these earlier periods.

Both the Puritans and the Victorians have been blamed for the uptight, sexually repressive views of past generations (Reiss 1960). However, when taking into account the standards of seventeenth-century European culture, we believe the Puritans had quite a healthy view of sexuality. Advocating a clear standard of celibacy for the unmarried and monogamy for married people, they proposed a liberated view of sexual pleasure in the marriage relationship. Sexual expression between spouses was regarded as good, natural and desirable for both spouses.

An example of this comes out of a New England Puritan church record in 1675 about a husband who confessed he was planning to abstain from having sex with his wife for one year as a personal repentance for disobeying God. Once the church elders heard this they pronounced that he had no right to deny his wife sexual pleasure because she, too, had rights to sexual fulfillment. In this case, sexual expression between spouses was not to be withheld for the purpose of repentance because it would deprive the wife of her inalienable right to marital sexual activity.

On the other hand, during the Victorian period there were many sexual taboos that gave repressive messages about sex. During this period of history anything that appeared to be sexual was covered up. For example, not only did people have to cover their arms and legs in public, but little skirts were placed over the legs of the chairs and sofas. Bare legs, whether on a person or furniture, were a symbol of sexual immodesty.

Also during this time of sexual restraint the "double standard" became the norm of how men and women were to express themselves sexually. It was generally agreed that since men had sexual needs, they were allowed to find a "bad" woman (prostitute) to take care of their sexual passions, but they would be socially allowed to marry only a "good" woman (virgin). This was a loud and clear message to both men and women that sex was not to be desired by pure or proper women, but was a passion in men that needed to be tolerated. This double standard held until the first half of the twentieth century, when it was replaced by a "permissiveness with affection" standard. This was the beginning of the so-called sexual liberation.

This new standard acknowledged that sexual desire and expression were no longer regarded as pathological for women, but acceptable and desirable for women as well as men. Therefore when two people loved each other and were committed to their relationship, it was now permissible to engage in sexual expression, including intercourse.

In the years following World War II, there was a period character-ized by a *preoccupation* with sex. This began with the publication of the Kinsey reports: *Sexual Behavior in the Human Male* (1948) and *Sexual Behavior in the Human Female* (1952). About the same time, Hugh Hefner left his job as a copy editor at *Fortune* magazine and started a publication known as *Playboy* magazine. The sexual freedom of this era took the "expression with affection" one step further by promoting the idea that it was permissible to have affection for a number of partners, not just the person you would marry. In addition, this second sexual liberation introduced the premarital sexual standard of "permissive-ness without affection." This set the stage for expressing sex as a recre-ational activity rather than a commitment to one particular person.

In the name of sexual liberation, sex became a glorified object, void of the meaning associated with personal commitment and intimacy. C. S. Lewis (1960) speaks about this in the following hypothetical illustra-tion of a society overly focused on sex. Suppose there is a place in which people pay good money to enter a room to view a covered platter sit-ting on a table. Then, at the assigned time and to the beat of the drums, someone slowly lifts the cover of the platter to expose what's under-neath. There, before the lustful and expectant eyes of the many specta-tors, is a luscious pork chop! He goes on to say that one would begin to wonder what was so desperately wrong with the eating habits of such a society. The point is well taken! We must ask the question, What are we to make of a society that has such a preoccupation with sex?

In many modern societies sex has even been taken a step further. Now the platter is no longer covered! In many ways, we have become saturated with sex. Sex is boldly presented as front-page news, no longer hidden at the bottom of the last page. We hear it over the radio in popular music, are bombarded with it in the advertising media and find it expressed as a major theme in movies and daytime soap operas. How much further can a society go before the pendulum swings back?

By 1980 we saw some backlash to this overexposure to sex in a trend toward a new virginity. Feminists began to question what they had bought into with their newfound sexual freedom, and many felt their relational perspective and desire for emotional intimacy had been sabotaged in the process. In fact, many college women began to wear large red buttons declaring "NO" to casual sex as a protest to this dehumanizing trend.

Also, about the same time, cable TV channels found a sharp drop-off in their late-night X-rated movie audiences. Raw, explicit sex had lost its appeal as a shock and stimulus, and some people were beginning to rebel against sex being depicted as entertainment and recreation. The "free sex" morality was also reexamined in the light of the AIDS epidemic. The fear of STDs (sexually transmitted diseases) caused many to reexamine these promiscuous sex standards. Promotion of safe sex practices became widespread. Monogamy resurged as a more sane way to express sexuality in today's world.

Yet, the current scene is still confusing. While we've witnessed conservative Christian young people marching on Washington making purity pledges, the rate of sexual intercourse among junior and senior high school students is increasing. We hear that monogamy is the norm, yet extramarital affairs are on the rise. The safe sex message is advocated by prominent celebrities in the media, yet many confess to making exceptions in their personal sexual encounters. We are encouraged on one hand by the message that mature sex has to do with responsible emotional and physical intimacy with one's life-time partner, yet many are engaging in casual sex or struggling with sexual addictions of one kind or another. As youth are exposed to the incongruent contemporary sexual attitudes, it seems they are growing up in an absurd and confusing world.

Social psychological level: Cultural scripting of sexuality. Right in the middle of a sexual revolution about attitudes and behaviors, there is a redefinition of gender roles. In the past, it was assumed that little girls would naturally grow up to be women, with certain well-defined "feminine" roles and identities, and little boys would grow up to be men, with corresponding roles and identities. We now realize that much of what was assumed to be "natural" is determined by sexual scripts that our culture assigns to girls and boys. From the time they are newborn babies, the traditional script for boys is physical courage, toughness, competitiveness, strength, control, dominance and aggressiveness, whereas girls are scripted to be gentle, expressive, responsive, sensitive and compliant. Social scientists find that much of the expressed difference between males and females is learned rather than genetic, and this has challenged the traditional definitions of masculinity and femininity. Rather than giving a detailed account of current changes in gender roles, we shall limit our comments here to those aspects of gender redefinition most directly related to sexuality.

Females have traditionally been regarded as "less sexual" than males. Evidence indicates, however, that this difference is due largely to greater sexual restraints being placed on females. As little girls grow up, parents take a more protective stance towards their daughter's sexuality. Girls are cautioned to show modesty in their clothes, to keep their dresses down and their breasts covered and to guard themselves against sexual advances. These messages are generalized and reinforced by society at large.

The messages boys receive from their parents and society are generally much less restrictive. Boys are given more freedom to uncover their bodies and to explore themselves physically. As boys grow into puberty, they often become part of adolescent male subcultures where they are encouraged to make sexual advances toward girls as a sign of their masculinity. This message about sexuality is reflected in the language of the adolescent male subculture. The boy who fails to "score" can be in danger of having his sexuality called into question. By the time adulthood is reached, males have traditionally been conditioned to be sexually active, while females have been culturally conditioned to resist sexual stimuli and advances.

It is also through culture that males and females come to learn which symbols and objects to associate with sexual meaning and stimuli. Male sexual stimulation is often considered to be more centered on sight, while female sexual response has more to do with touch. While there may be a physiological basis for this difference, crosscultural evidence suggests that it also may be culturally determined.

The following story, told by a female missionary on her first term in the mission field, illustrates the cultural basis for sexual arousal. While walking through a rural village for the first time, she realized that the men of the village were whistling at her. Since she was modestly attired, she was quite surprised by this reaction. An experienced missionary explained to her that men in this culture found plump legs to be a sexual stimulus. This demonstrates how a culture defines its sex symbols and corresponding response to these symbols.

The extent to which human sexual responsiveness is culturally conditioned can also be detected through the change in women's bathing suits over the last one hundred years. During Victorian times men and women were not permitted to bathe together on a public beach. Around the turn of the century, when mixed bathing finally became more acceptable, bathing suits covered the body all the way down to the ankles and wrists. During the twentieth century, bathing suits have steadily shrunk, exposing ever-increasing expanses of anatomy.

Increased exposure of the body has also diminished the sexual stimulus of various body parts. While a bare knee could have caused quite a stir around the turn of the century, it is not the focus of erotic attention today. To emphasize this point, suppose a young man living at the turn of the century were placed in a time capsule and transported to a typical bathing beach in the United States today. A man conditioned to sexual conventions of the 1890s would be totally shocked, to say the least! Thus, a person's sexual response can be understood in part by social and cultural conditioning.

Sociological level: Context of sexuality. The cultural meaning of sexuality resides within and is filtered through a variety of social structures. In *Journey into Sexuality* (1986) Ira Reiss presents a sociological explanation of sexuality. Reiss makes the assumption that sexuality is learned in a societal context. People learn about sexuality the same way they learn about friendship or love relationships. Sexual learning is especially potent, he suggests, because of the bonding that is created between persons when *physical pleasure* and *personal self-disclosure* accompany the sexual encounter. This partner bonding is what most societies wish to support. Sexual bonding not only promotes the formation of kinship ties but also helps form gender role concepts.

Based upon cross-societal evidence, Reiss suggests that in all societies sexuality is linked to three elements of the social structure: *marital jealousy, gender role power* and *ideology* (beliefs about what is normal).

Marital jealousy serves as a "boundary-maintenance mechanism" that aims at protecting relationships that society views as important. Powerful people in social structures will be more likely than those less powerful to be jealous of their partners and to react with greater violence and aggression. This is where *gender role power* comes in. Usually those who are in power have control over what the society views as important. Thus, since sexuality is viewed as important by the powerful, males will tend to demand and possess greater sexual rights than females, since males usually have more power.

The third element, *ideology*, refers to the shared societal beliefs about sexual normality and human nature. Sexual ideologies are subtypes of the general ideology in a society and revolve around two dimensions: (1) overall gender equality and (2) the relative sexual permissiveness allowed to each gender. For example, North American societies tend to promote partner equality and therefore emphasize the importance of mutual foreplay and orgasm during sexual intercourse, while such concepts are nonexistent in societies that fail to value equality between the sexes.

Understanding the importance of Reiss's writings is important when defining authentic sexuality. He not only gives a sociological explanation of sexuality but attempts to develop a sexual morality. Reiss believes we should hesitate to label as abnormal (or, in our words, inauthentic) any sexual act that can be found as an accepted act in another culture. Only sexual acts that are found unacceptable in all cultures will be deemed abnormal. In other words, Reiss argues that what *is*, is right! He states, "There may well be other scientific bases for defining a sexual act as abnormal, but until it is clearly established as such by scientific evidence and reasoning, we had better not use such labels freely if we are to avoid the politicization of therapy" (Reiss 1986:239). This is a good example of how a person with a naturalistic worldview makes moral decisions. Although it is important that Christians be informed by what is defined as normative in nature and nurture, we take the Holy Scripture as an ultimate basis for moral values.

The sociologist rightly observes that all societies have customs that provide boundary mechanisms around important relationships in order to preserve them. Upholding marriage as the place to engage in sexual intercourse and bear children organizes and provides stability in a society. It may simply be accomplished by means of jealousy norms that are taught to group members in a particular culture. The more powerful members learn to maximize their control of that which is sanctioned by their group. Hence, when one gender is more powerful, it is more likely that this gender possesses greater sexual rights and privileges. This, like most sociological explanations, deemphasizes the role of biology in explaining sexuality. As Reiss states, "There are biological tendencies, but they are demonstrably malleable if we are willing to pay the cost of shaping them in the directions we prefer."

One must distinguish between Reiss's sociological analysis of the formation of human sexuality and the values inherent in his interpretation of that analysis. One can accept normative behavior by studying all cultures without accepting carte blanche the value premise that what *is*, is right. We look for values that are based on a biblical understanding of sexuality. In addition, the social scientist tends to use culture as the normalizing base, while the biological scientist tends to use biophysical structure. In our view God is the creator of all things, and we dare not place a limit on the means (nature and/or nurture) by which God chooses to bring about authentic sexuality.

Partial and Holistic Explanations of Sexuality

Before considering a theological perspective on sexuality, let us visually illustrate alternative explanations of human sexuality. Figure 1.2 provides a summary of this chapter and an introduction to the next.

The three arrows in this figure leading from nature to human sexuality, from God to human sexuality, and from nurture to human sexuality represent three alternative single-factor explanations of human sexuality. Each one alone is an incomplete explanation because it fails to acknowledge the contribution of the others.

When one attempts to explain human sexuality by exclusively utilizing only one set of explanations, the result is a "deterministic" explanation of sexuality. Determinism is an explanatory approach that attributes a "one-and-only cause." Determinism is sometimes referred

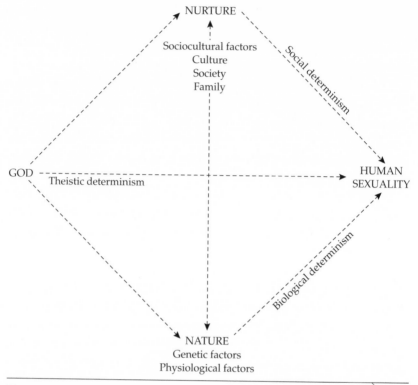

Figure 1.2.   Explanations of human sexuality

to as "nothing-buttery," since it proposes that nothing but the one factor is necessary and sufficient to explain a phenomenon (MacKay
1974).

As represented in figure 1.2, *biological determinism* explains human
sexuality purely in natural (physiological and genetic) terms, *social
determinism* attributes the development of human sexuality solely to
sociocultural factors, and *theistic determinism* claims that human sexuality is simply part of God's creation and not dependent on either
sociocultural or biological factors. The latter is a type of naive theistic
determinism and should be distinguished from a more sophisticated
theistic determinism that conceptualizes God as determining sexuality
through bio-psycho-sociocultural factors.

As an aside, it is interesting to note the relationship between one's
theological position and the relative importance one gives to sociocul-

tural and biological explanations of human sexuality. For example, people holding a more conservative theological position tend to emphasize biological factors when explaining male/female differences but focus on environmental factors and discount genetic explanations in reference to homosexual behavior. On the other hand, persons with liberal theologies tend to do just the opposite. They deemphasize genetic explanations for gender differences but embrace genetic explanations when addressing homosexual orientation and behavior. It is important to recognize how one's theology colors an acceptance or rejection of social and biological explanations of sexuality.

We believe that each of the deterministic positions yields a biased understanding of human sexuality and fails to provide an adequate grasp of authentic sexuality. Even though each approach explains an important aspect of human sexuality, when taken alone, the explanation is partial. The interactive effect between biological and sociocultural factors upon sexuality, indicated by the arrows leading from nature to nurture and from nurture to nature, represent a more elaborate connection between biological and sociocultural factors and how they both affect and are affected by each other.

A holistic understanding of human sexuality is much more complex than what is allowed in any of the single-factor approaches. Starting at the extreme left of figure 1.2, we recognize that God can act either directly or indirectly as the author and creator of human sexuality. We depict God acting indirectly by the arrows pointing from God but then *through* nature and nurture to human sexuality. It seems that God, in infinite power and wisdom, has chosen to use sociocultural and biological factors to bring forth the fullness of one's sexuality.

Therefore we should not feel uneasy about evidence that points to the influence of sociocultural and biological factors, thinking this undermines the role of God as the creator of human sexuality. Rather God has chosen to work through, and allow for, both biological and sociocultural factors in the formation of human sexuality. The formation of any individual's sexuality is due to a wide range of sociocultural and biological considerations. At the same time we solidly believe that God takes a direct role through biblical teachings that help us live out authentic sexuality in our heart's desires, mind and attitudes and through our behavior. We will elaborate on this in the following chapter.

An Interactive Developmental Theory of Authentic Human Sexuality

An adequate explanation of human sexuality must include both developmental and interactive aspects. Hereafter we use the term "interactive" to refer to the biological and sociocultural factors as they mutually affect and are affected by each other simultaneously throughout the life span of an individual. Figure 1.3 represents a graphic illus-

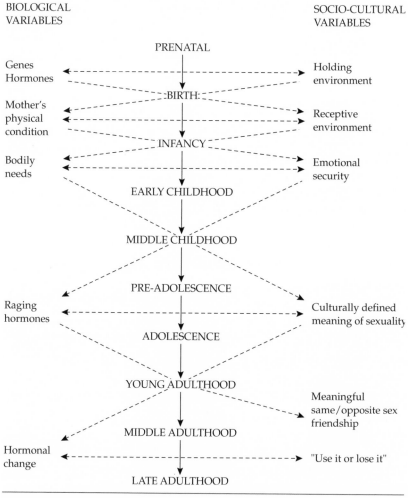

Figure 1.3. An interactive developmental theory of authentic human sexuality

tration of this continuous *interactive* process between biology and sociocultural factors as they affect sexual formation and development.

The stages of human development are represented from top to bottom at the center of the figure. At each stage of human development both biological and sociocultural variables play a significant role in sexual formation and development. Even before a child is born (prenatal stage) there are important interactive affects (represented by the top horizontal dotted line) between genes, hormones and the mother's womb as the holding environment. The vertical and diagonal dotted lines represent the idea that both biological factors and sociocultural factors affect the biological and sociocultural makeup of the individual in subsequent developmental stages and within each interaction (horizontal dotted line) with each other.

Figure 1.3 gives approximations of the bio-psycho-social dynamics of human sexual development and is not meant to be a description of stage-specific development. Thus, we point to such considerations as meeting basic bodily needs and providing emotional security during infancy as affecting the child's sexual development. Emerging from preadolescence into adolescence, increased hormonal levels and culturally defined messages about the meaning of sex contribute to the adolescent's sexual development. For example, sexually promiscuous teenage boys not only share common permissive home backgrounds but higher hormonal levels than those who are less promiscuous. As presented at the bottom of the figure, research shows that during later life stages, hormonal levels not only affect the rate of sexual intercourse, but engaging in sexual intercourse increases hormonal levels.

Perhaps the best example of this interactive effect between biology and sociocultural factors is the accumulated research evidence about the brain's impact on sexuality. In response to erotic arousal, the brain organizes bodily reactions that eventually lead to sexual satisfaction or lack of it. Incoming sensual stimuli are encoded in the cortex of the brain, and the hypothalamus determines whether the stimuli are painful or pleasurable. Once this is determined, the message is sent to the pituitary gland, which controls outgoing messages to the adrenal glands in the female and male gonads. If the pituitary gland receives the incoming sexual stimuli as pleasurable, it commands the necessary hormones to begin the sexual arousal process. However, if the message indicates pain, the pituitary gland will close down the sexual arousal system. Needless to say, the brain, as a biological sex organ, is greatly influenced and responsive to the social environment. Once again, it is the social and biological influences interacting together that make it difficult to separate the effect of each.

An example of the inseparable quality of biological and social factors is illustrated by the resent research showing brain differences between homosexuals and heterosexuals. Advocates for the gay community insist that this study provides irrefutable evidence that gender orientation is determined by biological rather than sociological factors. Yet, others argue that the differences found in the brain have been a result of AIDS which, of course, has to do with social factors.

The Meaning of Sexuality and Human Agency

Of all living creatures, the human infant is dependent upon adult care for the longest period of time. There is an inverse relationship between the dependence of the young upon adults within a species and the importance of biological (instinctive) factors in shaping sexual behavior. In other words, there is a positive relationship between the young being dependent upon adults in a species and how socio-environmental factors shape sexual behavior. So, we understand human sexual behavior as less directly "determined" by biological factors and more susceptible to influence and modification by social factors. Under control of the human brain, the biological base shares with·social factors and the cultural matrix as they blend together to form sexuality. All five senses—touch, sight, smell, taste and sound—are encoded on the cerebral cortex with corresponding cultural meanings.

In various societies, the sight of an exposed ankle is defined as sexually stimulating or nonstimulating, depending on the learned cultural message. Touch in the form of a caress, a kiss or hug is likewise judged sexually stimulating or not, depending on the culturally assigned meaning. Even human sound, like a deep moan or extended groan, is embedded in a social context that determines if one is experiencing pain or sexual pleasure.

So, in a thousand and one ways, the sexual makeup of any individual is formed in the context of this interaction between the biological factors, the social environment and the cultural context that give meaning to our sexuality. As children develop their sexual maps, they become increasingly complex and sophisticated in the manner in which their senses are categorized in the brain. But also with increased sophistication comes an increased ability to control what senses affect the brain. Moral development determines one's ability to make choices about sexual stimuli and behavior for which negative meaning has been assigned. This realization leads us to the importance of taking into account the agency nature of human beings.

Human beings are not merely reactive to biological and sociocultural imprints but are active participants in their own sexual development. Human beings are free to make choices. Freedom and human choice are even championed in one of the strongest empirically based models of personality, *social learning theory*. In his reciprocal determinism model Albert Bandura (1974) asserts, "Within the social learning framework, freedom is defined in terms of the number of options available to people and the right to exercise them. The more behavioral alternatives and social prerogatives people have, the greater is their freedom of action" (p. 865). This view is consistent with the conclusions we offered in our discussion of figure 1.3, that biological and sociocultural factors can either limit or expand the range of choices for any given individual. The greater the number of choices, the greater the range of freedom within which choices can be made.

From a biblical perspective, human choice is not defined solely by biology, psychology and sociocultural factors but also includes spiritual meaning and implication. Since we are created beings who have been given free choice by the Creator God, we propose a biblical perspective that embraces but is not solely determined by biological, psychological and psychocultural factors. We recommend *Whatever Happened to the Soul? Scientific and Theological Portraits of Human Nature* (Brown, Murphy and Malony 1998) for an in-depth consideration of these ideas. In the chapter "Brain, Mind, and Behavior," Malcolm Jeeves asserts, "It is at the level of our conscious experience that there is indeterminacy, irrespective of any indeterminacy at the level of the brain" (p. 97). In other words, the essence of human freedom is that it is the person and not the brain who chooses and decides. While we can explain sexual behavior in terms of brain activity, in doing so we must not explain away the conscious human beings who make and are responsible for the sexual choices they make.

From a Christian perspective, one can best understand sexual choice as a reflection of the meaning of sexuality that one holds as residing in familial and community contexts. Authentic human sexuality ultimately needs to be defined by a biblical understanding. In the following two chapters we develop a biblical approach to the deeper meaning of sexuality and sexual relationships.

Authentic Sexual Development: A Summary
This brief overview of the biological and sociocultural aspects of human sexuality provides a foundational understanding upon which to define authentic sexuality within a biblical perspective. As a basis for this task, we offer seven summary principles. These principles can serve as a guide in considering the interplay between biological, sociocultural and biblical contributions to the formation of authentic sexuality in the following chapters.

1. *The evidence is insufficient to make causal statements in explaining the development of authentic and inauthentic sexuality.* It can be noted that both biological and sociocultural factors contribute to rather than cause human sexuality. The wisdom within the philosophy of science dictates that to be considered a cause, it must be demonstrated that a factor is both necessary and sufficient for an ultimate explanation.

2. *Biological factors serve as necessary, but not sufficient, contributors to the formation of authentic human sexuality.* An adequate male or female biological package is needed in order for an individual to develop an authentic male or female sexuality. However, what is biologically given is not sufficient to ensure authentic sexual development.

3. *Sociocultural factors serve as the sufficient, but not necessary, contributors to the formation of authentic human sexuality.* An adequate biological package and adequate sociocultural factors are necessary to develop authentic sexuality. Defining what is "good enough" is the subject of future chapters.

4. *Authentic or inauthentic sexuality emerges as part of a developmental process.* Sexuality emerges from physiological, psychological, socialcultural and spiritual factors that each make a unique contribution at strategic points in a person's life.

5. *While biological factors are most crucial in establishing sexuality early in life, sociocultural factors become increasingly significant as the child matures.* As children develop the capacity to use language, they correspondingly learn the meaning of sexual attitudes and behavior. An understanding or lack of understanding of spiritual meaning for human sexuality becomes increasingly important as the individual constructs a purposeful life. The meaning of sexuality is gained within a social context; thus it is important for family and community members to live out and communicate God's designed meaning for sexuality and sexual expression.

6. *Social units, such as families, churches, communities and societies, will vary greatly in the degree to which they reflect God's design and meaning for human sexuality.* Since all individuals are members of various groups, many of which offer competing definitions and meanings of human sexuality, individuals can internalize contradictory meanings of sexuality. The more these significant membership groups consistently reflect God's ideal for sexuality, the more internally consistent will the development of authentic sexuality be in any one individual member. However, since each individual is a choice-making creature with emotive, volitional and moral values, authentic sexuality emerges from an interplay between the individual and the social environment.

7. *Authentic sexuality and inauthentic sexuality are dichotomous only in a moral sense and should never be used to describe given individuals.* Authentic sexuality is not totally represented in any one person. Being part of a fallen creation, all human beings are sexually broken and lack perfect wholeness in some way. In the following chapters, we hope to identify authentic sexuality within a Christian theological context and thereby provide a model for moving toward authentic sexuality as it is found and represented in the many arenas of daily life.

Suggestions for Further Reading

Brown, W., N. Murphy, and N. Maloney. 1998. *Whatever happend to the soul? Scientific and theological portraits of human nature.* Philadelphia: Fortress.

Byer, C., L. Shainberg and G. Galliano. 1998. *Dimensions of human sexuality.* 5th ed. New York: McGraw-Hill.

Reiss, I. 1986. *Journey into sexuality.* Englewood Cliff, N.J.: Prentice-Hall.

2

Principles of Authentic Sexuality

Chapter one revealed the complexity of a number of factors contrib-uting to the development of human sexuality. Even more challenging in this chapter is the task of defining authentic sexuality. We'll begin with a simple definition of authentic as "something that is genuine or real." Authentic sexuality, then, brings authenticity to ourselves and our relationships as it reflects God's divine intention for who we are and how we are to behave as sexual relational beings.

In our society of competing worldviews, a naturalistic assumption of biological and social scientists is to define authentic sexuality in terms of what *is*. The methodology of the social sciences is to compare and contrast crosscultural ethnographic evidence in order to determine normal as opposed to abnormal sexual behavior. Sexuality in this case is determined through crosscultural practices. In summarizing the work of Ira Reiss (1986), we see that he not only gives a sociological explanation of sexuality but uses naturalistic assumptions to propose a sexual morality. Reiss believes it is improper to label as morally abnormal (inauthentic) any sexual act that is acceptable in any culture. Therefore he limits his definition of inauthentic sexual behavior to only that which is unacceptable in *all* cultures. This naturalistic worldview develops a morality of sexuality that accepts everything as normal, until a behavior is clearly established by scientific evidence and reasoning as being "abnormal" (Reiss 1986:239).

Sexologists take both sociocultural and biological evidence into account when arriving at a definition of sexual normality. However, making judgments about what is sexually normal and abnormal gets a bit tricky since naturalists are only comfortable in developing a sexual construct that "points" to the normative. In our minds, this takes quite a leap of faith. It seems more accurate to look at sexual characteristics, orientation, attitudes and behaviors as more or less consistent with what *most* people report and experience. As with a bell-shaped curve, some individuals will be closer to the center of the curve, while others are more toward the extremes on any given sexual dimension. When restricted by defining sexual normality only in terms of what is culturally normative, what is obviously lacking is the divine purpose that provides intrinsic meaning to a definition of authentic sexuality.

While we should not ignore the reality of what is biologically or culturally normative, neither can we ignore the values inherent in the interpretation of the biological and cultural analysis. Clearly we gain an enormous understanding of what is "normative" sexual behavior by studying cultures throughout the world. But we can't stop here. We must faithfully seek out the biblical meaning and purpose of being created as sexual beings. We propose six basic biblical principles we believe lead to authentic sexuality. Principles one through four deal with creation; principle five, with the Fall; and principle six with redemption and restoration.

1. *Human sexuality is established in the differentiation between male and female and in the unity established between them.*

2. *Sexuality is a good gift meant to draw persons to deeper levels of knowing self, others and God.*

3. *Humans are born with an innate capacity for sexual pleasure, and human sexuality can best develop within an emotionally caring, trustworthy family environment.*

4. *Sexuality and spirituality are intricately connected.*

5. *After the Fall sexuality became distorted and in need of redemption.*

6. *Christ offers restoration and renews our potential for authentic sexuality.*

Differentiation and Unity

The starting point for this principle is found in the creative act of God noted in Genesis 1:26-28, 31: "Then God said, 'Let us make humankind in our image, according to our likeness, and let them have dominion.' . . . God created humankind in his image, in the image of God he created them; male and female he created them. God blessed them, and . . . God saw everything that he had made, and indeed, it was very good" (NRSV). First, we note the importance of the relational nature of the Godhead in the phrase "Let *us* make humankind in *our* image." Phyllis Trible (1987) makes a point that *humankind (hā'ādām)* in the first line changes to the singular pronoun *him* and finally to the plural form *them,* reinforcing "sexual differentiation within the unity of humanity" (p. 17). In these verses we recognize God's holy work in not only creating humankind but creating two distinct human beings, male and female. This places authentic being and sexuality in the context of male and female distinctiveness as well as in their unity and harmony.

Karl Barth expands this discussion: "Man never exists as such, but always as the human male or the human female. . . . Nor can he wish to liberate himself from the relationship and be man without woman or woman apart from man; for in all that characterizes him as a man he will be thrown back upon woman, or as woman upon man. The female is to the male, and the male to the female, the other man and as such the fellow-man" (Frazier 1986: 117-18). Paul Jewett (1976) takes a similar position when he writes, "Man, as created in the divine image, is Man-in-fellowship. . . . The primary form of this fellowship is that of male and female" (pp. 45-46). Jewett views differentiation as complementarity, correspondence and encounter.

Building upon these ideas, Ray Anderson (1982) argues that the created differentiation between male and female reflects a differentiation within the Godhead. He writes, "Human sexuality thus has a correspondence to the Godhead in that it is an encounter with a corresponding but different being. Not the 'mating' but the *meeting* is the essence, but one can't be separated from the other on the creaturely level. Human sexuality is the image of God" (p. 106). Differentiation makes unity a profound possibility.

Further insight on sexual differentiation is given by Phyllis Trible

(1987). In noting the shift in Genesis 1:27 from singular to plural pronouns, she draws several important conclusions in regard to sexual differentiation: first, that *hā'ādām* (humankind) refers to two creatures, thus disallowing an androgynous interpretation of the term; second, that the "singular word *hā'ādām* with its singular pronoun *oto* shows that male and female are not opposite but rather harmonious sexes"; and third, that "the parallelism between *hā'ādām* and 'male and female' shows . . . that sexual differentiation does not mean hierarchy but rather equality" (pp. 18-19).

The question about whether the man was created first and therefore is in a special position of authority over the woman is still debated in Christian circles today. Genesis 2:18 proclaims that it was not good for man to be alone, so a helper was made for him. This particular verse needs to be interpreted with care and clarity. According to Trible (1987), *helper* in the original language (*`ēzer*) refers to God as the helper of humankind fifteen of the sixteen times it is used in the Bible. This verse is the one exception in which it is used to describe the relationship between human beings, namely, Eve and Adam. Trible goes on to suggest that even the most inventive exegete would have to make a huge stretch to conclude that God, as our *`ēzer*, is subordinate to humankind and therefore beyond such an interpretation when it comes to subordination between the man and woman. It makes no sense to conclude that Genesis 2:18 implies subordination between the man and the woman.

Rather God gives Adam a helper who complements him and corresponds to him in mutuality and equality. Referring to Adam's first words upon seeing Eve, "This is now bone of my bones and flesh of my flesh" (Gen 2:23), Trible comments, "These words speak unity, solidarity, mutuality, and equality. Accordingly, in this poem the man does not depict himself as either prior to or superior to the woman. His sexual identity depends upon her even as hers depends upon him. For both of them sexuality originates in the one flesh of humanity" (Trible 1987:99).

A man finds his identity and meaning in being male, just as a woman finds identity and meaning in being female. Differentiation connotes "unique quality" rather than inequality! What is uniquely different enhances and expands the other. Based upon the Genesis account, and continuing throughout the Old and New Testaments, sex is simply taken for granted, and authentic sexuality is founded on two differentiated persons joining together in a sacred union.

As difficult as it is to develop an explicit "theology of sexuality," the scriptural view certainly presents sexuality as basic to our human existence and the very thing that informs our way of being in the world as embodied persons. Sexuality involves a whole array of feelings, thoughts, memories, self-understanding, attitudes and behaviors through which we express ourselves in relationship. As we will see in the next principle, our "God-designed" sexuality is meant to draw us into authentic relationship through connection, communication and communion.

Deeper Levels of Knowing

C. S. Lewis (1963) reminds us that physical pleasure is God's idea, not the devil's. We are created as sexual beings with sexual desire. As noted in chapter one, God not only made our bodies but equipped them with hormones, a nervous system, physical sensations, thought patterns and a psychological capacity to help us find connection with others. It seems we were made for each other! So, God didn't mean for man and woman to be alone, but created them in similar but uniquely different ways so they could engage soul to soul and flesh to flesh! How exhilarating it is to read that Adam received his companion with enthusiasm and eager anticipation as one who was mysteriously his equal. In such union of body, mind and soul, a relationship is solidified as each one expands the other through self-knowledge and understanding. Through the good gift of sex, each discovers more about themselves, each other and their Creator God.

We find it necessary to emphasize the good gift of sex, since sex has so often been viewed in negative ways throughout history. A "sex is bad" perspective can be traced back to Greek philosophy, as Platonic dualism made inroads into the early church pronouncements. While the spirit was pronounced as good, the flesh was denounced as bad. Sex, especially sexual desire, was considered fleshly and lustful, sinful and base.

Condemnation of sexual pleasure often corresponds with a theology that insists on procreation as the sole purpose of human sexuality. Holding to this view makes it quite impossible to attach sacred meaning to sexual desire and pleasure in and of itself. Theologies that uphold the goodness of the sexual union (Gen 2) emphasize the sealing of the one-flesh relationship. Therefore because procreation is *not* the exclusive reason for sexual expression, sexual desire and fulfillment between man and woman have divine meaning and purpose as well.

Let's imagine Adam and Eve gazing at each other in the garden, recognizing each other as "bone of my bones and flesh of my flesh." Their sexual nature moves them toward each other for a deeper level of knowing themselves and each other in the meeting. Their distinctive differences engage them in an emotional and sexual oneness they cannot find in themselves alone. Trible (1987) writes, "The result of this convergence of opposites is a consummation of union: 'and they become one flesh.' No procreative purpose characterizes this sexual union; children are not mentioned. Hence, the man does not leave one family to start another; rather he abandons familial identity for the one flesh of sexuality" (p. 104). Out of differentiation, two sexual beings, man and woman, find wholeness and one-flesh communion in their sexual consummation.

Deeply embedded within each one of us is a divine longing for wholeness that sends us reaching beyond ourselves to God and others. Sexual desire helps us recognize our incompleteness as human beings and causes us to seek the other to find a fuller meaning in life. The erotic generates creative energy and capacity for relationship growth and change. How unfortunate it would be if sexual attraction were just a restless urge for sexual release, for then one would be deprived of the greater satisfaction of deep emotional and sexual connection.

Sexual fullness is the reward of relationship vulnerability. Authentic sexuality urges us toward a rich sharing of our lives. Physical, emotional and intellectual openness is the basis for self-understanding that attracts us toward others, toward inner and outward harmony and responsiveness. A communion of trust and intimacy with God and others helps us take the necessary steps beyond our personal safety zone to risk honest expression of who we are. This intimate encounter has potential to transform.

The Genesis 2 passage concludes, "The man and his wife were both naked, and they felt no shame" (Gen 2:25). Authentic sexual interaction carries no shame, for it is entirely good for the man and woman to respond to each other openly. Sexual attraction, desire and engagement are part of God's sovereign plan. Trible (1987) refers to the Song of Songs as a symphony of love that gives us an important key to understanding and celebrating the Genesis concept of being naked and not ashamed. In mutual vulnerability and harmony, "This couple treat each other with tenderness and respect. Neither escaping nor exploiting sex, they embrace and enjoy it. Their love is truly bone of bone and flesh of flesh, and this image of God as male and female is indeed very good (Gen 1:27, 32). Testifying to the goodness of creation, then, eroticism becomes worship in the context of grace" (p. 161).

When we are bold enough to believe that God is at the center of our sexuality, we will discover ourselves anew and learn to be responsive and responsible in our relationships. In a similar way, our deep desire for Christ brings us to a deeper level of knowing ourselves. As we honestly examine our deepest cravings, we are forced to consider how to bring our lives into accordance with what we cherish and what God desires of us.

Capacity for Sexual Pleasure and the Family Environment

We have already discussed how children experience sexual feelings from the time they are born. The pleasurable feelings an infant experiences center on being held close, caressed and fondled. The parent's body gives sustenance, security and pleasure. Early on, young children also find pleasure through all their senses: smell, taste, touch, hearing and sight. God has created human beings with a tremendous capacity for taking in pleasure.

How sad it is that parents so often give children negative messages about bodily pleasure at a very early age. The genital area is either considered nonexistent (something to be ignored or avoided) or bad (something disgusting). The child begins to hear a different tone in the parent's voice, giving harsh reprimands and showing disapproval. "Bad boy! Off limits!" "Bad girl! Don't touch!" The shameful message communicated during normal curiosity and inquisitive touch leaves children feeling they have done something improper. What forms within children's minds is the sense that it is wrong to feel the slightest pleasure of a genital nature; hence, they repress the sexual in themselves.

Larry Friesen believes,

> It is precisely during the age from birth till six that presents the greatest opportunities to acquaint young children with a biblical basis for his or her sexuality. A parent can affirm pleasurable feelings generated by genital touch and the inherent enjoyment of one's sexual response by responding to the behavior in a loving and assuring tone of voice. In this way, a child learns that the pleasurable sexual feelings that are experienced are part and parcel of being an infant and growing child. This also opens up the opportunity to impress upon the child that, because of the sacred and precious nature of the pleasurable feelings, it is of utmost importance that such a treasure should be a private matter between the child and the heavenly Father, who is the giver of the gift. Sexual instructions to a child must be specific, according to the understanding of the child, and imbedded into a deeper acceptance that, from birth, sexual pleasure generated by the genital touch is precisely what the Creator had in mind when He drew the original plan. (Friesen 1989:322-24).

Receiving a positive message about the wonderful nature of pleasurable feelings, along with helpful guidance about appropriate ways and places to express such pleasure, provides an affirming security about one's sexuality. Self-pleasuring within the context of discretion and discernment offers an effective way to embrace one's sexual embodiment.

Perhaps it is difficult for parents to talk to their children openly about sex because negative connotations were attached to sexuality during their own development. If parents are able to affirm sex as a good and integral part of being created in the image of God, their children will be able to do the same. Sexual feelings and desires should be considered as something to protect and embrace rather than as something bad to deny and reject.

In fact, social scientists believe that human sexuality develops according to learned sexual scripts or cultural definitions of what is acceptable sexual behavior. Basically, people learn about sexuality in the same way they learn about other relationships. But, as Reiss noted, sexual learning is potent due to the bonding power created when physical and emotional pleasure accompany the interaction. Think for a moment about the parent-child bonding and the personal pleasure expressed between them. The closeness of bodies—the touching, stroking and nurturing—that takes place in this intimate interaction speaks volumes about love. Freud graphically reminds us that a baby sinking back satiated from the breast and falling asleep with flushed cheeks and a blissful smile is a prototype of sexual satisfaction in later life (Freud 1953).

Object relations theorists look at attachment and bonding experiences as foundational for forming intimate relationships in later life. In fact, if there has been a serious disruption in this bonding experience, children often exhibit deficits when it comes to knowing how to make significant connections with others. This theory recognizes that relatedness and relationship are central to the development of a person. When these basic needs are not met, the adult is uncertain, riddled with fears and incapable of trusting others. It is quite obvious, on the other hand, when sufficient attachment occurs, that children form a secure identity and have confidence in relating to others. A balanced, congruent self is the outcome of being nurtured, accepted, empowered and encouraged in a loving family environment.

Sexual health in the home develops through an integration of one's physical, emotional, intellectual, social and spiritual selves. Here we find the four guidelines about personal sexual health proposed by the World Health Organization to be most helpful:

☐ One's personal and social behaviors are congruent with one's gender identity and a sense of comfort with a range of sex role behavior.

☐ One has the ability to carry on effective interpersonal relationships with members of both sexes, including the potential for love and long-term commitment.

☐ One has the capacity to respond to erotic stimulation in such a way as to make sexual activity a positive, pleasurable aspect of one's experience.

☐ One has the maturity of judgment to make rewarding decisions about one's sexual behavior that do not conflict with one's overall value system and beliefs about life (Maddock 1975:52-53).

These guidelines helps us focus on the family as a context in which emotionally loving and supportive interactions help members develop a balanced and harmonious sexual self. A positive sexual identity and sexual value system give children an ability to embrace their sexual selves in ways that help them become congruent and authentic in their sexual attitudes and behaviors. Of course, children learn about the meaning of sexuality within the social context of the family as well as the wider community. The more these social contexts reflect God's ideal for sexuality, the greater the potential for authentic sexuality.

Parents can foster healthy sexuality by regarding sexuality as a vital, God-created good that draws their children into meaningful, caring relationships. In the best of all worlds, the family is the place where children gain a clear grasp of themselves as unique and separate sexual beings who are secure in a deep sense of family belonging. James Maddock defines healthy family sexuality as "the balanced expression of sexuality in the life of the family, in ways that enhance the personal identities and sexual health of individual family members and the organization of the family as a system, functioning effectively within its social and material environment" (p. 63). He goes on to describe the following characteristics of healthy family sexuality (Maddock and Larson 1995:64):

☐ "a balanced interdependence among all family members based upon respect for both genders as legitimate and valued, including their physical embodiment and ways of experiencing reality—regardless of perceived similarities and differences between males and females";

☐ "a balance between boundaries that defines individual family members and maintains suitable physical, psychological and social boundaries relevant to respective ages and stages of the life cycle while supporting appropriate gender socialization and personal erotic development";

☐ "a balanced (verbal and nonverbal) communication among family members that distinguishes between nurturing, affection and erotic contact while helping all of these to occur between appropriate persons in developmentally suitable ways";

☐ "shared sexual values, meanings and attitudes among family members, permitting a balance between shared family goals and activities, on the one hand, and individual decisions and actions, on the other"; and

☐ "balanced transactions between the family and its social and historical environments, reflected in reciprocity between family members' sexual attitudes, meanings and behaviors, those of their families of origin and those of their community."

Sexually healthy families engage in an interaction system that helps members accomplish acceptable transition to their social environment. As you will note, it may take different forms in different families, but the end result is a balanced position. Within these characteristics, there is high regard for gender variation, difference in individual development, appropriateness of boundaries to protect personal privacy, meaningful interpersonal closeness, honoring of requests for distance, and open channels of communication and negotiation. Individual and family sexual health go hand in hand. Positive patterns of interaction among family members create a network of shared meaning about sex and serve as a basis for defining behavior between members. The family is a unique unit that carries on the traditions, beliefs and values by interfacing with the larger community of which it is a part. Once again, the family has an impact on the community while being influenced by society as well.

Sexuality and Spirituality

We believe that spirituality is not just relevant but essential to working out an authentic sexuality. Some people are shocked to see "sexuality" and "spirituality" placed next to each other in a sentence, let alone to think of them as intricately related. Most of us have been taught to think of sexuality and spirituality as separate entities or exact opposites that have nothing to do with each other.

While the Bible affirms sexuality, our civilization has too often engaged in eroticism-hating sexual oppression or hedonistic, unsatiated sexual obsession. Both these extremes fail to acknowledge the personal and relational meaning at the core of sexual wholeness. A further separation between sexuality and spirituality goes back to ascetic practices. The denial of bodily pleasure was a common rule for spirituality. Sexual desires were historically considered as dangerous temptations that needed to be suppressed. Women too were suppressed since they were thought to be a primary source of sexual temptation. Early church leaders went so far as to consider sexual union as a temporary separation from the Holy Spirit. And, as little as a century ago, married people were advised not to have sex too often because intercourse was a disgusting act that led Adam and Eve astray (Hunt 1959).

Augustine is often faulted for cementing the body/soul dualism within the church. Among the erroneous beliefs that Augustine introduced into the church were that sexual intercourse was disgusting, that sexual lust and intercourse were the original sins of Adam and Eve and that the guilt and shame associated with this act passed on through inheritance (Hunt 1959:120). Prior to his conversion Augustine lived a sexually promiscuous life, and following his conversion he struggled with sexual desires and involvement, facts that help us understand why he took such a negative view toward sexuality.

According to the biblical account, sexuality is part and parcel of the creative act of God. Experientially, sexuality and spirituality may be considered analogous experiences. Sexual fulfillment is meant to be a climactic experience that takes place in a relationship between two people who totally give themselves to each other. The Christian concept of spirituality can likewise be thought of as yielding to and being filled by God's Spirit. The height of Christian spirituality is to be filled by God in such a way that one's own will has become God's will, and desire is an effortless experience of being in harmony with God's will.

Sexuality and spirituality are also analogous in that each can be approached either from a self-negating or self-affirming stance. Both of these approaches have been and still are represented within the church. What we need to understand is that each approach consists of a belief about how human wholeness is obtained and maintained. Each of these systems is capable of influencing a given type of person. The self-affirming system produces the well-integrated lover, the self-negating system produces the impotent lover, and the self-centered system produces the addicted lover (Schnarch 1997).

Due to historical factors, it may take a radical shift for many to define desire not as a sin but as a positive force that draws us to others and to God. Isn't it true that when we desire, seek and yield to God we experience our greatest transformation? John 15:5 indicates a mysterious union in which Christ abides within us and we in him to bring forth much fruit in our lives. In this sacred encounter we see ourselves in our Creator's eyes and we are changed.

Ironically, it's the lack of desire for God's grace and God's way that stagnates us. Spiritual apathy is what keeps us in a defeated and

self-negating place. Those who believe they are unworthy are likely
to be victims of life, lacking energy or passion for God, yet expecting
God to do miracles in their life. Spirituality out of emptiness is a desperate plea to fill up the hole and gaps, while spirituality out of the
fullness of God's grace leads to increased riches far beyond our
imagination. A passionate seeker of God is one who reaches out with
desire for growth as well as eagerness to cooperate with God in the
transformation. The impotent lover focuses on self-defeating faults,
wallows in self-pity and fears change.

Unless our theology affirms the goodness of desire, we will be reluctant to integrate sexuality with spirituality. Desiring, enjoying and
relating to a partner who is made in God's image affirms the sacred
meaning embedded in the sexual union. Our desire can lead us to profound places of growth, for it takes courage to open ourselves, recognize our vulnerable places and be changed as we struggle together in
our quest for wholeness.

Whether in the sexual or spiritual realm, our desire for God and others propels us to new places of ecstasy. In a spiritual sense, if people
hunger for merger with God as a way to satisfy emptiness, they have
missed the point. God has created us with the desire to be part of the
process, as we simultaneously work out our salvation while God
works within us to shape and transform our lives. Relationship
between desire and grace is a critical step, for it is when we actively
long for God to dwell within us that we have the impetus for wholeness. Desire leads to salvation and sanctification. We look for a super-
natural connection with the Holy Spirit, who empowers us to do God's
will. Sexuality is integral to spiritual wholeness and must not be dis-
paraged or glorified, but be in a balanced place as we seek wholeness.

Sexuality in Need of Redemption

How pure and uncomplicated human sexuality would be if it were not
for the entrance of sin into the world. God's good gift of sex as
described in the first two chapters of Genesis is quickly shattered by
what happens in chapter three. Sin puts a damper on things, and we
live with the consequences of the Fall. Life is no longer a perfect state
or a rosy existence; now there is turmoil and pain to contend with in
work, family and relationships between men and women.

Sexuality, a gift of God's perfect design, is now a part of our fallen nature and we must reckon with this truth. Sexuality suffers the consequences of sin, just as everything else does. There are many ways this good "gift of sex" has been perverted, distorted and warped. We all are prone to behave in ways that are contrary to God's. The Old and New Testaments describe how our fallen condition has disrupted relationships through jealousy, greed, murder, abuse, mistreatment, neglect, coveting and so on.

Mary Stewart Van Leeuwen (1984) puts it like this: "Our disturbed sexual natures are only one aspect of a disturbed and abnormal universe. Our understanding of this ought to keep us from overrating the seriousness of our sexual struggles. We should be no more surprised by the constancy and diversity of our sexual struggles than we are by our moral struggles regarding work, money, possessions, family obligations, or anything else that the Ten Commandments highlight as areas of life in special need of regulation." She continues, "None of us is going to live a risk-free morally neutral sexual existence in this culture or any other. The sooner we acknowledge this, the more likely it is that we can give support and counsel to one another in this area of our lives as in others" (p. 10).

We become acutely aware of our need for healing and redemption in our sexual attitudes, behaviors and strivings. We try to live out an authentic sexuality in the midst of a world that espouses inauthentic sexuality. Being created as sexual persons demands much more of us than an assent to a set of rules and regulations about sexual behavior and standards. It involves our very being and how we live in relationship to others. In authentic sexual interaction we are mutually responsible for building mature relationships that bring forth the best in us and each other. Each of us is responsible for our sexual attitudes, behaviors and interpersonal relationships, and when we compartmentalize rather than integrate our sexuality, we risk irresponsibility. It's not something that should be left to chance. We need to intentionally integrate our sexuality and spirituality by carefully assessing our attitudes and behaviors in terms of biblical values. It is a challenging task to achieve a level of integration that leads to mature, person-centered sexuality, but it is well worth the effort.

Restoration and Renewal

This good news is hopeful, because Christ came to earth not only to redeem us, but to restore us. The Holy Spirit is given to empower us to live out our broken life in a broken world. We are all in the process of trying to follow Christ and live the kind of person-centered sexual lives that God intended. Van Leeuwen (1984) points out that substantial healing is possible as we work toward that healing place. And, when we fall short, we are to share each other's burdens and "bear witness to our allegiance to the One whose incarnation has affirmed the worth of our bodily passions, and in whose resurrection we have the promise of all things made new" (p. 30).

God's grace keeps us reaching toward our all-knowing, loving God. Faith is a lifelong process. We must view ourselves as created in God's image and be constantly mindful of God's indwelling presence as we reach for wholeness. Recognizing we have a unique life to live that is not like any other, we must remain grounded in Christ in our particular life circumstances. We each have sexual wounds and struggles, disappointments and confusion, but God provides the light we need so we don't lose our way on that journey toward sexual authenticity. Our God is a generous guide and comfort, present with us through life's challenges.

When we can look at life with all its ups and downs, and trust God to transform us through it all, restoration brings us to new heights of wholeness. When we depend on God and are challenged to go beyond what we in ourselves are capable of doing, we experience how our sexuality leads us to a deeper spirituality. Most of us are quite content to remain in our safe and secure world rather than ask God to examine us so we can be accountable before God in this area.

In *The Mystery of Sexuality* Rosemary Haughton views sexuality as "a mystery at the heart of our familiar selves; it is ourselves as we live with other people we love" (quoted in Bender 1982:155). Through self-acceptance in Christ we find our familiar self, the self created by God to live in relationship with others. Knowing who we are in Christ, sons and daughters of God, leads to a deeper level of knowing how God's image within urges us to be rightly related to others. Therefore, spiritual desire leads to a fullness of God, and sexual desire leads to a full, meaningful life in relationship. As we struggle with the Divine about our sexual nature, we are brought to a deeper knowledge of ourselves. Likewise, the sexual relationship is an important place of self-discovery and growth. Our passion drives us to deeper, intimate encounters. When we not only know who we are but Whose we are, we meet life with a view toward growth and transformation.

We all have needs, deficits and wounds to heal, and our hope lies in the belief that our transcendent God wants to make "something new" because we are willing to die, over and over, to our old selves. We participate in the event as we obediently put on the new and take off the old so we can become more like Jesus. Substantial healing comes when we take an honest look at ourselves and ask God to correct us and give us courage to change.

Suggestions for Further Reading

Dawn, M. J. 1993. *Sexual character: Beyond technique to intimacy.* Grand Rapids, Mich.: Eerdmans.

Lewis, C. S. 1963. *The four loves.* London: Collins/Fontana.

Smedes, L. B. 1976. *Sex for Christians.* Grand Rapids, Mich.: Eerdmans.

Thatcher, A. 1993. *Liberating sex: A Christian theology.* London: SPCK.

Thatcher, A., and E. Stuart. 1996. *Christian perspectives on sexuality and gender.* Grand Rapids, Mich.: Eerdmans. See section 5, "Sexuality and spirituality," pp. 211-27.

Trible, P. 1987. *God and the rhetoric of sexuality.* Philadelphia: Fortress.

3

Toward a Theology of Authentic Sexual Relationships

How does one go about developing a theology of authentic sexuality? A common approach is to locate verses in the Bible that deal with sexuality, apply a careful exegesis to these texts, and make applications to sexual relationships. However, this method tends to focus on sexual morality rather than sexual authenticity in relationships.

In this chapter we attempt to build a theology of sexual relationships utilizing an analogical approach, within which appropriate biblical texts can be understood. We used this method to develop a theology of family relationships in our book *The Family: A Christian Perspective of the Contemporary Home* (Balswick and Balswick 1999). In the Bible familial terms are used to describe the relationship between the Creator God and we who are God's creation. The marriage analogy in the New Testament points to Jesus as groom of the church, and in the Old Testament God is pictured as parent to the children of Israel. A relational God establishes a model of human relationships in general and authentic sexual relationships in particular.

The four relationship themes—covenant, grace, empowerment and intimacy—are essential aspects of authentic sexual relationships. We propose that authentic sexual relationships must be *covenantal* rather than contractual, gracing rather than shaming, *empowering* rather than controlling and *intimate* rather than distant. In this chapter we'll specify how each of these relationship principles contributes to sexual authenticity and contrast how opposite transactions lead to inauthentic sexual relating.

Covenantal Commitment: To Love and Be Loved

The first principle is *an authentic sexual relationship is meant to be based upon an unconditional covenant commitment.* Although the concept of covenant has a rich heritage in Christian theology, its biblical meaning has often been eroded by thinking of commitment in contractual terms (McLean 1984:2). The notion of covenant includes contractual arrangements, but it involves much more. The core theme of covenant is an *unconditional commitment* that goes far beyond a simple social contract. We can best understand this deeper meaning of covenant by looking at the supreme acts of God in the Old and New Testaments. God established a covenant with Noah (Gen 6:18) and again with Abraham and his family in Genesis 17:4-9:

> I make this covenant, and I make it with you: you shall be the father of a host of nations. . . . I will fulfil my covenant between myself and you and your descendants after you, generation after generation, an everlasting covenant, to be your God, yours and your descendants' after you. . . . For your part, you must keep my covenant, you and your descendants after you, generation by generation. (NEB)

First, we see that God made a unilateral commitment. They had no choice in the matter, nor was the covenant determined by their response. That is, God was *not* saying, "I am going to commit myself to you *if* this is your desire," but God made a promise based entirely on God's sole commitment to them. God initiated and sustained the covenant as an independent action.

Second, although God desired and even commanded a response from Noah and Abraham, the covenant remained unconditional *regardless of their response.* It had nothing to do with Noah or Abraham keeping their end of the bargain. One might ask, "Was God 'free' to retract the offer if it was not reciprocated?" The answer is a resounding

No! The covenant that God gave was "an everlasting covenant," and God, being true to God's self, would faithfully carry out the promise.

Third, whereas the covenant was *not* conditional, the benefits or *blessings* of the covenant were conditional. While Noah and Abraham were completely free to receive or reject the offer, they would reap rewards from receiving what God had to offer. In other words, although the continuation of God's love was not based on their action, the blessings of the covenant were gained or lost depending on their response. The Old Testament stories show how Israel time and again failed to realize the blessing of God because they turned away rather than followed God's way. The relationship between God and the children of Israel seemed to follow a repetitive cycle of God reaching out, Israel choosing to go its own way and yet God continuing to pursue, forgive and attempt to restore the relationship.

In the book of Hosea this relationship between God and Israel is actually presented in terms of a sexual relationship. Israel is alternatively referred to as a "faithful lover" or as the "adulterer" who prostitutes herself by whoring after other lovers (gods). In fact, the breaking of the covenant is understood in terms of a similar sexual metaphor in Deuteronomy 31:16: "And the LORD said to Moses: 'You are going to rest with your fathers, and these people will soon prostitute themselves to the foreign gods of the land they are entering. They will forsake me and break the covenant I made with them.'"

Israel is frequently warned *not* to go whoring after other gods (Ex 34:15–16; Lev 17:7; 20:5; Num 15:39; 1 Chron 5:25; 2 Chron 21:13). The book of Judges records how Israel "did not listen even to their judges; for they lusted after other gods and bowed down to them" (2:17 NRSV); and "As soon as Gideon died, the Israelites relapsed and prostituted themselves with the Baals, making Baal-berith their god" (8:33 NRSV). The psalmist refers to Israel's behavior in similar terms, "They defiled themselves by what they did; by their deeds they prostituted themselves" (Ps 106:39).

The prophet Ezekiel expressed God's sorrow at Israel's behavior, "I have been grieved by their adulterous hearts, which have turned away from me, and by their eyes, which have lusted after their idols" (6:9). Note the strong sexual language in the prophetic warning in Ezekiel 23:29–30, "They will leave you naked and bare, and the shame of your prostitution will be exposed. Your lewdness and promiscuity have brought this upon you, because you lusted after the nations and defiled yourself with their idols."

Faithfulness and *unfaithfulness* are concepts throughout the Scriptures used to describe covenant or the lack of covenant commitment. The pattern of Israel's unfaithfulness and God's continual response to restore the relationship is clearly seen throughout the book of Hosea: "Go, take to yourself an adulterous wife and children of unfaithfulness, because the land is guilty of the vilest adultery in departing from the LORD. . . . I will betroth you to me forever; I will betroth you in righteousness and justice, in love and compassion. I will betroth you in faithfulness, and you will acknowledge the LORD" (1:2; 2:19-20).

Embedded throughout the entire Bible are examples of God moving toward the created ones with extended arms. Ultimately, God's faithful commitment is seen in the incarnation event and the sacrifice of Christ on the cross at Gethsemane. In this final act of love, God's Only Begotten Son gave himself for all who would believe. Although God stretches out in every way to pursue with enticing covenant love, humans have the freedom to respond to or reject that love. God never overtakes in the pursuit, but faithfully beckons the created ones to respond to the life-changing love of Jesus.

In the New Testament the marital analogy symbolizes the relationship between Christ and the church. When John the Baptist explains that he is not the Christ but sent to proclaim the one who is, he says, "The bride belongs to the bridegroom. The friend who attends the bridegroom waits and listens for him, and is full of joy when he hears the bridegroom's voice" (Jn 3:29). Also, in response to queries about why Jesus and his disciples did not fast, Jesus answered, "How can the guests of the bridegroom mourn while he is with them? The time will come when the bridegroom will be taken from them; then they will fast" (Mt 9:15).

The nature of the conjugal relationship between Christ and the church is recorded in Ephesians 5:25-27, "Christ loved the church and gave himself up for her to make her holy, cleansing her by the washing with water through the word, and to present her to himself as a radiant church, without stain or wrinkle or any other blemish, but holy and blameless." Revelation 21:2 refers to the church in its perfect condition

"coming down out of heaven from God, prepared as a bride beautifully dressed for her husband." The obvious symbolism is the anticipated union between the bride and groom.

Do you grasp the picture of God in covenant relationship? God reaching out with an everlasting commitment of love and loyalty is a model
for authentic human relationships. The marriage union is rightfully held
up as a reciprocal (two-way) unconditional covenant commitment. One
of the deepest desires in life is to love and be loved unconditionally, and
in the context of a committed, trustworthy relationship a couple has the
richest possibility of achieving this. In fact, covenant commitment provides the security and safety in which people can see themselves as wor-
thy of love in ways that move them to intimate connection. Faithful
nurture, protection and affirmation of a sexual partner are basic to deepening covenant commitment. Out of this sanctity of marriage comes a
capacity to make covenant commitment to others.

People who lack a trustworthy environment will have a difficult
time believing they deserve to be loved or that they have a capacity to
love. In fact, they may be starved for love out of deprivation and yet
actually not be able to receive affection due to mistrust. Some have
learned that the best way to survive is to defend against further disappointment by remaining distant and removed. While they may engage
in sexual behaviors or even be promiscuous, they are extremely careful
not to give their hearts away. There is little joy or emotional depth in a
sexual relationship that is devoid of covenantal love.

One major boundary given in the Scriptures concerning sexual
intercourse is abstinence prior to marriage. Some may wonder why
this is such a sacred boundary and ask questions about why a person
should wait for marriage to express this ultimate "one-flesh" union.
We believe that the primary reason has to do with the quality of the
marital relationship. The demands of lifelong relationship take an
intentional mutual covenant between two people who are supported
by a loving community. A solid commitment keeps spouses from leaving prematurely when the going gets rough. The personal promise to
stand firm in one's commitment to the spouse and relationship—no
matter what the circumstances—creates a strong bond of shared
meaning and trust. This kind of covenant supports the marriage bond,
sustains the relationship and promotes deeper sexual fulfillment. Cov-

enant commitment safeguards love's highest qualities by establishing a secure trust that energizes a couple to invest themselves in it for the long haul. Covenant love provides a resilience that sustains a couple through the inevitable stresses of life. Even after a covenant has been made, however, spouses will continue to fail each other and are in constant need of grace.

Grace: To Forgive and Be Forgiven

The second principle is *offering grace rather than placing blame or shame leads to healing and renewal in sexual covenant relationships.* By its very nature, covenant *is* grace. From a human perspective the unconditional love of God makes no sense unless experienced through grace. Grace is a relational word because the goal is to restore connection when there has been a breach between people due to human failure or sin. It is the promise of grace that holds out hope for reconciliation and renewed relationship.

Relationships lived out in an atmosphere of grace bring life and acceptance, whereas a critical, perfectionist environment suffocates and constrains the relationship. The grace dimension is clearly evident in the relationship between God and Israel. God is painfully aware of Israel's rejection in Hosea 2:13: "'She decked herself with rings and jewelry, and went after her lovers, but me she forgot,' declares the LORD." Then, in the very next verse, we hear God's compassionate response, "Therefore I am now going to allure her; I will lead her into the desert and speak tenderly to her. There I will give her back her vineyards." Grace culminates with a reaffirmation of God's unconditional commitment: "I will betroth you to me forever; I will betroth you in righteousness and justice, in love and compassion. I will betroth you in faithfulness, and you will acknowledge the LORD" (2:19-20).

Hosea's marriage paralleled God's relationship with Israel. Gomer, an unfaithful wife, sought out other relationships, yet God asked Hosea to continue to pursue her, to give her his love, his home, his name and even his reputation. Although Gomer continued in unfaithful living, the LORD told Hosea, "Go, show your love to your wife again, though she is loved by another and is an adulteress. Love her as the LORD loves the Israelites, though they turn to other gods and love the sacred raisin cakes" (3:1). Hosea entreats Gomer with acceptance and accountability, "You are to live with me many days; you must not be a prostitute or be intimate with any man, and I will live with you" (3:3). This relationship is a symbolic message that conveys God's action with Israel. The Lord not only loved his covenant people but would take them back. Going astray certainly had its negative consequences, but the Lord's compassion and faithful love continued to show forth in forgiveness and mercy.

Not all relationship difficulties stem from a failure as disconcerting as adultery. Sexual interaction can be less than ideal or disappointing in a number of ways. When failure occurs, the temptation is to blame the partner by pointing out their inadequacies. The shaming/blaming becomes a one-up/one-down mental game, and the injured person can in turn injure through an unforgiving and righteous attitude.

To fully understand the destructive consequences of shame in sexual relationships, it is necessary to distinguish between shame and guilt. Most of us will agree that guilt is a natural human response that occurs when a person does something wrong. Guilt urges one to acknowledge mistakes in order to correct the wrongful behavior. Shame, on the other hand, relays the message that one has not just done something wrong, but, deep inside, the person is bad and can never measure up. Believing one is bad to the core leads to a defeatist position since there is no way to ever right the wrong.

Shaming messages are often given about sexuality. Strict religious values based on perfectionistic and unrealistic standards will inevitably leave one feeling unacceptable and unredeemable as a sexual person. Since one can never measure up or be forgiven, the person either strives harder to be perfect or stops trying at all! Since one is defined as bad and obviously unable to meet the standards, why try to fight the inevitable? This deafening, self-defeating message leads to a continuous cycle of shame.

Most people enter adulthood with certain degrees of sexual shame. A damaging aspect of shaming sexual messages is their potential to undermine one's sexual self-worth. If a person has been profoundly shamed in this area of life, it may be more difficult to develop an authentic sexual self.

Acceptance of oneself as a sexual person is basic to authentic sexuality. Recognition and affirmation of one's unique sexual embodiment must be regarded with deepest respect. Acceptance comes through embracing one's gender and one's sexuality. Sexual vitality is inhibited when shaming, degrading messages are inflicted by self or by others. Rejection of one's sexual self is a form of denial that can leave a deeply felt schism in oneself. Jesus accepts us just as we are as sexual persons, declared by God as good.

It would be inaccurate to think of grace as wishy-washy. Grace rightly expressed is consistent, strong and demanding. Anyone who confesses and honestly seeks forgiveness will find healing and restoration. Grace does not tolerate dehumanizing sexual messages or behaviors but challenges anyone who tries to undermine what God has determined as good. Grace rightly expressed leads to personal empowerment.

Empowering: To Serve and Be Served

The third principle is that *a sexual relationship is one in which personal resources and gifts are used to affirm the other rather than control.*

Covenant is the vow to love, grace is the ability to forgive, and empowerment is the action of using power to affirm and strengthen others. Jesus Christ modeled empowerment. The celebrated message of Jesus was that he had come to empower: "I have come that they may have life, and have it to the full" (Jn 10:10). The apostle John puts it this way: "But to all who received him, who believed in his name, he gave power to become children of God, who were born, not of blood or of the will of the flesh or of the will of man, but of God" (Jn 1:12-13 NRSV).

The power given by Jesus is power of the personal order, power to build up the powerless. In our sinful and powerless condition, God gives us the power to become children of God. The supreme example of empowerment is seen in Jesus, who gave his life for others and chose to serve rather than be served. Jesus redefined the understanding of power through his teaching and actions to put the best interest of others at the forefront. What Jesus taught about power was so central to his mission that it serves as an ideal for all human relationships. In Mark 10:43-45 Jesus says, "Whoever wants to become great among you must be your servant, and whoever wants to be first must be slave of all. For even the Son of Man did not come to be served, but to serve, and to give his life as a ransom for many." Jesus rejects the use of power to control others, and affirms the use of power to serve others, to lift up the fallen, to forgive, to encourage responsibility and maturity.

A common definition of power is simply the ability to influence another person. Using power in a healthy manner is not yielding to the wishes of another person or giving up power in a relationship but an active, intentional process of building up resources and strengths in one's partner. The individuals who are empowered have gained power because someone believes in them and sees their potential. In a very real sense, sexual empowerment is "love in action." Power is a major component of the sexual relationship. When one person attempts to manipulate or coerce another in sexual matters, it is a violation of power. Those who feel powerless in relationships may use sex as a way to gain power in the relationship.

Inauthentic sexual behaviors are organized around using power to *control*. For example, note how the popular male image of the playboy lends itself to control and disempowerment of the female. As epitomized in *Playboy* magazine, the playboy is depicted as a shrewd, resourceful man who remains emotionally detached when interacting with a woman. He remains in control by "playing it cool" and being independent. In a nonfeeling mode of operation, he treats the woman as a commodity to be enjoyed. By reducing her to a nonperson whom he can control and handle, she becomes a playboy accessory. In fact, she becomes a "playmate" who, in our disposable-oriented society, can conveniently be discarded when playtime is over. He manipulatively tells her what she wants to hear, but they are empty words uttered as a means to his own selfish end.

The "playboy philosophy" gives advice to insecure males in our society about how to conquer a woman. Males who are terrified of interacting with a real live female are told what clothes to buy, what music to play on the stereo, which drinks to serve, when to turn the lights down and how to talk seductively. In short, these are instructions about power, that is, how to get the woman to bed, have sex with her and then be rid of her. In fact, a successful "love affair" is one in which the bed is shared, but the playboy emerges free from any personal involvement. The playboy really does not care about the woman, only about the sex she can provide. Everything is done to control the outcome of the sexual encounter for his own pleasure. If the playboy were to lose his heart to the woman, this would be considered a huge mistake.

Some males may exert power over females by considering them as a possession. Since power in our culture is seen as strength, violence is often tolerated. Using brute force or abusive put-downs to get one's way is common. Usually persons who resort to such offensive behavior actually lack self-esteem. Control over someone who is physically or emotionally weaker gives a false impression of being in a "one-up" position, but in actuality it points out a serious weakness. Some partners learn to accept such coercive actions in a relationship out of dependency needs or low self-esteem. Often boundaries are nonexistent, and there is little if any regard for individual rights or personal choice.

When mutual empowerment reigns supreme, however, maleness and femaleness are affirmed, and sexual potential is enhanced! Mutual affirmation of physical and emotional pleasure enhances one's authentic sexuality. Each partner respects and maintains suitable physical, psychological and social boundaries in the relationship. These boundaries define individual space and personal sexual development. Partners are responsible for their sexual behavior in relating to each other.

Personal empowerment means that sexual decisions are congruent with one's value system and moral beliefs. Shared sexual values, meanings, attitudes, beliefs and goals give the relationship a solid interdependency. Individual expression is welcomed, and one is accountable to others for choices made in the sexual relationship.

Affirming self and others as unique sexual persons who are in the process of becoming authentic sexual beings is empowering. Dependency issues between people are addressed so that interdependence becomes the goal. There is no need to coerce, control or manipulate the other when expressing one's own needs and desires. Neither is it necessary to place oneself in a superior position over the other, since regarding the other's needs and desires on par with one's own means there is respect and desire for mutual giving. When uniqueness is verified in the context of the relationship, it is possible to be self-assured and competent as a sexual person. The empowering event is a reciprocal process in which each person is able to become more of who God intends them to be, and the relationship is built up as a mutually fulfilling union.

God's resources are inexhaustible! The fruit of the Spirit is offered to all believers. God gives strength and power to interact in extraordinary ways. Two persons sufficiently differentiated will build each other up in their masculinity and femininity. Out of covenant security, gracing acceptance and mutual-empowerment intimacy blossoms.

Intimacy: To Know and Be Known

The fourth principle is *a sexual relationship is meant to deepen one's experience of knowing and being known.* One of the incredible truths of Scripture is that God knows us intricately and desires that we know him more deeply. We are encouraged to share our deepest thoughts and feelings with God in prayer as the Holy Spirit speaks through groanings that are too deep for words (Rom 8:26-27).

In the Garden of Eden, Adam and Eve were naked but felt no shame (Gen 2:25). In this perfect place they stood before each other and before God, completely open and transparent. Nakedness in this passage must be understood as more than physical. Exposed in every way, they faced each other in their vulnerability and felt absolutely no shame in each other's presence. In this heavenly environment, there was no need to hide or cover up; there was no desire to keep secrets, pretend or put on airs to impress each other; there was no reason to play deceptive games or control the other. They were authentic in their identity, in their sexuality, in their relationship.

Genesis 1:27 speaks of differentiation in their male and female embodiment. A man knows his manhood as distinct and in relationship to woman just as the woman knows her womanhood as distinct and in relationship to man. It is a complementary, intimate process of becoming known. Differentiation is what frees them to leave home and stand on their own. Thus they open themselves wholeheartedly to the other to come to know themselves more deeply through a full expression of that self in relationship. In *Constructing the Sexual Crucible* David Schnarch (1991) proposes that a person's capacity for sexual intimacy is directly related to that person's degree of differentiation. Schnarch defines differentiation as "the process by which a person manages individuality and togetherness in a relationship" (p. 198).

Genesis 2:24 states, "For this reason a man will leave his father and mother and be united to his wife, and they will become one flesh." The action verb *become* refers to a sexual knowing, but intimacy also entails an emotional and intellectual knowing. It seems that differentiation is predicated on one's ability to leave (father and mother) before he or she can cleave rightly. Modern systems theorists describe this as *developmental differentiation*. In fact, one of the factors that contribute to a strong relationship bond is the establishment of a sufficient self.

Murry Bowen emphasizes the need for an individual to be *emotionally* differentiated from parents in order to maintain a healthy balance of individuality (separateness) and togetherness (connectedness) in subsequent relationships (Bowen 1978, Kerr and Bowen 1988). More recent writings have emphasized the need for a strong "differentiation of self" before one is ready to enter a relationship as emotionally demanding as marriage. David Schnarch concludes, "Differentiation permits a person to function individually and yet be emotionally involved with others, and to do both simultaneously at profound depth. Differentiation of self is a critical task that ideally precedes adult attempts at intimacy, for it is differentiation that permits one to be intimate rather than 'closed' or fused" (p. 198). He believes that the degree of sexual intimacy is directly related to the intimacy possible in a relationship. Where differentiation is low, sexual intimacy is also low due to fears of being engulfed, entrapped, exploited or abandoned. Satisfying sexual encounters are based on two strong individuals who are full, not empty, so they are secure enough to give and receive in mutually *interdependent* ways.

The capacity for differentiation is often lacking in immature persons who mistakenly believe that mutual dependency or fusion is what makes a relationship strong. Yet, just the opposite is true, for leaning heavily on each other or family support, rather than establishing a mutual interdependency between two strong selves, only weakens the union. Erik Erikson acknowledges that adolescence is a time when persons work out identity and intimacy skills. Identity must be established during adolescence so one can successfully move into intimate connection at the young adult stage. The high rate of failure in teenage marriage (eight out of ten end in divorce) may point to insufficient development in identity and intimacy tasks. However, "collective" cultures, which give primary loyalty to the group, do not hold individuation at such high value. Therefore the concept of differentiation must be understood within a particular culture's framework.

Sexuality and intimacy are intricately connected. Becoming "one flesh" involves knowing and being known in the act of intercourse as well as in the act of melding two lives together through a growing covenant commitment. It takes a mutual giving and receiving of oneself in reciprocal vulnerability to discover the fullness of intimacy.

A crucial ingredient for becoming intimate in a sexual relationship is communication. Humans are unique among living creatures in their ability to communicate elaborately with each other through language, a capacity that makes it possible for humans to know each other intimately. The "bone of my bones and flesh of my flesh" (Gen 2:23) response between Adam and Eve was possible because they could communicate thoughts, feelings, desires and wants in a way that was not possible with any other living creature.

Honest communication is the key to authentic sexual transactions. Each partner must freely express and discuss sexual feelings, desires and struggles without feeling shame. Freedom and spontaneity come with being comfortable with one's body and having the ability to respond to touch, nurturance, affection and erotic expression.

Emotional distancing in relationship most likely occurs due to a fear of intimacy. Sex becomes a vehicle for meeting one's sexual needs, but fails to grasp emotional knowing and being known. The superficial sexual connection leaves one feeling isolated, restless and lonely. With nowhere to turn for interaction and communion at a personal level, some may turn to addictions to numb the pain or offer symptom relief. This does not solve but simply perpetuates the problem. The name of the cover-up game is keeping secrets; denial becomes a vicious cycle leading further and further away from the emotional connection that could make a difference.

Adam and Eve responded with blame, shame and fear after distancing from God. "Then the eyes of both of them were opened, and they realized they were naked; so they sewed fig leaves together and made coverings for themselves. Then the man and his wife heard the sound of the LORD God as he was walking in the garden in the cool of the day, and they hid from the LORD God among the trees of the garden" (Gen 3:7-8). It was only after their disobedience that Adam and Eve tried to hide from God because they felt their nakedness and shame. Shame is always a barrier to open communication. Persons who feel unworthy of being known try to hide themselves rather than disclose themselves.

Only when sex is woven into a wider fabric of communication between two differentiated lovers can it bring them to the deepest places of knowing. The vulnerability that comes from being open, honest and self-reflective helps the couple find more of themselves in the context of their union. Sex in and of itself cannot get one to this deeper level of intimacy. However, sexual intimacy that is based on emotional intimacy carries the relationship to new levels of growth and passion.

Emotionally satisfying sex is best when there is committed love. The capacity for partners to freely and openly express sexual love for each other is contingent upon their mutual trust and responsible actions of faithfulness. John gives us insight into this in 1 John 4:18: "There is no fear in love. But perfect love drives out fear." God expresses perfect love so we can respond to that love without fear, shame or hiding. This brings us back to the first of our principles: an unconditional love commitment, the cornerstone for God's ideal in sexual relationships.

Summary

We have suggested that a theology of sexual relationships involves four sequential but nonlinear principles: *covenant commitment, gracing, empowering* and *intimacy.* We depict these principles in figure 3.1 as spiraling inward because they deepen authenticity in sexual relationships. Note that an authentic sexual relationship does not emerge fully developed but is a process of two people intentionally moving into deeper levels in these relationship dimensions.

Growth in a sexual relationship can be blocked or retarded at any point when a person is unable or unwilling to follow the biblical relationship principles. We might think of the spiral as a clock spring that unwinds in a counterclockwise direction toward deteriorating levels of couple functioning. The relationship stagnates because one or both partners are unable to risk what it takes to move in the direction of growth, especially if the couple seeks out a "tit for tat" arrangement that says, "I'll share if you share," "I'll forgive if you forgive," "I'll make a commitment as long as you make one first," or "I'll empower you when you empower me. "

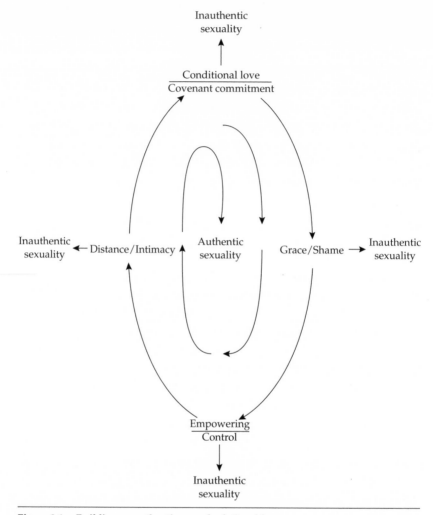

Figure 3.1. Building an authentic sexual relationship

A standoff like this may occur at any point or time in the cycle due to broken trust, disappointments, hurt or angry feelings, misunderstanding or a number of things that prevent a forward movement. Pain in one's past may hinder that person's capacity to trust or love unconditionally. It may be that well-kept secrets or shameful behaviors are hindering relationship growth. Insecurity may lead a partner to control the other, or lack of self-esteem may prompt manipulative behaviors.

Or a man may not know how to be intimate due to social conditioning that cautions men to keep their emotions to themselves to prove they are strong. Most of us constantly struggle with our human tendencies to be conditional in our love, to shame or blame those who fail or disappoint us, to use our resources and power to control or manipulate others and to disengage or distance ourselves rather than risk personal vulnerability. There is a myriad of reasons why things go wrong in relationships; this is why it takes courage to step out, take risks and seek biblical ways of being. It's not a matter of changing the other person, but being changed by the power of the Holy Spirit so one acts out of the fullness of being differentiated in Christ rather than out of a self-centered emptiness.

The vitality of a sexual relationship is dynamic. Thus, we believe that as either partner moves in the direction of commitment, grace, empowering and intimacy—refusing to become sidetracked by contracting, shaming, controlling or distancing—there is great potential for sexual authenticity. May we be strengthened by God's Holy Spirit to move in God's direction of authentic relationship.

Suggestions for Further Reading

Balswick, J., and J. Balswick. 1999. *The family: A Christian perspective on the contemporary home.* Grand Rapids, Mich.: Baker.

Grenz, S. 1997. *Sexual ethics: An evangelical perspective.* Louisville, Ky.: Westminster John Knox.

Jewett, P. K. 1976. *Man as male and female.* Grand Rapids, Mich.: Eerdmans.

Schnarch, D. 1991. *Constructing the sexual crucible.* New York: W. W. Norton.

4

Homosexuality

The Complexity of Explanations

Being attracted to persons (same or opposite gender) who share similar ideas, feelings, vision and passion for life is one of the great blessings of being authentically human. Most certainly, we experience expressions of love with same-sex persons (siblings, parents and friends) at deep levels of caring. In fact, the love between same-gendered persons is often considered a "pure form of love" because it is not complicated by romantic or erotic overtones. It is "soul-mate" friends who bring out the truth of who we are by opening us up to express our honest thoughts and secret emotions. For the majority of people, these same-sex relationships do not include an erotic dimension. The purpose of this chapter is to examine same-sex erotic attraction. Before doing this, however, we will point out the four critical criteria that determine one's sexuality.

Dimensions of Sexuality
In chapter one we suggested natal sex, sexual identity, gender role and sexual orientation are criteria that might be used to understand the complexity of sexual development. While sexual orientation is best

understood as only one of these four dimensions of sexuality, it is conventionally used as the reference point in any discussion of homosexuality. The four types of sexual orientation are heterosexual, homosexual, bisexual and transgender. The first three describe individuals who have erotic attraction for the opposite sex, the same sex and both sexes; while *transgender* is an umbrella term used to describe individuals who cross or transcend culturally defined categories of sex and gender. Following are six categories of transgender orientations:

☐ A transsexual desires or has undergone hormone therapy and/or sex reassignment surgery to resolve an extreme conflict between gender identity (basic conviction of being male or female) and sex assignment at birth (natal sex based on male or female anatomy).

☐ A transvestite likes to wear clothing associated with another sex, for a variety of reasons. Sometimes referred to as cross-dressers, these persons are not dissatisfied with, nor do they have a desire to change, their natal gender, sexual identity or sexual orientation, but like to occasionally present themselves as the opposite gender. Some transvestites may be sexually ambiguous in sexual identity or sexual orientation.

☐ A transgenderist lives in the gender role associated with another sex without going through sex change surgery.

☐ A bigendered person identifies as both male and female and has attraction to both.

☐ A drag queen/king is a gay or lesbian who "does drag" by dressing up in women's/men's clothes for exhibitionistic reasons.

☐ A female/male impersonator mimics the opposite gender for entertainment purposes.

These descriptions indicate how difficult it is for some individuals to be aligned on all four dimensions. It is not a clear-cut process for them, but may take years of struggle to finally find a satisfying and congruent sexual authenticity.

At this point we will focus more specifically on homosexuality. We begin with a historical perspective, provide a definition of homosexuality and summarize various theories that attempt to explain the causes of homosexuality. We conclude this chapter with an integrative model that includes an interactive process of bio-psycho-social and human agency.

Historical Perspective on Homosexuality

Erotic sexual activity between same-sex persons has occurred throughout recorded history. According to Scanzoni and Mollenkott (1978) the
following well-known people may have had a lifelong homosexual orientation: Erasmus (1466-1536), a scholar and editor of the Greek New
Testament; Leonardo da Vinci (1452-1519), the artist who gifted the
world with the moving portrait of Christ in *The Last Supper;* James I of
England (1566-1625), who commissioned the translation of the Bible
that bears his name; Michelangelo (1475-1564), the creator of the beautiful sculpture *The Pieta* as well as the magnificent frescoes on the ceil-
ing of the Sistine Chapel; Sir Francis Bacon (1561-1626), an outstanding
essayist and scientific theorist; Mary II (1689-1694), Queen of England,
Scotland and Ireland; Walt Whitman (1819-1892), the famous American
poet; Peter Ilyich Tchaikovsky (1840-1893), the great composer; and
Henry James (1843-1916), an outstanding American novelist (pp. 32-
37). This list, which is by no means exhaustive, is a reminder that persons with homosexual orientation (known and unknown) can and do
live productive lives and contribute in significant ways to our world.

The response to homosexuality throughout the ages has ranged
from outright condemnation and punishment to tolerance, acceptance
and even celebration. The obvious stigmas and sweeping stereotypes
attached to homosexuality have created fear, social distance and contempt between homosexuals and heterosexuals. Not until the 1800s
was a distinction made between homosexual orientation (an attraction
to the same sex) and homosexual behavior (engaging in sex practices
with someone of the same sex). Before that time, homosexuality, along
with all forms of mental illness, was categorized as a sin or heresy.
However, beginning in the twentieth century, this view was replaced
by the medical model, in which mental disturbance, and homosexuality in particular, was considered a sickness or mental illness. Homosexuality was included in the *Diagnostic and Statistical Manual of Mental
Illness* (DSM) as a sexual deviance. During the 1970s homosexual
groups began to contest this view. The debate continued for approximately a decade. Later, embarrassed by the lack of a secure scientific
explanation, the American Psychiatric Association stopped identifying
homosexuality as a mental disorder, removing it from the DSM. The
current manual, DSM-IV, retains dystonic homosexuality as a cate-

gory only for those who are in conflict about their sexual orientation and desire to change. By the 1980s the majority of health care professionals started viewing homosexual orientation as a fact of life rather than a problem to treat. Homosexual orientation and behavior became an acceptable lifestyle rather than a shameful pathology. The homosexual community saw this as an important political victory. No longer was homosexuality diagnosed as a congenital anomaly, a major neurosis, a sexual perversion or a moral deviation. In fact, many therapists now question the appropriateness of putting a homosexual under the psychological duress of working toward change. Compassion was felt for many who had tried everything they knew to change, but were unable to solidify a change over time. This led to a renewed interest in understanding the complex factors that contribute to a homosexual orientation.

Homosexuality Defined

Arriving at a clear definition of homosexuality is a bit tricky, since homosexuality can be described as an orientation and as a behavior. For instance, those with a homosexual orientation may be erotically attracted to persons of the same sex, but never act on that attraction. On the other hand, some persons define themselves as heterosexual in orientation but at times choose to express sexual eroticism through homosexual encounters. Also, some people define themselves as bisexual, meaning they are equally attracted to and can be erotically engaged with persons of either the same or the opposite sex. Situational homosexuality is a common occurrence for heterosexuals under certain circumstances when opportunities for heterosexual contact are not possible. For example, there is a high incidence of homosexual behavior reported by inmates in prison.

As you can see, even defining homosexuality becomes a complicated task. We cannot automatically assume that all persons with homosexual orientation are exclusively attracted to or engage in sexual behavior with the same sex. Nor can we consider persons of predominantly heterosexual orientation to be exclusively sexually involved with the opposite sex. For this reason, sexual attraction is sometimes described along a continuum ranging from exclusively heterosexual at one extreme, attraction to either sex (bisexuality) in the middle and exclusively homosexual at the other extreme. And there are all kinds of combinations in between. Some will never be attracted to or involved with same-sex persons, and others will never feel the slightest attraction to or engage in sexual behaviors with the opposite sex. Those in between may feel attraction to either gender without ever engaging in sexual behaviors, while others may engage in sexual behaviors with both but have a strong preference for heterosexual or homosexual involvement.

The ten percent solution. You can begin to understand why it is difficult to estimate the exact number of homosexuals in the population. Alfred Kinsey (1948, 1952) estimated that approximately 10 percent of the American population was homosexual. However, this figure has been questioned in *Kinsey, Sex and Fraud: The Indoctrination of a People* (Reisman et al. 1990). The authors claim that Kinsey's findings were skewed due to a sample that included a disproportionate number of subjects from a prison population, thus inflating the percentage.

A host of studies have suggested a much lower rate of those who report homosexual orientation or expression in the general population. Hirschfield, as early as 1920, and Ellis, in 1936, reported the rate of homosexuality to be just under 2 percent. In 1943 the Army noted that only 1 percent of servicemen had a homosexual orientation. Of course, this figure may be low due to the ramifications of admitting the truth in light of the Armed Service stance on homosexuality. Revealing such information could lead to dismissal.

Among the most representative current public opinion polls are surveys conducted by the National Opinion Research Council. Based upon these surveys taken between 1970 and 1990, Rogers and Turner (1991) found that 5 to 7 percent of adult males reported "some" homosexual contact, but only 1 to 2 percent of these men said they had been active during the preceding year. In a study of 34,706 adolescents Remafedi et al. (1992) found that 1 percent of all adolescents and 2.8 percent of 18-year-olds had experienced "some" homosexual contact. However, adolescent sex experimentation is common and often includes same-sex contact. Finally, a survey of 3,321 American men ages 20 to 29 (Billy et al. 1993) found that 2.3 percent of their sample reported some homosexual activity over the previous ten years, while 1.1 percent were exclusively homosexual over those past ten years.

The University of Chicago study (Laumann et al.) conducted in 1994 and reported in *The Social Organization of Sexuality* is the most recent comprehensive study on human sexual behavior. Based on a random sample of nearly 3,500 Americans ages 18-59, this study found that 2.7 percent of men and 1.3 percent of women reported having engaged in homosexual sex in the past year. It should be noted that these studies refer to homosexual behavior and not homosexual orientation. Undoubtedly there are persons who may have homosexual attractions (orientation) but choose not to act on them. Therefore, it is likely that the percentage with a homosexual orientation is somewhat higher.

The available research in other countries estimates that the rate of homosexuality is approximately 2-5 percent. In a survey of 480 British males, Forman and Chilvers (1989) found that 1.7 percent of their subjects had "some" homosexual contact and less than 1 percent engaged in exclusive homosexual contact. In a random sample of 18,876 men in the United Kingdom, Johnson et al. (1989) found that 6.1 percent reported "some" homosexual contact and 1.1 percent had been sexually active with more than one same-sex partner in the preceding year. (A paper presented by Court and Whitehead at the 23rd International Congress of Applied Psychology in 1997 indicated that similar results were reported in forthcoming studies conducted in Canada, Norway and Denmark.)

Explaining Homosexuality

Explanations about homosexuality come from two basic perspectives: one that focuses on psychosocial factors (nurture) and another that focuses on biological factors (nature). Psychosocial explanations of homosexuality can be further divided into social learning theories and neopsychoanalytic theories.

Social learning theories. There are several social learning theory explanations of homosexuality that have common themes. One theory points to a lack of adequate heterosexual experiences during childhood as a cause; it explains homosexuality as a deprivation of adequate heterosexual experiences. According to this view, a young person never learns how to adequately relate to persons of the opposite sex and therefore channels his or her efforts toward the same sex. A second explanation is an inverted version of this theory. Here it is presumed that homosexuality results from negative experiences one has with members of the opposite sex. In this case, the young person does relate to opposite-sex persons, but experiences a series of negative responses in the process. Therefore erotic attraction for persons of the opposite sex is repressed and they turn to more satisfying experiences with same-sex persons.

A third explanation has to do with early experiences and contact with homosexuals. Proponents of this theory argue that early sexual contact with a homosexual serves to reframe a young person's sexual orientation. One study reports that although homosexual males were more likely to experience homosexual sex prior to their first heterosexual sex, or homosexual sex only, lesbians were more likely to report heterosexual sex prior to their first homosexual sex (Cook, Boxer and Herdt 1989). In addition, most adult males, heterosexual and homosexual, report a homosexual encounter during childhood or adolescence. This explanation therefore seems less than complete.

A fourth theory looks at homosexuality with a developmental lens in terms of the rate of sexual maturation in adolescents (Storms 1981). Up until about age twelve, both boys and girls are in what is termed a homosocial stage, in which they associate quite exclusively with persons of their own sex. Following puberty, each gender becomes much more interested in the opposite sex. The sex drive of most young people emerges *after* they have left their homosocial stage for the heterosocial stage of adolescence. But for some youth, the sex drive emerges earlier. The explanation proposes that when the sex drive emerges while a youth is still in the homosocial stage (twelve and younger), the youth is more likely to develop a homosexual orientation. Proponents of this view explain that there are more male than female homosexuals precisely because the sex drive among males emerges earlier on the average. Thus, there is a greater pool of boys than girls who begin to experience their sex drive during a time when the vast majority of their social relationships are with persons of the same sex.

One can easily recognize the social learning aspect of these various explanations and, while they seem to make sense, the evidence to support these theories is far from conclusive.

Neopsychoanalytic theory. The most popular explanation of homosexuality, psychoanalytic theory, came in the first half of the twentieth century. According to this theory, the origin of same-sex preference is an aberrant psychosexual development that occurs during the genital stage of development at ages four to six. This is an age when children work through the Oedipus or Electra complexes, in which they have an unconscious desire to defeat their same-sex parent in order to gain exclusive access to their opposite-sex parent. Ironically, if the opposite-sex parent encourages this kind of singular attachment, coupled with a cool and distant relationship with the same-sex parent, the child becomes confused about his or her own sexual identity and later on has a deep craving for connection with a person of the same sex.

A major effort to test a psychoanalytic theory of homosexuality was conducted by Irving Bieber (1962, 1976). He compared the family patterns of 106 male homosexuals and 100 male heterosexuals who were receiving psychoanalysis. The study found that homosexuals, more than heterosexuals, tended to have a dominant, overprotective and overly close mother along with a weak or passive father. Charlotte Wolff (1971) reported similar conclusions in a study of over 100 nonpatient lesbians and a matched group of heterosexual women. Wolff's major findings show that homosexual more than heterosexual women were reared in families where the mother was rejecting or indifferent and the father was distant or absent. Wolff concluded that, in seeking love from other women, lesbians are really seeking the love they failed to get from their mother. She also theorized that lesbians have difficulty relating to men because they were deprived of a warm, loving relationship with their father.

Several psychologists have offered a revised version of classical Freudian explanations of homosexuality. Two influential writers, Elizabeth Moberly (1983a, 1983b) and Leanne Payne (1984), believe that homosexuality is based on certain deficiencies in the parent/child relationship. The primary cause of homosexuality emerges out of deficits in a child's relationship with his or her parent of the same sex. Parents are normal sources of love to their children, so when love is withheld and replaced with hostility and anger, the same-gender child/parent relationship is gravely disturbed. In such situations, children cannot relate to their same-gender parent, resulting in intrapsychic damage at the deepest level. Moberly is careful to point out that the disruption is not merely due to father absence (which she believes rarely results in such severe woundedness) but an *active destructive* relationship with the same-sex parent who is present in the home.

The damage caused by such disruption is referred to as *defensive detachment*. Defensive detachment emerges in the form of authority problems between parent and child, along with parent resistance to attachment attempts. A son or daughter who needs the security of an authority figure as parent can be overly dependent and at the same time resistant to bonding with that parent. Defensive detachment leads to an ambivalence toward the same-sex parent, which ultimately shows itself in *avoidance-approach conflicts*. Such conflict can be portrayed as a push-pull interaction. The child has the desire to be close to the parent, yet when closeness is obtained, the child pushes away in fear of being hurt.

Children need to be attached in healthy ways to the parent of the same sex. Among males, defensive detachment blocks the normal identification process with masculinity, resulting in an expressed effeminacy. Among females, the blockage against normal identification with femininity results in an expressed masculinity. Defensive detachment represents an unmet love-need which, when it reemerges, is known as homosexuality.

Proponents of this neopsychoanalytic theory help us see that the desire to fulfill this unmet parent love-need is *natural*. There is nothing "unnatural" about it, until the love-need has such a grip on a person that he or she compulsively seeks to get this need met through erotic means with a same-sex person. The impulse to eroticize the same-sex love-need is referred to as *cannibal compulsion*. Like the cannibal who desires to eat the flesh of a strong person in order to gain strength, this theory believes the homosexual male wants to sexually consume the same-sex person who possesses the traits he desires. This is why, it is argued, homosexual men are attracted to strong, good-looking, self-assured men. This is the image they want to incorporate into themselves. The homosexual, then, has normal needs that he attempts to meet through sexual involvement with a same-sex person. However, the lack of fulfillment as a child has now become an abnormal obsession that cannot be fulfilled through sexual encounters alone. There is a deeper need for emotional bonding and affection through nonerotic expression.

Although proponents of neopsychoanalytic explanations offer a wealth of clinical case studies to support their theory, empirical research to back up these explanations of homosexuality has been mixed. One study compared the family backgrounds of heterosexual and homosexual females in five countries on twelve familial factors that should be relevant to neopsychoanalytic theory (Whitam, Daskalos and Mathy 1995). Of these twelve familial factors—normal family, absent mother/father, warmer parent, stronger parent, hostile father, hostile mother, detached/distant father, detached/distant mother, seductive mother, seductive father, father's attitude toward sex and mother's attitude toward sex—five were found to be somewhat significant but inconsistent in all five societies. The study concluded that there is "little support for the role of familial factors in the development of female homosexual orientation" (p. 59).

A study comparing samples of homosexual and heterosexual females found no difference in childhood experience of physical or sexual abuse (Steele 1992), while another study comparing homosexual and heterosexual college males found gay males to have been more frequently abused and to have poorer relationships with fathers (Harry 1988). In response to these challenges Whitehead (1996) argues that such survey-based studies are inadequate to test for the importance of familial contributions to homosexuality. He concludes that "family factors and childhood experiences are still important in the genesis of homosexuality" (p. 322), and can be demonstrated through in-depth, qualitatively based research. The question of research support for neopsychoanalytic theory aside, proponents have developed a commendable redemptive ministry to homosexuals, which we will discuss later in this book.

Biological factors. Support for a biological explanation of homosexuality can be categorized as genetic, constitutional, endocrinological or ethological (Herrn 1995). Beginning in the 1950s, genetic studies reported that identical twins were usually of the same sexual orientation (Kallman 1952). This finding had been refuted by Heston and Shields (1968), but was more recently confirmed by Bailey and Pillard (1991) and Buhrich, Bailey and Martin (1991), in two articles comparing fifty-six gay men who had an identical twin brother and fifty-four gay men who had a nonidentical (fraternal) twin brother. While 52 percent of identical twins were themselves gay, only 22 percent of the fraternal twins were gay. Further, only 11 percent of the adoptive brothers of gay men were gay. Hamer (1993) claimed some progress in an

attempt to show a linkage between DNA markers on the X chromosome and male sexual orientation. These correlational data suggest the
important contribution of biological factors for homosexuality. Several
studies have found that homosexuals have a significantly higher proportion of homosexual siblings than heterosexuals (Bailey and Bell
1993, Pillard and Weinrich 1986), a finding that might be due to either
familial or biological influences.

Dorner (1976) reported that hormonal divergence during fetal development can result in genetic males having female genitals or vice versa.
One could speculate that hormonal discrepancies during fetal development might therefore contribute to homosexuality. Based on their hormonal research, Ellis and Ames (1987) conclude that the critical time for
sexual orientation determination is between the middle of the second
month and the middle of the fifth month of fetal development. Some
have speculated that hormonal factors during this crucial time may
determine homosexuality. Yet in a more recent review of these studies,
Doell (1995:345) finds "little evidence" for the hypothesis that "hormonal influences during fetal life 'organize' certain parts of the brain
which thus become centers for sexual orientation and behavior later in
life." Likewise, in a review of relevant studies, Banks and Gartrell
(1995:247) conclude that "the studies as a whole do not support a causal
relationship between postnatal hormone levels and sexual orientation."

Based on research with pregnant rats, Ward (1974) reported that
severe stress to a mother during pregnancy tends to produce homosexual offspring. Building on Ward's finding, Dorner et al. (1983) asked
mothers of male homosexuals, bisexuals and heterosexuals to recall
stressful episodes that occurred during their pregnancy. Approximately
two-thirds of the mothers of homosexuals, one-third of the mothers of
bisexuals and less than one-tenth of the mothers of heterosexuals
recalled stressful episodes. Another study that compared mothers of
lesbians and heterosexual women found no significant differences in a
mother's stress factor during pregnancy with their lesbian daughters
(Ellis et al. 1988). Bailey et al. (1991) also found no evidence of prenatal
stress effects on the sexual orientation of either males or females.

Other research has suggested that there are anatomical differences
between the brains of homosexuals and heterosexuals that may
account for differences in sexual orientation. The most publicized of

these studies is Simon Le Vay's (1991) report on differences between certain cells in a portion of the hypothalamus. However, since most of the homosexuals in the sample had died of AIDS, the anatomical differences between gays and straights could very well have been attributed to AIDS.

There have been a number of studies investigating the possibility of differences in testosterone (male hormone) levels of male homosexuals and heterosexuals. Results, to date, suggest a relationship with sexual orientation, even though the results have been contradictory and inconclusive. Writing in the *Scientific American* William Byne (1994:50) concludes, "What biological evidence exists thus far of innate biological traits underlying homosexuality is flawed. Genetic studies suffer from the inevitable confounding of nature and nurture that plagues attempts to study heritability of psychological traits. Investigations of the brain rely on doubtful hypotheses about differences between the brains of men and women. Biological mechanisms that have been proposed to explain the existence of gay men often cannot be generalized to explain the existence of lesbians (whom studies have largely neglected). And the continuously graded nature of most biological variables is at odds with the paucity of adult bisexuals suggested by most surveys."

Finally, a number of studies suggest that although homosexuality may have a biological base, where biological factors are important they will more likely contribute to general tendencies rather than determine sexual preference. Green (1987) believes that there is a genetic receptivity factor that encourages homosexual behavior in gay males. He concludes that if there is a biological precursor, it is most certainly combined with certain cultural factors. In the same vein, John Money (1987) concludes in his review of research that although there are prenatal hormone effects on sexual orientation, postnatal socialization influences are also important.

Based on interviews with 979 homosexual and 477 heterosexual men and women, Bell, Weinberg and Hammersmith (1981) reported that their data do not support traditional psychoanalytic explanations of homosexuality. Nor does their study support psychosocial explanations of homosexuality that claim lack of adequate heterosexual experiences during childhood, negative experiences with members of the opposite sex or early experiences and contact with homosexuals.

Their most consistent finding was that one-fourth of the gay males in their sample reported a tendency *not* to engage in traditional masculine types of behavior as children. Gay men reported a childhood preference for girl's activities, coupled with the feeling that they were not very masculine, a finding also reported by Zuger (1988). The one social psychological factor that seems to be somewhat important is that homosexual men, more than heterosexual men, reported having a cold and detached relationship with their father.

Lesbians reported having engaged in homosexual activity during adolescence, and they also expressed gender nonconformity or dissatisfaction with their gender more often than the heterosexual women in the sample. Bell, Weinberg and Hammersmith (1981) conclude that there are no firm links that establish the origins of heterosexuality or homosexuality, but state that biological factors "are not inconsistent with what one would expect to find if, indeed, there were a biological basis for sexual preference" (p. 216).

In an evaluation of biologic theories regarding sexual orientation, psychiatrists Byne and Parsons conclude "that although recent studies postulate biologic factors as the primary basis for sexual orientation, there is no evidence at present to substantiate a biological theory, just as there is no compelling evidence to support any singular psychosocial explanation (1993:228)." And again, based on an overview of the current state of the art of biomedical research on homosexuality, Schuklenk and Ristow (1996) conclude that "so far the cause(s) of homosexuality is (are) unknown and that biomedical research has failed to provide evidence for a possible causation of homosexuality" (p. 5).

Explaining Homosexuality: An Integrative Model

Given the present state of knowledge, no one theory or set of explanations, in and of itself, is capable of explaining the emergence of homosexuality. Our conclusion is supported by others who have examined the existing evidence. In his examination of the causes of sexual orientation Haynes (1995) concludes, "No one theory has proved to be satisfactory" (p. 91). A study reporting on 508 psychiatrists' attitudes with regard to the causes of male homosexuality is likewise inconclusive. Among the twelve theories evaluated, the five highest-ranking theories are biological rather than psychological. Genetic inheritance theory was the highest ranking, followed by prenatal hormone development theory. The highest-ranking psychological theory was the dominant mother theory, followed by the weak father theory (Gallagher, McFalls and Vreeland 1993:1).

Perhaps because of invested interests, it seems difficult for many to move beyond single-factor explanations of homosexuality. As Bermant (1995) has stated, "Unfortunately, the physical versus mental and nature versus nurture controversies remain alive, well, and mischievous in regard to the correct understanding of human sexuality" (p. 343). We recommend a healthy suspicion of any person who claims to know *the* cause of homosexuality. Instead we need a model that integrates both biological and psychosocial factors. Bermant (1995) believes that "Sexuality emerges from the interdependencies of biology, awareness, and the facts and artifacts of public life" (p. 343). As an attempt to take all of the accumulated evidence into account, we offer two models, which must be taken as tentative and subject to progressive refinements as additional knowledge is accumulated in the coming years regarding the explanation of sexual orientation.

Biology as necessary and sociocultural as sufficient contributors. In chapter one we suggested that biological factors might best be considered *necessary* and sociocultural *sufficient* contributors to the formation of human sexuality. We suggest that this model can also be utilized to explain homosexual orientation. Byne and Parson (1993) cogently express a similar point of view when they state, "Genes or hormones do not specify sexual orientation per se, but instead bias particular personality traits and therefore influence the manner in which an individual and his or her environment interact as sexual orientation and other personality characteristics unfold developmentally" (pp. 236-37). In a similar manner, Paul (1993) suggests that any potential biological factors contributing to sexual orientation "must be mediated by a complex sequence of experiences and psychosocial factors" (p. 41).

By using figure 4.1 as a reference point, we suggest that an individual must possess, as a necessary contributor, a genetic or hormonal package, either at birth or through the process of physical maturation, that renders that person susceptible to a homosexual orientation. On the other hand, it may be highly improbable that other individuals will ever

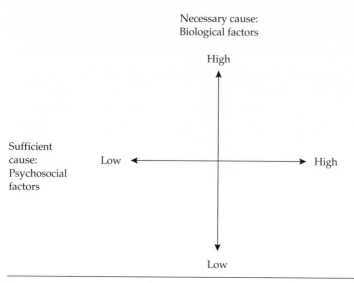

Figure 4.1.   An integrated model of authentic human sexuality

develop a homosexual orientation because their genetic/hormonal package is loaded against this. The genetic or hormonal makeup might be considered a necessary condition that needs to be present in order for a homosexual orientation to emerge. However, biological factors are insufficient in and of themselves to produce a homosexual orientation.

What is needed besides a biological predisposition toward homosexuality (the necessary contributing factor) is the presence of psychosocial factors (the sufficient cause). As represented in figure 4.1, the proportion of necessary (biological) contributors to a homosexual orientation is represented from *Low* at the bottom to *High* at the top. The proportion of sufficient (psychosocial) contributors to a homosexual orientation is represented from *Low* at the left to *High* at the right.

When there is a high presence of a biological package rendering one susceptible to homosexuality, combined with a high incidence of psychosocial experiences, there is a greater likelihood for a homosexual orientation (upper right corner of figure 4.1). Persons who are low in biological susceptibility and low in incidence of psychosocial experiences are unlikely to develop a homosexual orientation (lower left corner).

This model also suggests different "paths" to homosexuality, or possibly even different types of homosexuals. The upper left corner of the figure represents individuals who might be considered susceptible to a homosexual orientation, but do not have this orientation because of an insufficient presence of psychosocial contributing factors. The lower right corner represents individuals who are exposed to all of the psychosocial conditions that could result in them becoming homosexuals, but they do not have this orientation because of the absence of biological-genetic factors that would render them susceptible.

Daryl Bem (1996) has recently presented a developmental theory of sexual orientation that gives a similar interpretation to the role of biological and sociocultural factors. We present the basic points of his theory in summary form, but recommend a thorough reading of this creative piece of work.

Bem's theory is based on an understanding of how a temporal sequence of events leads to the development of sexual orientation. Bem (1996) believes that five sequential events act as *causal antecedents* that culminate in a natural erotic/romantic attraction to opposite- or same-sex persons. "The first causal antecedent consists of biological variables such as genes and prenatal hormones that code for childhood temperaments like aggression or activity level" (p. 321). Bem is careful to say that these biological factors do not code for sexual orientation directly but, as we shall see, are the beginning of a chain of sequential events that eventually lead to one's sexual orientation.

Childhood temperaments (the second sequential phase) predispose some children to enjoy active contact and competitive play, which come to be regarded as "male-typical" activity. Other children prefer quiet social interaction and play, which are associated as "female-typical" activities. The sex-typical/atypical activity and playmate preferences lead to the third sequential stage. Children seek out other children who share similar activity preferences. Children who prefer sex-typical activities and same-sex playmates are defined as gender conforming, while children who prefer sex-atypical activities and opposite-sex playmates are referred to as gender nonconforming.

This sets the stage for the fourth important sequential event in the development of sexual orientation. Children who are gender conforming will feel different from opposite-sex peers, "perceiving them as dissimilar, unfamiliar, and exotic" (Bem 1996:321). Correspondingly, gender-nonconforming children will feel different from and even alienated from same-sex peers, perceiving them as dissimilar, unfamiliar and exotic.

When these feelings of dissimilarity and unfamiliarity produce heightened autonomic arousal, the fifth important sequential event occurs. Chronologically, this corresponds to latency, that period of time when male-typical boys feel antipathy when girls are present. Boys who are too much like the unfamiliar and rather strange girls are labeled as "wimps" or "sissies." Female-typical boys feel apprehensive in the presence of other boys. Also, nonconforming girls are ostracized by their female peers because of their "tomboy" behavior. Nonconforming children come to experience a strong sense of fear or anger in the presence of their own gender. Both conforming and nonconforming children experience "heightened, nonspecific autonomic arousal in the presence of peers from whom [they] feel difference" (Bem 1996:321), whereas among most children this arousal will not be consciously felt.

The sixth event, sexual orientation, is the emergence of erotic/romantic attraction to opposite- or same-sex persons. This occurs when childhood autonomic arousal is transformed into erotic/romantic attraction. In short, the exotic, that which is viewed as different, is transformed into the erotic.

The strength of such models is that they have moved discussion beyond single-factor explanations of homosexuality. Further movement is needed, however, because such models are limited by being *linear* and *additive*. Bem's theory is linear in the sense that biological factors are considered to make important initial contributions to *subsequent* psychosocial factors. This results in overstating the importance and invariance of biological factors as contributors to sexual orientation. In the interactive model of human sexual development that we introduced in chapter one and which we will apply more directly to the development of sexual orientation below, biological and sociocultural variables are conceived as continually being affected by and affecting each other.

An interactive developmental model. We propose that a more adequate explanation of homosexual orientation conceptualizes biological and psychosocial factors as *interactively* related, meaning that they are mutually affecting and being affected by each other simultaneously and continually. Biological factors don't just make their appearance at stage one; rather the biological organism is continually changing throughout the human life cycle. Temperament and involvement in sex-typical or atypical activity may be formed in childhood, but it is far from fixed, capable of dramatic changes at different stages of life. What is needed is a model that recognizes biological variables that "kick in" in the same way that the sociocultural variables kick in throughout the human development process. We propose that the effects of biological and sociocultural factors are not additive, but *interactive,* in their effect on the development of sexual orientation. These factors both affect and are affected by each other on a continuing basis throughout the human developmental process.

A homosexual orientation emerges as part of a developmental process in which both biological factors and psychosocial factors kick in or fail to kick in at crucial points in the individual life developmental process. Figure 1.3 (see page 30) represents our attempt to graphically illustrate this interactive developmental process.

At conception there may be genetic factors that contribute to sexual development. During the prenatal period both congenital conditions (environmental) and endocrinological factors may interact in forming the sexual development of the unborn child. During the early years of life the quality of the emotional bonding with parents may contribute to sexual development. But even here, genetic or hormonal factors may have indirect effects. As Bem (1996) suggests, due to the genetic/hormonal makeup, a young boy may show signs of gentleness and sensitivity rather than aggressive "masculine" behavior. His father or peers may define him as "effeminate" and attempt to "correct" this behavior by taunting, teasing or general condemnation of his behavior. This results in the boy feeling rejected and shamed by both father and peers. The impact of this compounds the problem, leading the son to seek fulfillment in his relationships with male friends. Correspondingly, a girl who acts like a "tomboy" may experience similar treatment. However, we must move beyond Bem's "one-way" explanation, which conceptualizes biological factors as influencing psychosocial development, by recognizing that biology (the body) can also be affected by psychosocial factors.

Biological and psychosocial factors contribute both independently and interactively to the nature of a child's sexual development. Sexual abuse during any period of childhood, as well as hormone activation, or lack of it, during puberty, can both independently and interactively affect sexual development. By the end of puberty the bulk of factors contributing to the development of sexual orientation may have played their role, but the interactive effect of biological and psychosocial factors continues throughout an individual's life span.

Human agency. Although the next chapter will focus on a Christian response to homosexuality, before ending our discussion of the factors that contribute to homosexuality we need to return to the idea of human agency introduced in chapter one. This centers on the question of whether a homosexual orientation is a matter of choosing to have sexual desire for a same-sex person. The short answer is that although a person decides whether to act or not act on these desires, a person with a homosexual orientation is *not* responsible for the sexual desire any more than a heterosexual person is responsible for sexual desire directed toward an opposite-sex person.

This is not to say that human beings are merely passive agents and therefore pawns of biological and psychosocial influences. Human beings come to be choice-making creatures through the process of moral development. This primarily involves learning the meaning of sexuality in a social context. As individuals grasp the spiritual meaning of sexuality in terms of being drawn into significant relationships with others, they develop a self-structure that becomes increasingly capable of making choices. As we develop, we are not merely reactive to the forces of environment but have a capacity to act on our environment and even participate in the creation of that environment.

An understanding of the development of sexual orientation, as with the development of any other aspect of the psychosocial self, must acknowledge human agency within that human being. This assumption is made not only by theologians but by behavioral psychologists as well. In social learning theory, which is the theoretical offspring of behaviorism, deterministic assumptions are rejected. The major contributor to social learning theory, Albert Bandura (1978), allows for human agency in what he refers to as reciprocal determinism: "In their transactions with the environment, people are not simply reactors to external stimulation. . . . The extraordinary capacity of humans to use symbols enables them to engage in reflective thought, rather than having to perform possible options and suffer the consequences of thoughtless action. By altering their immediate environment, by creating cognitive self-inducements, and by arranging conditional incentives for themselves, people can exercise some influence over their own behavior. An act therefore includes among its determinants self-produced influences" (1978:345).

We hasten to add that social learning theory doesn't view human agency as a radical freedom, but more in terms of individuals having choices within a range of possibilities. Bandura (1974) concludes, "Within the social learning framework, freedom is defined in terms of the number of options available to people and the right to exercise them. The more behavioral alternatives and social prerogatives people have, the greater is their freedom of action" (p. 865). We believe that a theological discussion of human freedom must take into account the evidence that both biological and sociocultural factors can greatly expand or limit human choices that are framed in terms of human freedom. In that regard, differences in human constitutions, which reflect biological and sociocultural influences, mean that some individuals are more free than others.

We suggest that biological and sociocultural contributors to human sexuality, as applied to an understanding of human sexual development, operate to either increase or decrease the range of choices individuals have in regard to their sexuality. Some individuals are more limited in their range of sexual choices due to the limiting conditions set by biology and social environment. Freedom in making sexual choices can be limited in a variety of ways. Behavioral deficits restrict possible choices and may curtail opportunities in realizing one's possibilities. Growing up in an emotionally cold or hostile social environment can produce internal fears and stringent self-censuring ideas that restrict the effective range of activities and possibilities. We suggest that an array of sexual problems and addictions might be of this sort, and sex therapy or spiritual healing may become an opportunity to restore or expand one's personal choices and freedom.

A truly integrative theory of homosexuality will go beyond biological and psychosocial factors as the only focus. The development of moral character and responsible choice is a crucial aspect of sexual maturity and authenticity for all persons. Whereas deficiencies in bio-psycho-social input presents certain challenges and struggles for individuals as they seek sexual congruence and authenticity, everyone must come to grips with the deeper moral and spiritual meaning involved in sexual decision-making.

God created human beings as choice-making creatures with the ability to act as well as react. Human beings are not only acted upon, but are capable of making needed adjustments to biological and sociopsychological constraints. This brings us face-to-face with the more difficult question about how persons with homosexual or bisexual orientations make responsible choices about sexual behavior. In the following chapter we address this more directly and present a Christian response to homosexuality as well.

Suggestions for Further Reading

Bem, D. 1996. Exotic becomes erotic: A developmental theory of sexual orientation. *Psychological Review* 103 (2):320-35.

Laumann, E., et al. 1994. *The social organization of sexuality: Sexual practices in the United States.* Chicago: University of Chicago Press. See chapter 8.

Riesman, J., et al. 1990. *Kinsey, sex, and fraud: The indoctrination of a people.* Lafayette, Ind.: Huntington House.

5

Homosexuality

A Christian Response

A serious issue being debated in churches today is how the Christian community should respond to homosexuality and homosexual people. Given the complexity of the issues and the competing explanations about the causes of homosexuality, it is not surprising that vastly different positions are taken by Christians within and between denominations. The responses generally reflect people's understanding of what causes homosexuality and their beliefs about what Scripture teaches. Having considered various explanations of homosexuality in the previous chapter, we shall now focus on the specific biblical references relevant to homosexuality. Then we will describe various ministry approaches.

One's interpretation of Scripture about homosexuality and one's view of the biological and social scientific explanations of homosexuality are mutually intertwined. Personal bias and values are also persuasive factors that enter into the mix. For instance, while conservative Christians often accept biological explanations for gender differences, they tend to reject biological explanations of homosexuality; liberal Christians may reject biological explanations for gender differences but are more prone to accept these explanations for homosexuality. Before elaborating on how a Christian defends a particular position, we focus on the several references in the Bible concerning homosexuality.

What Scripture Says and How It Is Interpreted

While many biblical passages deal with sexuality in general, there are only five specific references to homosexual behavior. The Bible makes no definite statement about homosexuality as an orientation, but only to homosexual behavior. The widely differing ethical positions held within the Christian community center on these few verses, and interpretations are often hotly debated. In presenting the following biblical references, we will limit our comments to contextual observations, reserving exegetical interpretations for the section in the summary on alternative responses to homosexuality.

The earliest scriptural reference to same-gender sexual behavior occurs in the story of Sodom and Gomorrah in Genesis 19, which describes the depravity of this community. God had confided in Abraham that these cities would be destroyed because of their sins. Lot, a godly man, offered his hospitality and therefore his protection to the two angels sent by God to investigate the situation in Sodom and Gomorrah. The wicked men of the city proceeded to surround his house demanding that these two strangers be released to them to suffer a degrading rape. Lot refused to let his guests undergo the humiliation and violence of this act of homosexual rape. If we allow Scripture to interpret Scripture, we note that in the four later references about the destruction of Sodom and Gomorrah, homosexuality is not specifically mentioned as the reason for God's judgment. God had been long-suffering over the 400 years these cities' residents chose to reject God and follow their own ways. They warranted God's judgment and were conquered and destroyed. Ezekiel mentions God's rejection of Sodom and Gomorrah, and the book of Jude refers to the sexual immorality and unnatural lusts of Sodom and Gomorrah. According to discoveries of archaeologists, promiscuity, incest, pedophilia and bestiality were common practices during this time. The homosexual behavior was condemned by God as one of the many sins and shouldn't be elevated to a significance that God himself does not emphasize. The focus is on the despicable gang rape, shame and humiliation as the condemned sin rather than homosexual behavior per se.

Peter refers to the condemnation of these cities and the ungodly people who inhabited them, speaking of their lawless deeds, as well as their indulging in depraved lust and despising authority (2 Peter 2:6-10). God rescued Lot, a righteous man who had endured the torment of living among lawless people with such distorted values. Here is an example where the Lord delivered godly people, punishing the unrighteous for their reprehensible, exploitative acts and holding them accountable until the day of judgment.

In Judges 19 violent rape is described as a despicable evil. By this time in Israel's history, they had adopted all the immoral behaviors (including sex acts) of the Canaanites. God's judgment and comment on this account is not a single condemnation of homosexual behaviors, but of a total moral anarchy in which "every man did what was right in his own eyes."

The Holiness Code in Leviticus addresses same-gender sexual behavior. Leviticus 18:22 reads, "Do not lie with a man as one lies with a woman; that is detestable," and Leviticus 20:13 directs Israel, "If a man lies with a man as one lies with a woman, both of them have done what is detestable." According to the Jewish code, "they must be put to death; their blood will be on their own heads." While this was a clear and serious judgment, Christians disagree on the application of Levitical law since Christ came to abolish the law. There are other parts of the Holiness Codes that are no longer observed in today's world, because of Paul's teachings about our newfound freedom in Christ.

Other passages in the New Testament that may apply to homosexual behavior are lists of various immoral sexual acts. In 1 Corinthians 6:9-10 we read, "Neither the sexually immoral nor idolaters nor adulterers nor male prostitutes nor homosexual offenders nor thieves nor the greedy nor drunkards nor slanderers nor swindlers will inherit the kingdom of God." Some take these words literally, while others believe that the two Greek words, *malakoi* and *arsenokoitai,* from which "male prostitutes," "homosexual offenders" and "perverts" are translated, have imprecise meaning. It is thought that this refers specifically to sexual relationships between men and boys, which would be a coercive and perverted relationship. First Timothy 1:10 says that the law was made "for adulterers and perverts, for slave traders and liars and perjurers," indicating that it is the power differential of these sexual acts that make them despicable. Taking a power advantage over another is the perversion that is rightly condemned here.

The most noteworthy New Testament reference to same-sex behavior is found in Romans 1:26-27, "God gave them over to shameful lusts. Even their women exchanged natural relations for unnatural ones. In the same way the men also abandoned natural relations with women and were inflamed with lust for one another. Men committed indecent acts with other men, and received in themselves the due penalty for their perversion." These verses quite clearly address homosexual behavior, yet the language of natural and unnatural become part of the debated interpretation. For some theologians, unnatural refers to perverse and hedonistic sexual practices, *not* the mutually loving interaction that occurs between same-sex consenting adults. Therefore it is argued that the persons with a homosexual orientation are *not* going against *natural* tendencies. Of course, one must then define perverse sexual behaviors for both heterosexual and homosexual people to determine what authentic sexuality means in God's grand design. In the following section, we consider some alternative responses to homosexuality.

Alternative Responses

Although a multitude of responses toward homosexuality could be identified within the Christian community, we will represent four categories of alternative responses. Figure 5.1 represents a continuum along which four alternative responses to homosexuality can be understood. We shall briefly describe the positions at each of the extremes and then present more detailed descriptions of the two central response positions.

Responses at the extremes. Represented at the extreme left of figure 5.1 is the view that sex is a pleasure to be enjoyed in the same way one enjoys recreation. For both heterosexuals and homosexuals, sexual intercourse is held to be ethical and legitimate if it is between consenting adults. In this position's most extreme form, sex is a desired good in and of itself and there is no need for commitment or even affection between persons. This secular position on homosexuality seems to be beyond even the most liberal of Christian theologies.

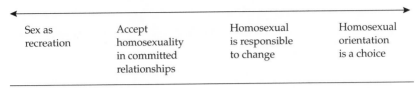

Figure 5.1.   Alternative responses to homosexuality

The position at the far right of the figure represents persons who believe that a homosexual orientation is a result of personal choice. In this view's most extreme, every homosexual impulse is an individual choice and the person is completely responsible for his or her sexual orientation as well as sexual behavior. A more tempered view recognizes potential psychosocial contributors to homosexuality, but discounts the magnitude of those influences in the face of the individual responsibility, even for one's formation and development. People holding this view believe that homosexuals should be judged and condemned, and often believe that the AIDS epidemic is evidence of God's judgment.

Committed gay relationships. The centralist position left of center accepts homosexual behavior in a committed, monogamous relationship as being morally right. This is the position generally defended within more liberal Christian theologies. Although most mainline Protestant denominations have not formally adopted this position, nearly all are currently debating the issue. Strongly organized proponents of this position are pressuring denominations to accept this stance under the theme of biblical justice, calling their churches "reconciling churches."

The injustice experienced by women in patriarchal society and the injustice experienced by gays in a homophobic society are equated as comparable examples of injustices that need to be eradicated. The logical extension of this view is the formal legitimization of same-sex marriages. Some churches have established lifelong commitment ceremonies for gay couples who desire to make such a covenant sanctioned by a community of believers.

A number of openly gay Christians find acceptance within their local worshiping communities, and some choose to worship in a gay church. The Universal Fellowship of Metropolitan Community Church was established in the early 1970s by Reverend Troy Perry, a homosexual Pentecostal minister in Los Angeles. These congregations have spread throughout the United States.

Due to the high view of scriptural authority held by many of the founders of the gay church, the theology is decidedly more conservative than some more liberal denominations who advocate openly for "gay rights." One major difference between gay churches and other evangelical churches has to do with the interpretation of Scripture when it comes to the promotion and defense of homosexual behavior. The gay church takes great pains to explain its understanding of the key biblical passages on which its morality of homosexuality rests.

The linchpin in response to the Sodom and Gomorrah account is the argument that God's judgment was upon the people for the violent rape and inhospitality of the people rather than the specific act of homosexual behavior. Pointing out that hospitality was viewed as a sacred duty in ancient Hebrew culture, it was the degrading sexual acts that were of great offense to God. The intent of these heterosexual men of the city was to sexually rape the strangers in order to humiliate and shame them. This is a far cry, they argue, from being involved in a loving, mutually expressive homosexual relationship.

Those who accept homosexual behavior between consenting adults generally believe that a person's sexual orientation is determined quite early in life. Thus, sexual expression between same-sex persons is accepted as a normal and essential part of one's life. Since it is "natural" for persons with a homosexual orientation to express themselves sexually with members of the same sex, it would be completely "unnatural" to engage in heterosexual union. The scriptural passage in Romans 1 condemning "unnatural" affections between people would therefore not apply. They believe this passage condemns persons who are heterosexual by nature, but turn against their natural sexual inclinations in sexual behaviors. They further assert that the major thesis in Romans 1 is Paul's declaration that *all* people have sinned and are in need of salvation, rather than the specific issue of homosexuality.

While the gay church condones homosexual behavior, they promote a standard of committed monogamous relationships for both heterosexual and homosexual couples. They believe it is against God's purpose to engage in casual or promiscuous sexual lifestyles. Whereas the gay church teaches sympathy and care for AIDS victims, they join with conservative Christians in pointing to the AIDS epidemic as a tragic result of promiscuous misuse of a God-given sexuality.

Stranger Outside the Gate (White 1994) describes the depth and sincerity of one person's genuine faith, as well as his tormented experiences growing up in a society that condemns a Christian with a homosexual orientation. Mel White, a well-known evangelical Christian who grew up in a Christian home, was deeply involved in the church, a Youth for Christ leader, a seminary professor, a producer of evangelistic films, pastor of a large church and ghostwriter for such people as Billy Graham and Jerry Falwell. After years of struggling to change his sexual orientation, from the time he was a young boy until he was an adult ready to end his life in suicide, Mel writes, "I can't explain why the comfort I find in a gay man's arms is greater than I could find in those of a heterosexual woman. It's not an act of sex. It's an act of love. It's not about sexual gratification. It's about spiritual survival" (p. 164). After a twenty-five-year marriage, several children and grandchildren later, White came to the conclusion that one's sexual orientation must be accepted as a gift of God so that he or she can exercise that gift with integrity, creativity and responsibility. Lila, his former wife, agrees and supports Mel with this testimony: "After all those decades of trying, we discovered that no one can choose or change his or her sexual orientation. Mel had no choice about being a homosexual. Believe me, if he had a choice, I know he would have chosen his marriage, his family and his unique ministry; for Mel's values, like most of the gays and lesbians I know, are the same as mine and my heterosexual friends: love, respect, commitment, nurture, responsibility, honesty, and integrity" (p. 5). No one is to blame, Mel asserts; he believes homosexual orientation is part of God's plan. He laments that so many Christians deny historic, cultural and linguistic evidence that would help them see the meaning of the biblical passages on homosexuality in a different light.

Sexual abstinence or change. The position right of center as represented in figure 5.1 holds the view that although homosexuals may not be responsible for their orientation, they are responsible for homosexual behavior. This is the most popular position taken by those who hold to conservative or evangelical theologies. One group holding this centralist position agrees with the idea that most persons with homosexual orientations will not be able to change their orientation. However, this group believes that even if this is the case, gay Christians should then practice sexual abstinence. They point out that many single heterosexual Christians want to marry but must adhere to a standard of abstinence as well.

Another group holding this centralist position believes that not only *can* persons with homosexual orientations change, but that they must *will* to change. Thus, there is strong support among these people's churches for ministering to homosexuals who want to change their sexual orientation. Most of these ministries have enormous compassion for the brokenness in our world that has contributed to broken sexuality and view healing as a lifelong process. The reality that homosexual orientation is not something that gets magically converted into a heterosexual orientation means there must be a purposeful and God-inspired way of moving from one to the other. So, using a developmental model, these ministries usually work toward gradual change, which comes through a prescribed and well-conceived structure. Basically a small group and individual counseling model, along with involvement in a caring community of believers, homosexuals learn about intimacy and authentic sexuality in a supportive, accountable environment.

The view of instant healing from homosexual to heterosexual is considered by this group as misguided. The wounds resulting from the guilt and shame heaped upon these homosexuals' already fragile psyches and low self-esteems by such messages are disheartening. A responsible ministry involves an open mind and open heart to receive the homosexual person with God's love and mercy. In this group are two main approaches for a homosexual who desires change. One is through an individually oriented and small group reparative psychotherapy, the other through a "redemptive ministry" approach that includes active participation in a vital spirit-filled community of faith.

Redemptive Ministries

In this section we draw upon materials from the Desert Stream and Living Waters ministries founded by Andy Comiskey, two of the largest redemptive ministries to homosexuals in the world. Based on a biblical model, their approach emphasizes truth and grace. They focus on striving for God's intended design for heterosexual marriage. Finding the way back to God's truth through Christ's atonement and redemption is the intention.

The creation purpose. The theological starting point is the Genesis 1:27 account of creation: "God created man in his own image, in the image of God he created him; male and female he created them." Being a part of God's image as male and female is seen as a sacred expression of heterosexual "one-flesh" relationship. In fact, this holy union represents the sacred fullness of God's creation. The complementary nature of male and female is crucial since each is incomplete without the other. Therefore same-gender sexual unions fall short of this intended reflection of God's image and thus the Creator's ultimate desire and purpose for one's life.

The gay church also acknowledges this creation purpose but believes male and female interaction happens as they are united in a spiritual realm as brothers and sisters in Christ. This is true of unmarried heterosexuals who develop spiritual and emotional connection in the body of Christ.

The Fall and redemption. Redemptive ministries have an especially high regard for the mystery reflected in a one-flesh heterosexual union. Because of the Fall, the perfect relationship between man and women was blemished by sin. Adam and Eve sinned against God, which led to alienation and distortion in their relationship. When exposed, they were ashamed, but tried to hide and place blame outside themselves rather than take responsibility for their disobedience against God. One way in which they suffered consequences in their relationship (Gen 3) was to bypass the Creator and go their own way. Men and women need Jesus and the truth of the gospel to find their way back to God's way.

Through the loving act of God, Jesus seeks to renew a right spirit of truth. In Christ Jesus homosexuals can reach their full potential through the power of the Holy Spirit to reconcile their lives to the glory to God. The goal is for homosexuals to develop rightful *same-* and *opposite*-sex relationships according to God's initial creation purpose. Through nonerotic intimate relationships with same-sex friends, the homosexual begins to see new possibilities for genuine connection and love. Whether the person makes a choice for celibacy or eventual heterosexual marriage, the person is brought back to a sexual authenticity as God intended.

One of the more controversial aspects of redemptive ministries by gay organizations is the claim that people can change their homosexual orientation to a heterosexual one. Social psychologists recognize two models of change: change in attitude and change in behavior. The debate has to do with whether changing attitudes ultimately changes behavior, or if changing behavior will result in a change of attitudes. A scriptural basis is found in the statement made by Christ, "Where your treasure is, there your heart will be also." Here it seems that Jesus is teaching that one's actions determine their attitudes. Redemptive ministries start with behavior change, believing it eventually changes attitudes and beliefs. It is not a simplistic ministry, but one that includes a variety of healing principles of change.

New relationships. In order to change a homosexual mindset, one starts by making a clear distinction between homosexual orientation and the homosexual lifestyle. The homosexual must not only want to change but begin by changing specific behaviors. One must cut off all former homosexual relationships. The homosexual is asked to take responsibility for his or her *behavior,* regardless of what thoughts, desires or feelings he or she might have. Past gender wounds must also be dealt with so one can grasp a deeper understanding of the gender confusion and make reconciliation. The next important step is to establish nonerotic relationships with straight persons of the same sex. Small group interaction with people of the same sex can lead to an emotional intimacy, which is believed to be the basic longing that can never be satisfied through sexual encounters. Since homosexuality is viewed as a developmental problem, it is solved through healthy, caring relationships. When the homosexual experiences covenant love with same- and opposite-sex persons in the context of a community of faith, healing takes place, according to this approach.

New desires. Disengaging from homosexual behavior is the initial step that enables one to grow beyond homosexual desires. Change will most likely be a slow process, accompanied by realistic goal setting. When homosexuals break off long-standing relationships, they must be supported through this time of grief and loss. The group and personal counseling provides a safe place to deal with the struggles, express feelings, forgive others, face self-hatred and shame, and ask the inevitable "why" questions of God. The battle is fierce, and one must actively draw upon God's power. As Paul tells Timothy, one must *flee* evil, *follow* Christ, and *fight* a fight of faith (1 Tim 6:11-12). Even after the emergence of heterosexual desires, the battle is not over; homosexual thoughts can pop up at the most inopportune moments. The person needs to constantly rely on God for spiritual help and presence to deal with the temptations. Through Bible study, prayer and Christian fellowship, individuals are supported and held accountable.

The ability to resist temptations and follow through on the behavioral commitments comes through reliance on the Holy Spirit. A strong focus of this ministry is to tap into the rich resources in Jesus Christ and to claim the promise given in 2 Corinthians 12:9 that God's strength is made perfect in our weakness. As one finds a new identity in Jesus Christ, there is reason to move away from the homosexual self-image toward God's truth.

The identity as gay or lesbian is often a painful process of discovery. An early awareness of being "different" from peers, along with the fear of being found out, labeled, teased and rejected, keeps people on edge and anxious prior to declaring themselves homosexual. The thought of being different keeps them from revealing true feelings, and isolates and distances them from others. Cruel labels like "queer" keep them hiding this aspect of their identity from themselves and others for as long as they can. It is extremely difficult to be congruent or authentic as a sexual being when hiding or pretending to be something you are not. Gay youth are two to three times more likely to attempt suicide because of the tremendous guilt and condemnation of parents, peers and society in general. Knowing how painful the past has been and how difficult it is to trust others, the process of healing takes time and cannot be rushed. A crucial part of the process is spending sufficient time with others who make a covenant to listen with compassion and care as the homosexual reveals struggles, guilt and suffering. Through friendship, compassion and acceptance one finds mercy and hope.

New community. New relationships and a new identity can best be cultivated in a caring community of faith. Engaging a new community is a two-step process. Primarily, one must dispel the myth that a romantic/sexual attraction with a person of the opposite sex is what is

needed to awaken a homosexual from his or her homosexual orientation. The first step is to establish caring relationships with emotionally
and spiritually mature straight men and women. The next step is to
develop *casual* opposite-sex friendships. Internal healing takes place
through small, predictable steps, setbacks and gradual movement forward. Prayer is a strong component of psychological and spiritual
healing that takes place in this supportive community of faith that
embraces rather than condemns, giving homosexuals hope of finding
authenticity in their sexuality.

Conclusion

Having considered the alternative Christian responses to homosexuality, we now return to the question raised at the conclusion of chapter
four: How do homosexual Christians take personal responsibility for
their sexual orientation and subsequent behavior? Considering the
multiple factors involved in homosexual orientation, by now we hope
the reader realizes it is not a simple matter of *choice.* Such a response is
analogous to explaining poverty as the result of a series of bad choices
made by poor people. While personal choice is an important dimension in understanding any type of human behavior, it is necessary to
consider the profound influence of the biological, psychological and
sociological factors involved. When individuals, through little or no
determination of their own, receive a biological package rendering
them susceptible to homosexuality, combined with wounding familial
and social experiences, their "choice" is much more restricted. On the
other hand, persons who receive the biological givens that determine
heterosexual orientation, along with a nurturing family and social
environment leading to heterosexual congruence, will have an easy,
natural inclination toward heterosexuality.

Responsible choice for heterosexuals, bisexuals and homosexuals is
made in the context of a supportive family and community who keep
us accountable for our choices. In this regard, we suggest that there is a
communal as well as a bio-psycho-social dimension to homosexuality.
The communal aspect of homosexuality is especially important in
understanding why some persons with homosexual orientations
choose to engage in homosexual behavior and others do not. It is a
sociological truism that the greater the availability of a supportive

homosexual community, the greater the likelihood that a person with a homosexual orientation will be drawn to homosexual relationships. The homosexual community provides an ideological and plausibility structure that encourages and justifies homosexual activity. On the other hand, a person with a homosexual orientation who chooses celibacy or change will most likely seek a Christian community that encourages, supports and empowers them in that choice.

While we do not believe homosexuals are responsible for their orientation, they must decide before God how they will respond and behave. The same is true of heterosexuals, both married and unmarried, who search out a supportive community to help them grapple with various sexual struggles. In order to be authentic sexual persons, we must address our sexual desires, temptations and behaviors in light of God's Word. In working out a compassionate sexual ethic, the Christian community must be careful not to hold a double standard. If chastity prior to marriage is the sexual norm, then heterosexuals as well as homosexuals and bisexuals should be asked to abide by that standard.

In the Genesis account the ideal prototype is the male and female becoming "one flesh" for love, intimacy, union and procreation. This persuades us to uphold the male and female union as God's intended design for authentic sexual union. Our theology of sexuality, then, is based on the premise that God created us to show forth God's image as male and female in relationship. The directive to replenish and subdue the earth (rightful dominion) and to be in authentic relationship (rightful sociability) leads us to a heterosexual norm. In moving together as male and female, married and single, homosexual and heterosexual in order to promote God's kingdom on earth, we find our holy calling. We firmly believe that the capacity for living in meaningful covenant relationship is a spiritual journey that brings forth God's image.

However, we are also acutely aware of how all of creation was altered after the Fall. Therefore none of us achieves sexual wholeness in accordance with God's highest ideals. Many have been damaged in sexual ways and now struggle with sexual intimacy, some are denied sexual expression even though they long to be married, others have natural attraction for a same-sex partner. Homosexuals, bisexuals and heterosexuals must strive to find a wholeness in their lives before God in a less than ideal world. We all struggle, in our own ways, for sexual authenticity. We believe that God is an essential part of this ongoing process and leads each one on a journey of sexual authenticity. We acknowledge that this will be a more painful and difficult road to travel for many. We grant to all Christians the privilege of walking through that process with Christ and in the context of a loving community of faith.

A key factor in the development of a healthy, authentic sexuality is the integration of sexual behavior within a biblically based personal value system. We are called to be compassionate and gracious to ourselves and others on that path to wholesome sexuality. We believe that the Christian community must model compassion and care for homosexuals, resting in the fact that God is at work in all those who love and desire to serve their Lord.

We acknowledge that some gay Christians may choose to commit themselves to a lifelong, monogamous homosexual union, believing this is God's best for them. They believe that this reflects an authentic sexuality that is congruent for them and their view of Scripture. Even though we hold to the model of a heterosexual, lifelong, monogamous union, our compassion brings us to support all persons as they move in the direction of God's ideal for their lives. Only through God's grace and the power of God's Holy Spirit do we have the courage to keep moving toward that goal. A suffering Jesus knows the way, embraces us where we are, forgives us when we fall, heals us when we're broken and longs to meet us where we are to deepen our intimacy with our living Lord.

Suggestions for Further Reading

Comiskey, A. 1989. *Pursuing sexual wholeness: How Jesus heals the homosexual.* Lake Mary, Fla.: Creation House.

Hays, R. 1996. *The moral vision of the New Testament.* San Francisco: HarperCollins. See chapter 16, "Homosexuality," pp. 379-406.

Moberley, E. 1993. *Homosexuality: A new Christian ethic.* Greenwood, S.C.: Attic Press.

Nicolosi, J. 1991. *Reparative therapy of the male homosexual.* Northvale, N.J.: Jason Aronson.

Payne, L. 1984. *The healing of the homosexual.* Westchester, Ill.: Crossway.

Scanzoni, L., and V. R. Mollenkott. 1978. *Is the homosexual my neighbor?* New York: Harper & Row.

Stott, J. 1998. *Same sex partnerships: A Christian perspective.* Grand Rapids, Mich.: Baker.

White, M. 1994. *Stranger at the gate.* New York: Simon & Schuster.

Worthen, A., and B. Davies. 1996. *Someone I love is gay: How family and friends can respond.* Downers Grove, Ill.: InterVarsity Press.

Part II

Authentic Sexuality

6

Sexual Intimacy
& Singleness

In 1960 Paul Goodman wrote a book about coming of age in the United States, which he aptly entitled *Growing Up Absurd.* Not least among the absurd aspects of growing up is how to behave sexually. Exposed to the electronic media, singles are bombarded with an onslaught of messages enticing them to act out sexual impulses, yet the Christian community continues to uphold the standard of sexual abstinence before marriage.

Asking unmarried singles to control their sexual impulses for longer and longer periods of time is a fairly new phenomenon in our culture. This has been brought about by an earlier-age onset of puberty combined with later-age marriages. Throughout history, young people in most societies married just before their sexual and reproductive capacities were developed. Around the middle 1800s girls reached menarche between ages fifteen and sixteen and married around that same age. Today the onset of menarche has dropped to between ages twelve and thirteen, while the median age at first marriage is 23.6 for women and 26.9 for men. The combination of early hormonal development coupled with a culture that encourages sexual involvement during dating makes it even more difficult for singles to remain celibate prior to marriage. The early awakening of sexuality through the constant bombardment of messages about sex in modern culture is cause for most singles to consider celibacy an absurd request that is quite impossible to manage during this ten- to twenty-year waiting period before marriage.

We start with the assumption that sexual feelings are extremely powerful, but a person has a clear choice about sexual behaviors. We need to teach teens that it's all right to have sexual feelings and desires but that they must learn to contain them. The media counter this message by teaching youth that if they have sexual feelings they should act on them. We need to develop media awareness programs to train teenagers to recognize how they are being manipulated by the media and how they can take constructive steps to counter its destructive messages. One needs only to understand the economics of eroticism to realize why teenagers are among the most manipulated groups in society today. It is enormously profitable for the media to provide sexually titillating and erotically suggestive messages to a large group of voracious consumers whose hormones are raging.

Sadly, many churches and parents turn a deaf ear to this dilemma, refusing to address the difficult questions about sex and singleness. Although rarely articulated, two messages seem to be given to teenagers and singles. Perhaps the most common message is, "Don't ask, don't tell." This response is actually a nonresponse. The other message, "Just say No!" may reflect a stance that ignores the struggle of living in a sexually saturated culture.

Singles need to feel understood as well as receive helpful guidelines in their desire to follow a standard of abstinence. Pretending that young people are not sexual leaves them in a quandary concerning how to be an authentic sexual person in today's world. They need to know how to exist in a singles' subculture that endorses premarital sex, while holding on to the Christian belief in celibacy before marriage. Significantly, the two types of behavior most correlated with teenagers delaying sexual intercourse are religious behaviors like *praying* and *attending church*. The church and biblical teachings are great resources for singles as they develop sound reasons for cultivating person-centered relationships.

In this chapter we present a brief historical outlook on sexual standards, then offer a biblical perspective and give some practical suggestions about how to affirm sexuality while remaining true to biblical standards.

Premarital Sexual Standards

There are four recognized premarital sexual standards held in the United States today: *sexual abstinence, double standard, permissiveness with affection,* and *permissiveness without affection.* Although the idea of sexual abstinence continues to be a primary sexual standard when it comes to beliefs about sex before marriage, it is not the actual behavior reported by the majority of singles. The double standard, on the other hand, which accepts sexual intercourse outside marriage for males but not for females, has continued to decline during the past sixty years.

Permissiveness with affection is the most practiced sexual standard when it comes to actual behavior. Many young adults believe that sexual intercourse between two consenting individuals is permissible when they are "in love" and have committed themselves to one another. Society generally accepts this arrangement when couples are in exclusive dating relationships or engaged or living together. However, there is still a societal sanction for legal marriage when a couple decides to have children.

Some confusion comes into play with the "permissiveness with affection" standard. There are those who practice what might be called serial monogamy in that they are true to one partner at a time, yet change partners every few years. They have affection for the partner during the sexually exclusive relationship, but they will move on to another partner when they "fall out of love" or become attracted to a new partner. In another scenario, singles report having affection for the partners they have sex with, but that affection may extend to several partners at the same time. As you can see, there is a wide variation in how this standard is interpreted. It can be justified to fit most any situation where there is an intentional relationship.

Permissiveness without affection, although less acceptable as a standard when attitudes are surveyed, has become a fairly common practice in the past thirty years. This view considers sexual intercourse to be a casual, recreational experience between two consenting adults. The recent AIDS epidemic has jolted many into rethinking this standard, due to the serious ramifications of such a promiscuous sexual lifestyle.

There are obvious reasons to consider the grave consequences of engaging in sex with many different persons for whom one has no affection, both from a physical and psychological perspective. Because of HIV, relationships from the past may have infected a person with a life-threatening illness in the present. Thus, casual sex for the sake of sexual pleasure has been questioned increasingly in recent years. However, there is not only concern about the increased risk of contracting sexually transmitted diseases but also about the emotional impact of being sexually intimate with a number of different partners for whom there is no affection.

The social context of premarital sex. A study of 1,925 seventh- and eighth-grade students revealed that males were more likely than females to have engaged in sexual activity and to hold more permissive attitudes towards sexual involvement (De Gaston, Weed and Jensen 1996). "Females were more committed to abstinence, less permissive in their views of premarital sexuality, less likely to view access to birth control or being in love as a justification for sex, and more likely to view sexual urges as controllable and adolescent sexual activity as an impediment to future goal attainment" (p. 217).

Evidence exists that attitudes of parents and peers influence adolescents' sexual attitudes and behavior. De Gaston, Weed and Jensen (1996) found that girls perceived less peer pressure for sex and more support for postponing sex than did boys. Girls were more likely to discuss sex and dating practices with their parents, but also viewed their parents as having more rules and being less approving of their sexuality.

A study of over 1,000 high school students helps us understand the circumstances under which adolescents experience their first sexual intercourse (De Gaston, Jensen and Weed 1995). When first sexual intercourse occurred, 50 percent of the students were going steady, 25 percent were dating someone they knew well, 20 percent reported that drugs or alcohol were used, and 75 percent were at home or a friend's home. Nearly 50 percent reported that they wished they had waited longer before having sex.

Ninety percent of persons who engage in premarital sex do so in their teenage years. The average age for boys' first sexual experience is sixteen, and for girls it is seventeen. These figures are only one year younger than in 1970. A study of 1,167 high-school students revealed that once sexual intercourse activity was initiated, it was persistent for most adolescents (Tubman, Windle and Windle 1996). Boys were nearly twice as likely as girls to be at high levels of sexual risk by having sex with multiple partners. Repeated intercourse with multiple partners was associated with antisocial behaviors and substance abuse.

The earlier the use of alcohol, cigarettes, marijuana or other illicit drugs, the greater the risk of sexual activity prior to age 16 for both males and females (Rosenbaum and Kandel 1990). Youth who begin sexual activity at an early age run a higher risk for a premarital birth (Miller and Heaton 1991). The single most powerful predictor of adolescent pregnancy is to have been sexually abused. Sixty percent of children born to adolescent girls are fathered by adults.

Other research indicates a great deal of struggle and sexual conflict in sexual encounters between adolescent males and females. While a boy is more likely to coerce a girl into having sex by lying or attempting to get her drunk or high, girls are more likely to stress the need for commitment and investment in the relationship as a basis for having sex (Eyre, Read and Millstein 1997). A study of English youth also confirmed the use of alcohol as a means of lessening a girl's resistance to having sex. Donovan (1996) reports that young women indicate that alcohol consumption would make them more likely to have sex with somebody for whom they felt attraction. Chapter twelve goes into more detail about inauthentic sexual behavior in social dating.

In light of this diversity in sexual standards, Christian singles must decide about a standard for themselves. We will present scriptural support for abstinence as a standard and then ask some critical questions about making sexual choices.

The Case for Abstinence

Sexual intercourse is carefully placed within the context of marriage throughout the Scriptures. This idea is so strong that unmarried persons who engage in intercourse are regarded as entering into a one-flesh union similar to marriage. In 1 Corinthians 6:17 the apostle Paul reminds us that when two become one flesh it is similar to uniting oneself with Christ's spirit. Paul dares to suggest that sexual oneness established between two people is comparable to the unity we are meant to experience with Christ!

Marriage is that time when two persons (1) base their relationship on a mutually shared covenant commitment and (2) consummate their relationship in sexual union. The sealing of the marriage covenant is likened to a sacred mystery in which two individuals become "one flesh" (Gen 2:24; Mt 19:4-6). The act of sexual intercourse carries with it the deeper notion of uniting two persons in the spiritual, emotional, intellectual and physical aspects of their relationship.

Premarital sex is defined as sexual intercourse between unmarried persons who do not share a mutual covenant commitment. This is referred to in the Bible, depending on the translation, as "fornication" or "sexual immorality" (Acts 15:20; 1 Cor 5:1; 6:13, 18; 7:2; 10:8; 2 Cor 12:21; Gal 5:19; Eph 5:3; Col 3:5; 1 Thess 4:3). One could argue that there is no such thing as "premarital intercourse" because the act of intercourse itself, according to the bottom-line position, seals the union whether or not the couple intends to marry (Friesen 1989, Olthuis 1975).

An obvious question for couples who forgo marriage but share a covenant commitment is whether they are free to engage in sexual intercourse. Whereas God alone judges the hearts and intentions of any committed couple, it is clear that sexual intercourse is meant to seal their marriage vows as they promise before God to be faithful to each other for a lifetime. On a practical level, merely making a mutual covenant does not automatically imply that the couple should move on to sexual intercourse. In a social psychological sense, there is a right and wrong time to marry. The right time is when two people are prepared to take their committed love and live together in a responsible, mutually satisfying relationship. A more complete discussion of the wisdom of this position will be given in the next chapter on cohabitation.

Genesis 2:24 indicates that the right time for marriage is when a couple is able to "leave, unite and cleave" in a newly established union. Until both partners have a sufficient sense of self that allows them to separate from their parents/family of origin, we believe that they are unprepared to enter such a demanding relationship as marriage. Then, when two persons love each other and make a covenant commitment to each other, they are mature enough to consider what is in the best interest of their partner as well as what is in the best interest of the relationship before making decisions about sexual intimacy or when to marry. The uniting of two lives involves a spiritual union that goes far beyond the two of them. It is vowing before God to put Christ at the center as they bind their lives together in the meaningful purposes of work, procreation, family and friendship ties, recreation and service to church and community.

Singleness and Moral Decision-Making

In this age of tolerance, it is increasingly difficult for Christian singles to simply accept the admonition, "The Bible says it, I believe it, that settles it!" The fact is, when it comes to specific sexual behaviors, the Bible is not so clear-cut. This leaves room for various interpretations, increasing the confusion in terms of what are the convincing arguments and whose opinions one chooses to follow. We believe it is more helpful to offer a series of questions that single persons can honestly ask themselves as they develop a moral basis about these gray areas concerning sexual behavior.

Do I have the right reason? Asking the question "What is the right reason?" helps one face some hard facts head-on. Even though pleasure and enjoyment may be a good reason, the potential harm of sexual involvement for a partner, yourself or your particular relationship must also be considered. "Will either of us get hurt by the sexual behaviors we engage in at this time?" "Are we emotionally ready to deepen our relationship at this level?" "Do I have a sufficient self to make a covenant commitment to this person?" "What happens if either of us wants out after we become sexually intimate?" "Will the emotional pain of breaking up after being this involved cause either of us psychological harm?" "What happens if a pregnancy occurs? Will the unborn child be hurt by this choice? Would we be able and willing to care for a child? What would be the effect of putting a child up for adoption? Would we ever consider abortion and how would that affect us?" "Will being involved sexually at this time hurt our parents, siblings or family in any way?" We could go on and on, but you get the idea.

There are many crucial questions to consider about the level of one's sexual involvement in a relationship before proceeding. Being honest about possible emotional complications keeps denial at bay. Singles, whether young or old, need to ask themselves if they have the right reasons to be involved with a partner sexually, then determine if these reasons are congruent with their psychological development, physical and emotional readiness, and Christian value system.

Will it enrich our relationship? If a couple decides they do have the right reasons for increasing the level of their sexual involvement and are assured neither of them will be hurt by it, the next step is to consider the impact on the relationship itself. Because they love each other, are deeply committed and believe that good will come out of the mutual decision for increased sexual intimacy, the question here has to do with whether it will enrich their relationship. The point of these questions is to keep the relationship in focus and to assume mutual responsibility for it. "Will sexual intercourse enhance or take away from our committed love?" "Is it the right time for us to be this involved sexually, for example, how far away is the wedding day?" "Are we committed to the point that we would marry should a pregnancy occur, and how would that affect our relationship?" "Can we trust each other to be faithful throughout the years to our covenant love when we can't postpone our passion now?" "Can we maintain our personal freedom along with paying attention to our partnership commitment?"

We realize that a couple may answer all these questions in the affirmative. It may confirm that they have the right reasons for themselves, each other and the relationship. On the other hand, they may see the need to look more realistically at potential complications should they increase the level of sexual involvement to their relationship at that point in time. Most important, if they've done this honest soul searching now, keeping unforeseen consequences in full view, they'll be at a better place to take responsibility for their decisions.

We know of an unmarried couple who decided to live together because they believed it would enhance their relationship. However, they didn't anticipate how difficult it would be for their families when church friends unknowingly asked questions that were too hard to cover up. So the couple stopped going to church. Then they began having difficulty working out finances and blamed each other for not pulling their share of the load. Soon, they were at each other's throats, and neither family was willing to bail them out. Finally, they terminated the living arrangement because they were basically unable to manage their relationship. The breakup was painful and each suffered emotionally. They were embarrassed about failing at something they were sure they could handle. Each one struggled to work out the relational consequences of being so involved sexually and now to be totally apart. A decision they thought would enhance their relationship actually became its demise. This was a difficult and painful experience for all involved.

Is it the right time? Biblical norms about sexual intercourse aren't meant to deprive one of sexual pleasure, but to ensure the sanctity of a mysterious union embedded in a deeply satisfying covenant relationship. We recognize that some Christians have made a full covenant to each other before God and engage in sexual intimacy prior to marriage. And they seem to do this with few complications. In these cases it precedes marriage that is lasting and fulfilling. However, this is quite a different situation from those who engage in impersonal, indiscriminate sex with a number of different partners without any sense of commitment.

Jennifer and Daniel were in an exclusive relationship for four years. After thoughtful discussion, they finally decided to include intercourse as part of their sexual intimacy with each other. They were secure in their pledge to an exclusive love and eventual marriage. Even though they weren't prepared financially to establish a household for at least another year, they felt they were ready for sexual intercourse at this stage in their courtship.

We can certainly have compassion for this couple who believed they made a choice for the right reason, yet the decision was premature due to their financial unsteadiness. Even though they had worked hard to establish independence from their families of origin and had achieved a level of emotional maturity, they remained dependent when it came to money issues. This not only put a strain on their relationship with their parents, who were paying the bills, but caused tension in their relationship as well. Therefore instead of enhancing the relationship, the added stress left them estranged from each other and their parents.

Did sexual involvement stymie the future of the relationship? By choosing to engage in sexual intercourse, a couple may shortchange themselves of the total package. For example, intercourse for Jennifer and Daniel diminished their relationship because they weren't able to fully enter into all aspects of married life. They ended up living out only part of their dream, so to speak. Emotional bonding occurs through the planning and setting up of a household together. Sexual involvement may help them feel physically close, but focusing on this aspect may disrupt the full meaning of their covenant. So, they limp along without the benefit of an all-encompassing relationship.

We believe that sexual intercourse loses its deeper meaning when it is not an integral part of the total life of the couple. The mutual joy, pain, vulnerability and accountability in all aspects of married life deepen the relationship and bring validation to the union. When bonding is limited to the sexual realm, partners are likely to hold back disclosing all of themselves. This robs them of a daily meshing of their lives through the thick and thin, the essential joys and difficult days of life together. Married life as a total package brings a couple to a higher level of intimacy and commitment.

In another case, Marsha and Gregg had both engaged in sexual intercourse with several partners before they started going steady. Neither had thought very much about their sexual choices or prior indiscriminate sexual behavior. So, when they came together, it was an automatic assumption that intercourse would be part of their relationship. Neither of them discussed what the sex meant to them, nor did they ask any of the questions about it being for the right reasons for either themselves or the relationship. Since they did not know much about making a covenant commitment to each other, they each longed for a deeper level of emotional intimacy to match their sexual involvement. Their relationship remained on a fairly superficial level, and they began to feel the same dissatisfaction they did with other partners. A crucial piece was missing, leaving a tremendous gap in their sexual union.

Marsha and Gregg engaged in sexual activity for the wrong reason ("it's just the thing people do when they're together") at the wrong time ("we're together because it's convenient"). They need help in developing a more satisfying relationship, but when bonding is not solidified in one's family of origin it is difficult to grasp an understanding of what it means to make a covenant. If one does not have a sufficient self, it is near to impossible to put the best interests of the other or the relationship on par with one's own interests. While we can agree that sexual involvement will not meet the deeper longings of their life, it's more difficult to help them discover the deeper meaning of sexual union and covenant commitment.

Wrong Reasons for Sexual Involvement

While some singles, like Jennifer and Daniel, may have believed they engaged in sex for good reasons, many more have sex for reasons that are wrong—and unhealthy—from the beginning.

Sex used as a substitute for emotional needs. The single life can be one of loneliness and self-doubt. Singles may long for emotional love, but due to low self-esteem they believe there is nothing in themselves that is lovable. So, they decide to give their bodies as a substitute for what they don't have to offer emotionally. However, the few moments of pleasure never deliver what they truly desire in meeting emotional needs. Sadly, such persons may go from one sexual relationship to another looking for love in physical terms, only to perpetuate the belief that there is nothing of their personhood that attracts others. Their self-esteem declines even more when they perceive they are nothing more than a sex object.

Singles who are underdeveloped in relational skills will find it hard to make satisfactory connections and are actually fearful of emotional closeness. They deceive themselves into thinking that physical intimacy equals emotional intimacy. Hiding behind this illusion when a partner asks more of them emotionally, they run in the opposite direction because they can't deliver something they don't have to give. They're likely to dump that person and get involved in another sexual encounter without ever developing in the emotional realm.

Insufficient ego strength—can't say no! Some persons don't have the ego strength to say *no* to sexual approaches, so they give in even when they don't want to be sexually involved. They don't really enjoy the sexual interaction; however, they are unable to assert themselves, so they tolerate the intrusion. Some may believe they don't have a right to keep sexual boundaries, others fear rejection or ridicule, so they say yes when they want to say no.

When working at a large university, Judy saw how this inability to say no to peers became a tragedy for a college freshman. Dormmates had learned that Dennis was a virgin and began teasing him mercilessly about it. They set him up with a girl for the purpose of "helping him become a real man." There was a big party on the fourth floor that night to celebrate his lost virginity. The dormmates felt triumphant, but Dennis was crushed by his failure to resist their pressure. Extremely guilty about what had happened, he condemned himself harshly for not standing up for what he believed. He was so distraught about going against his personal and religious standards, he attempted suicide the next day. We are saddened about the circumstances that led to the inability of this young man to combat these peer pressures.

When ego strength is underdeveloped, testing a person's sexual values can be a tremendous challenge. Dennis found it especially tough to assert his values in a non-Christian environment. In this case, physical sex with the girl involved proving something to his dormmates rather than coming out of a desire to express affection to someone he loved. The girl was also an innocent victim of this cruel setup. Single persons need to know they *always* have the right to say no at any time, so they will never feel obligated to anyone.

Using sex to control or coerce. Sex can be used in an effort to control, coerce or trick a person. Kristin remembers going to the college prom with Chuck and being so "in love" with him that night. They came home at midnight and slow danced to records in her living room. Kristin felt a nervous, butterfly sensation in her stomach and thought for sure this was a sign of true love. One thing led to another and soon they were petting heavily, just short of intercourse. The next few weeks Chuck and Kristin spent every waking moment together. Chuck began pushing for more physical involvement just when Kristin wanted to back up a step or two.

That's when Chuck started giving her guilt trips about what she owed him. After all, he said, they'd been physically involved and she was obligated to marry him. His constant pressure made Kristin want to run, but she felt trapped by her prior behavior. She couldn't see that if he really loved her he would not want to badger her into doing things she didn't want to do. If he truly cared about her well-being, he'd be thrilled that she wanted to complete college and prepare herself for a professional career.

When someone in Kristin's situation pulls away, the coercive partner usually becomes even more desperate, creating ugly, embarrassing scenes in front of others. At this point we can see how the one's pulling away threatens the instability of the one who clings and how that leads to more forceful attempts at control. This person manipulates out of personal need, not out of love for the other.

Rape and sexual violence are other examples of hostile, coercive sex. Perpetrators have one focus in mind, to satisfy their own needs without regard for the person they victimize. Sex is used to reassure themselves of their adequacy, for they are filled with self-hate, a topic we'll discuss in more depth in the chapter on sexual violence. At this point, we simply want to point out the potential danger in the contemporary singles scene where power and control are used in sexual encounters. Emotionally inadequate males tend to be especially susceptible to coercing their dates into having sex against their will.

Sex for sexual pleasure alone. When sex becomes an idol that supposedly satisfies all needs, persons expect too much too soon from sex. Engaging in sex in order to reduce boredom, pain, loneliness or anxiety is an attempt to escape problems in life. Expecting sex to alleviate these problems leaves one constantly dissatisfied. Trying and trying again for instant cures, this person is continually disillusioned because sexual solutions never satisfy the deeper longings in life.

Sex for the sake of sex is about bodily pleasure without caring who brings the pleasure. It's like having a penis and vagina get together without the persons attached. While it may bring a few minutes of orgasmic sensations, it is devoid of relational meaning. Having sex for pleasure can become such an obsession that one fixates on the external "high" of sex rather then seeing it become a pathway to internal and relational satisfaction. Thinking that it is the sexual pleasure that satisfies, people are desperate to get more of the thing itself, rather than more of the relationship. This person may have little to give, but has a big appetite to take.

Frederick Buechner (1992) makes the following comments about an "anything goes" perspective on sexual behavior. He believes that it's not just a matter of mutual consent or mutual affection or that no one is going to get hurt psychologically, emotionally or spiritually.

> What makes this a tragic situation, I believe, is not so much that by one set of standards or another it is morally wrong, but that in terms of the

way human life is, it just does not work very well. Our society is filled with people for whom the sexual relationship is one where body meets body but where person fails to meet person; where the immediate need for sexual gratification is satisfied but where the deeper need for companionship and understanding is left untouched. The result is that the relationship leads not to fulfillment but to a half-conscious sense of incompleteness, of inner loneliness, which is so much the sickness of our time. The desire to know another's nakedness is really the desire to know the other fully as a person. It is the desire to know and to be known, not just sexually but as a total human being. It is the desire for a relationship where each gives not just of his [her] body but of his [her] self, body and spirit both, for the other's gladness. (p. 264)

Singleness and Physical Affection: Some Guiding Principles

What can couples do when they want to show affection and express themselves sexually while remaining true to the biblical standard of celibacy prior to marriage? We believe that celibacy does not mean sexual *inactivity*. Quite the contrary, it is important for singles to express themselves in wholesome ways as authentic sexual persons. The capacity to respond to others in a positive, pleasurable way is congruent with a healthy sexuality. Physical expression requires self-awareness, knowledge, discipline and a godly value system.

Christians in the New Testament were told, "Greet one another with a holy kiss." Admittedly, the holy kiss is not clearly defined, but this verse at least alludes to the fact that people can appropriately express affection for each other with physical contact. It is difficult to set up hard and fast rules of premarital sexual involvement due to the many factors that enter into such a decision, such as age and maturity, level of commitment, length of engagement and the closeness to the marriage ceremony.

At this point we offer some guiding principles in the area of dating, courtship and sexual expression. We reason that it is natural and good for single persons to physically express their affection to the one they love. People need to be affirmed and touched by others. Lack of touch, in fact, makes us "skin hungry" because touching is a basic human need and an important means of communicating acceptance, love and care toward others. Children, for example, are unusually free to express themselves through touch and ask for touch from others. Unfortunately, adults are sometimes fearful of touch and withhold this expression of love and affirmation.

The discerning question about physical touch is the point where physical touching becomes sexually arousing. We must be aware of our responsiveness to touch so we can make good decisions about appropriate touching—what kind, how much and when. The two people involved *must* agree together about the degree of involvement. Here are some guiding principles that may be helpful in making these decisions.

The first principle is that *the degree of sexual intimacy will correspond to the degree of love and commitment present in the relationship.* Where there is no love or commitment in a relationship, a high degree of sexual intimacy is inappropriate because the focus is on the physical dimension rather than the relational dimension. Physical intimacy was meant to enhance the expression of the love and commitment toward the beloved. The committed lover seeks the other because being with that special one is more important than the physical pleasure between them. Covenant love involves a commitment to both the person and the relationship, and this commitment takes precedence over the sexual expression between lovers.

A second helpful principle is the *law of diminishing returns.* As a principle in physics, the law of diminishing returns means that in order for the same stimulus effect to occur over time, a stronger force must be applied. Think of the effect that the very first kiss has on a person. *Wow!* It is usually an exhilarating experience. However, as time passes and one becomes used to kissing, the effect of the same kind of kiss is diminished in terms of the amount of stimulus it has upon the couple. Over time, people tend to desire more intensity in the physical lovemaking in order to achieve the same stimulus threshold. The goal of increased sexual expression is to ultimately gain a certain sexual response. The closer the couple gets to the point of orgasm, the harder it is to return to a reduced state of arousal. Every couple, then, needs to be aware of this principle so that they can determine appropriate guidelines for their physical involvement. These guidelines need to correspond to their level of commitment and the developmental stage of their relationship (as stated in the first principle).

The third principle is that *each partner must test their personal motive for the physical involvement and activity.* Is the motive for physical involvement an expression of affection or a desire to sexually excite the other and oneself? It does something for the ego of both men and women to know that they can sexually arouse another person. Most people feel a sense of power and control when they can get another person to the point where they cannot be resisted. Such ego gratification can be the motive behind physical involvement and is more of a self-desire than a desire for the partner. Such motives have a way of separating sex from personhood since the goal does not lead to a deeper personal relationship with the other, but satisfies ego needs.

A fourth principle is that *the two persons involved in the relationship will continually communicate about all areas of the relationship.* A caution should be raised for a couple when the physical dimension of a relationship develops out of proportion to the social, emotional, psychological and spiritual dimensions of the relationship. When the sexual aspect dominates a relationship, the couple is lopsided. The other important dimensions are undernourished and the relationship is soon weakened. The fullness of a relationship comes through a communication process in which both partners share and get to know each other in all aspects of their lives. Getting to know another person intimately requires that a person appreciate all dimensions of the beloved. The hunger is to be in the presence of the beloved so that one can experience the multifaceted parts of that person. The relationship itself becomes strengthened in the process of such intimate sharing. It is a time of learning to play together, to plan and dream together, to enjoy mutual activities together and to work toward future goals and life meaning together. The spiritual oneness comes as these two persons seek God's presence in seeking God's blessing for the future union.

A fifth principle is that *both members will take responsibility for establishing guidelines and setting physical limits in the relationship.* Christian males must reject the societal norm that endorses the protocol that males should go as far as they can sexually, leaving it up to the female to set the limits. Both partners are responsible together for their sexual involvement in the relationship. The couple needs to discuss the issue of limit setting at a neutral time and place so they can agree on mutual boundaries and guidelines. One partner may be more capable of keeping that limit at any particular time, but since they have both committed to the standard ahead of time, upholding the standard is a way for each to respect the partner and the relationship. There is nothing to be argued in a passionate moment, since the commitment was mutually agreed to ahead of time. Honoring the commitment is honoring their partnership. This agreement eliminates a spontaneous changing of rules in the heat of passion that both partners will regret later.

Of course, there are times when a couple may want to rethink an already established boundary, to set either a looser or a more stringent limit. In this case the couple needs to find a place and time where they can honestly look at the pros and cons of such a proposed change in standards. In this way a mutual agreement is made where both views are respected and considered. It is splendid to practice mutual decision-making like this, for this will be an ongoing process throughout the life of any couple.

A sixth principle is that *each partner agrees to commit to following the standard of the person with the strongest felt limits.* This is a position of respect and caring that places the person above the desire for a certain sexual activity. In an authentic relationship, neither person will try to intimidate the other by judging their standards as prudish. It takes an understanding person to want to find out what that particular limit means to their partner. It also takes courage to honestly express one's ideas about a personal value system and what it means. In the end, honoring the limitation of the other indicates that the person is valued and cherished. This brings about a deepening of trust. Also important is that the person who has more freedom in a particular standard not be judged for this. The essential thing is that each partner listens, understands and tries to be understood. Partners open up to each other when they recognize differences without making judgments and accept and respect these personal value systems.

The seventh principle provides an overview of these guidelines: *use Scripture as your guide and recognize your freedom in Christ.* In 1 Corinthians 6:12-13 Paul says, "I can do anything I want to if Christ has not said no, but some of these things aren't good for me. Even if I am allowed to do them, I'll refuse to if I think they might get such a grip on me that I can't easily stop when I want to. For instance, take the matter of eating. God has given us an appetite for food and stomachs to digest it. . . . But sexual sin is never right: our bodies were not made for that, but for the Lord" (LB).

We must refrain from exaggerating or minimizing sexual sin. When Paul talks about immorality, he lists many different kinds of problems that keep us from God's way. When we magnify sexual sin out of proportion to other wrongs in our lives, we can get frozen in our tracks and stuck in our hopelessness to change. When we minimize sexual sin and yield to the temptations that pull us in the direction away from God, we start down another path that leads to destructive sexual behaviors.

The idea is not to establish unreasonable rules, but realistic ones to govern premarital sexual involvement in which one makes responsible decisions in accordance with God's word. Not everything is good or beneficial for every person or couple. You must be honest with yourself and your partner about problematic sexual behaviors that may have a grip on you. This is preventive medicine. When we strive for authenticity, we are seeking to be congruent with ourselves before God. Letting our partner know where we are vulnerable allows him or her to understand us more deeply, to help us in personal temptations and to keep us on the path toward God's way. Discovering more about how we work to empower each other in our sexual journey is what helps us make decisions that are in the best interest of ourself, our partner and the relationship.

Claiming Victory in Christ

While one can never erase the past, single persons can always reaffirm their virginity and recommit themselves to celibacy again. We make this suggestion based on our understanding of the encounter Jesus had with the adulterous woman (Jn 8:3-11). The Pharisees quoted Mosaic law as commanding that such women should be stoned. Jesus, however, did not condemn her but told her to go and sin no more.

Showing compassion does not mean compromising standards. We must ardently uphold the standards we think are right, articulate the biblical principles behind them and move toward God's way with God's help. We need to support one another in our common humanity and our common hope as we strive toward authentic sexuality.

Walter Trobisch gave readers three important reasons to keep sexual intercourse for the covenant of marriage: *the richness of love, the richness of sex* and *the richness of marriage* (Trobisch 1968).

The *richness of love* has to do with keeping focus on the person (beloved partner) and priority on the committed relationship. C. S. Lewis (1963) describes eros beautifully in *The Four Loves:*

> Very often what comes first is a delighted pre-occupation with the Beloved—a general unspecified pre-occupation with her [him] in total-ity. There is no leisure time to think of sex. He [she] is too busy thinking of a person. . . . One is full of desire, but the desire may not be sexually toned. If you asked him what he wanted, the true reply would often be, "to go on thinking of her." (pp. 86-87)

> Eros, though the king of pleasures, always (at its height) has the air of regarding pleasure as a by-product. . . . Desiring a human being is dis-tinct from desiring the pleasure that person can bring. . . . Love makes one want not *a* person, but *one* particular person. . . . Eros wants the beloved! (pp. 88-89)

Romantic attraction certainly leads us to want a particular person. This is evidenced in the Song of Songs, where the two lovers boldly declare, "I am my beloved's and my beloved is mine . . . his [her] desire is for *me.*" These lovers are full of love for each other, and take great delight in the other. Their eyes are for each other and their desire is to give and receive of themselves in person-centered intimacy.

One of the richest aspects of love is the intimacy that comes out of sharing without fear one's thoughts, feelings, dreams, fears, secrets and yearning. Commitment to the person safeguards the highest and deepest qualities of love. The couple desires to know each other in the deepest ways possible. One of the misconceptions about falling in love is that it just happens. We think that when we are mesmerized by the other or smitten with love we are not volitional in our pursuit. How-ever, just the opposite is true. It is precisely in that falling-in-love stage that two persons intentionally pursue each other. They can't get enough of each other and spend hours talking in order to get to know the other person more fully. Such attraction involves conscious deci-sions and purposeful action.

Bonding with each other in the richness of love makes the couple eager to want to seal it forever. The *richness of sex* is intricately related to the richness of love. Good sex has to do with person-centered love. Expressing sexual love to that beloved partner brings delight to one's soul. In the movie *Phenomenon* the sensual response between the lead characters as she gently shaves his face and cuts his hair is obvious. Yet, the attraction is so clearly about the person. Even when sexual desire is an obvious part of allure, it does not overtake them in this intimate exchange. There is no push for sexual involvement, even though he readily acknowledges his sexual interest in her, because it's much more important that she respond to him from the core of her being. It is because sex is so rich that sexual passion is rightly anticipated as the reward of a permanent relationship.

When two lovers give themselves to each other in this manner, it truly is a mystical union of bodies, minds and souls that goes far beyond sexual pleasure. It is more than one body entwined in the other; it is a union of heart and soul. While the couple will gladly acknowledge that they enjoy the sexual interaction, they will be quick to add that it's because they adore each other.

Granted, not everyone who engages in sexual intercourse experiences such a full, life-giving relationship. Many find it difficult to understand that it takes time to get to know and understand another person at an intimate level. The pleasure of making the most of the encounter comes out of a mutual passion that is well worth waiting for. Listen to these phrases from the Song of Songs to grasp this more completely: "I found . . . him and would not let him go. . . . You have stolen my heart. . . . I opened for my lover. . . . Your love is more delightful than wine. . . . How beautiful you are and how pleasing. . . . This is my lover, this is my friend." We listen to the erotic language and can visualize the passion expressed between these lovers. It seems to come out of pure joy for the other that brings their bodies and souls into a harmonious rhythm. Sexual fulfillment can be like this! Person-focused passion is an interaction that involves all levels of responsiveness between the lovers.

C. S. Lewis (1963) makes the observation that sexual desire is a fact about ourselves like every other desire about us, but when sexual desire is about the beloved, it "has the air of regarding pleasure as the by-product" (p. 89). It takes little effort to simply have a genital experience with someone, but making love to a multidimensional person requires attention, responsive interaction, sensitivity, time and commitment.

The *richness of marriage* is the final reason to keep sex a sacred part of the marriage bond. God ordained marriage as a covenant relationship between two people who will live out their lives in the context of a supportive community. Marriage is not just an event between two individuals, but it is a joining of two families, two sets of friends and the community who stand with them in their commitment to each other. It's a private and yet public affair. In the Old Testament a marriage was consummated when the couple began to reside together and had their first sexual union. Whether it was an agreement between the parents with the customary exchange of gifts or a wedding feast in which joining hands in the presence of witnesses made the union public, the community pledged to support the couple in their vows of commitment.

It is quite a remarkable thing that two people exchange vows and promise to love each other unconditionally for the rest of their lives. Agape love calls for the extraordinary self-sacrifice that puts the best interests of the other as priority. Some argue that only God is capable of such a covenant, but with God's help, along with the support of a committed community, agape love truly keeps the couple working toward this goal. It is what keeps a couple going through the thick and thin of marital disappointments and struggles. It is what brings hope during days of discouragement.

Covenant love is the highest response we can give to another. We vow we will be faithful to our promises and agreements, we will be invested in our partner's well being, we will be involved in mutual interdependency.

Love demands security if it is to flourish. Lifelong commitment is the anchor in the midst of the unknowns of life. It is a place to make mistakes, to change, to develop, to take risks, to go on when we fail. Marriage offers a place of ongoing respect, devotion, trustworthiness and gracing ways. Covenant marriage gives the context where the highest possibilities of love are possible. It is the *more excellent way!*

Suggestions for Further Reading
Balswick, J., and J. Balswick. 1994. *Raging hormones: What to do when you*

suspect your teen may be sexually active. Grand Rapids, Mich.: Zondervan.

Grenz, S. 1997. *Sexual ethics: An evangelical perspective.* Louisville, Ky.: Westminster John Knox. See chapters 9-10.

Jones, S., and B. Jones. 1993. *How and when to tell your kids about sex.* Colorado Springs: NavPress.

Thatcher, A., and E. Stuart. 1996. *Christian perspectives on sexuality and gender.* Grand Rapids, Mich.: Eerdmans. See section 10, "Sexuality and singleness," pp. 411-37.

7

Premarital Cohabitation

Cautions & Concerns

Few developments have been as dramatic as the rise of premarital cohabitation. While only 2 percent of women born between 1928 and 1932 cohabited before marriage, 40 percent of those born between 1958 and 1962 chose to cohabit (Schoen and Owen 1992). Macklin (1983) discovered that approximately one-fourth of college students in the United States have lived with someone prior to marriage. According to the U.S. Bureau of the Census (1989), the number of unmarried couple households in 1980 was 2.6 million, a substantial increase of 117 percent from 1970 to 1980. Based on their survey of 13,000 persons ages nineteen and older, Sweet, Bumpass and Call (1988) projected that almost half the population of the United States would choose to cohabit some time prior to their mid-thirties. In a comprehensive review of recent research on cohabitation, Popenoe and Whitehead (1999) report, "By 1997, the total number of unmarried couples in America topped 4 million, up from less than half a million in 1960" (p. 2).

Given the fact that one-third to one-half of all marriages end in divorce, there are also numerous post-divorce cohabiting couples. As might be expected, people who cohabited with their first spouse prior to marriage have a greater propensity to cohabit with another person after a divorce (Wu 1995). Those who lived together prior to marriage had a 50 percent higher hazard rate of divorcing after marriage than those who had not cohabited.

Our goal in this chapter is to develop a Christian perspective on the topic. We draw on existing research, mainly self-reported responses to survey research questionnaires or interviews, to address the question "Why do people choose to cohabit?" We then examine its effect upon marriage and give a response to cohabitation that is informed by both biblical and social scientific literature.

Why Cohabitation?

McRae (1997) suggests that cohabitation serves as a type of "trial marriage" or "marriage preparation," which can best be understood as a stage between courtship (mate selection) and marriage. In this case, cohabiting gives the couple a chance to test the degree of compatibility in the relationship. If they conclude that their personalities "fit" with one another, they then proceed to marriage.

Premarital cohabitation is actually not a new idea. As early as 1966 anthropologist Margaret Mead tried to address the situation by proposing a two-step plan for single adults. The first step would be a "trial marriage," in which the couple would determine whether they were compatible. The second step would be for those couples who wanted to legalize the union when they had children. Taking it a step further, Scriven (1968) proposed a three-stage plan whereby a relationship progressed from sexual satisfaction, to social security, to sensible spawning. Cadwallader (1966) believed that cohabiting would free couples from feeling "trapped for life." He suggested that couples establish contracts for stated periods of time, which would be periodically renewed.

These views stretched trial marriage about as far as it could go, eventually leading to the concept of premarital cohabitation. It has only been within the past 30 years that cohabitation has become popular among the middle classes. Cohabitation originated among lower-class and disadvantaged youth (Thorton, Axinn and Treachman 1995; Bumpass, Martin and Sweet 1991).

Today, many couples admittedly choose to cohabit for the convenience and companionship of being in an exclusive sexual relationship with a chosen partner. There is not necessarily any intention for the arrangement to lead to marriage. Bumpass and Sweet (1989) found that the majority of cohabiting relationships end within 2 years, with couples spending on average 1.3 years together in a cohabiting arrangement. In a study of over 1,500 Canadian divorced persons, Wu and Balakrishnan (1992) concluded that postmarital cohabitation was chosen as an alternative to remarriage.

A study comparing dating, cohabiting and married women found that "cohabitation, in terms of sexual commitment, is more similar to dating than marriage" (Forste and Tanfer 1996:33). However, what distinguishes cohabiting relationships from married ones is not only the lack of commitment to sexual exclusivity, but also greater illicit drug use (Yamaguchi and Kandel 1985); lower age, education level, employment status and economic well-being (Glick and Spanier 1980); minority racial status (Clayton and Voss 1977); and lower mental health (Horwitz and White 1998). Seventy percent of all cohabiting relationships fail to culminate in marriage, typically terminating after a little over a year (Bumpass and Sweet 1989, Surra 1990).

All of these differences between cohabitation and marriage could be taken as indirect evidence that cohabitation is not to be understood as an alternative to marriage. Given the present state of knowledge about cohabitation, it is probably wise to recognize that for some couples, cohabitation is an *alternative* to marriage and for other couples it is a *stage* in a relationship that leads to marriage. Each interpretation might be true of different individuals and both might be true of the same individuals at different times in their life.

What does love have to do with it? This rather cool and detached analysis of the function of cohabitation causes us to ask, "What does love have to do with it?" What distinguishes modern forms of mate selection is the freedom youth have to pursue sexual/romantic relationships without parental involvement. No longer is marriage an economic arrangement, controlled and arranged by parents, but a participant-run system in which love drives the relationship.

Being in love carries a variety of meanings such as mutual attraction, strong sexual feelings, commitment and enjoying each other's company. Romantic love had its beginnings in European societies during the eleventh century. At that time, "courtly love" became well known among the privileged class. Courtly love usually involved a romantic relationship between a married aristocratic lady and an unmarried knight or troubadour. As portrayed in literature, the stereotypical courtly love involved a dramatic story in which the knight goes forth into battle motivated by the love of his lady, or a mandolin-playing troubadour sings love songs to a young lady in a balcony on a moonlit night. In this early version of romantic love, it was believed that true love is free of the restrictions of sex or marriage.

The development of courtly love relationships served to introduce tenderness and affection into male/female relationships. This was an uncommon experience for most married persons, who were usually united in marriage for economic reasons. From the eleventh to the sixteenth century, the nature of these love relationships changed to include sexual involvement between the lady of nobility and her "true" love. During the sixteenth and seventeenth centuries the middle classes of European society came to value romantic love but still held to faithfulness in marriage. This dilemma was solved when the love object of the single male changed from the married woman to the single woman. For a period of time during the seventeenth and eighteenth centuries, parental-arranged marriage and romantic love existed side by side. As Western societies moved into the twentieth century, the custom of a man asking the father for his daughter's hand became a formality.

During the first half of the twentieth century, the irrational "head-over-heels" concept of romantic love reached its zenith. Confusion over the exact meaning of romantic love made it difficult for persons to really know if true love was present in their relationship. Psychiatrist Erich Fromm recognized this fact when he wrote *The Art of Loving* (1956). Fromm made the observation that most people see the problem of love primarily as that of being loved, rather than loving the other. He argued that modern persons need to *learn* how to love in the same way they learn how to play a musical instrument. He contended that love is an art to be practiced, and it requires discipline, concentration, patience and supreme concern. When people start "working at love," the noticeable active elements will include behaviors like giving, caring, responsibility, respect and knowledge.

During the 1950s the mate-selection process in Western societies moved to a new stage, referred to as rational/romantic love. This type of love included a strong dose of the participants' rational consideration of their compatibility with their true love. Although few people would marry someone they did not love, it is now true that few people will marry *only* on the basis of love. Rational/romantic love is especially common among college-educated persons who decide to marry after their education is completed. Today marriage is as much a rational decision as it is a head-over-heels response to the partner.

Three kinds of love. Roger Sternberg (1987) attempted to sort out the complexity of what our society calls romantic love. Based on research, he believes that love includes three dimensions: *commitment,* the cognitive component of love; *intimacy,* the friendship factor and emotional component of love; and *passion,* the motivational component of love. We suggest that these three ingredients of love are quite similar to the three types of love known from Greek culture: *agape, philia* and *eros* (Balswick and Balswick 1999). C. S. Lewis (1963) has written eloquently about this in *The Four Loves.* The self-giving agape corresponds to commitment; philia, the brotherly/friendship love, corresponds to intimacy; and eros, the love one feels for the beloved, corresponds to passion.

The correspondence between these descriptions of love provides a basis from which to discuss the place of cohabitation in a mate-selection system. From a biblical perspective, we believe a *complete love* embraces all three loves; commitment/agape, intimacy/philia, and passion/eros. However we know this is not always the case, as any one of these types of love can dominate a relationship.

If only one type is to be dominant, it seems that it should be the self-giving, commitment/agape love. The vow to be faithful in marriage is the desired prerequisite in most societies, and commitment is considered a critical factor in arranged marriages. Note that a lower proportion of arranged marriages end in divorce than those that are based on romantic love. However, this should not imply that parent-arranged marriages are more likely than love-based marriages to achieve a Christian ideal. The strength of the courtship and premarital relationship involves a commitment that can bring together friendship, emotional intimacy and passion that grow into maturity in marriage. While there may be a potential for intimacy and passion in arranged marriages, the familial structure may actually hinder the formation of these relationship qualities. The commitment that keeps these marriages together may be less a "self-giving" commitment to one's spouse than it is a commitment to the extended family and community.

The emergence of cohabitation may be symptomatic of a problem in Western-style mate-selection systems in which commitment is not given a primary place in defining love. In chapter three we asserted that unconditional commitment is the foundation of a biblical understanding of love. Most typically in Western courtship systems, passion is likely to dominate at the beginning of a relationship, followed by emotional intimacy and finally commitment.

The least stable of all cohabiting relationships are likely those based on passion/eros. Most relationships get off to a passionate start out of physical attraction and sexual vibes. Such passionate impulses may override the emotional core and commitment stability needed to sustain a relationship. Since *passion* by itself cannot usually carry a relationship over time, the passionate relationship often burns out before a commitment occurs.

Other cohabiting relationships are based largely on friendship *intimacy*. Although few relationships move into marriage on the basis of friendship alone, it has been found to be an essential factor in marital satisfaction. Persons often describe their spouse as their "best friend," connoting a "soul mate" connection and emotional companionship that they value.

Although cohabiting couples represent combinations of all types of love relationships, by its very nature premarital cohabitation is a relationship in which intimacy and passion rather than commitment are the strongest elements. Cohabitation conveniently allows for the fulfillment of passion and intimacy, but commitment is often a low priority. This is verified by the fact that the majority of cohabiting relationships (70 percent) fail to culminate in marriage and end in a little over a year.

Does Premarital Cohabitation Lead to Better Marital Adjustment?

In this section, we consider the impact of cohabiting on subsequent marital success. When premarital cohabitation became fairly widespread in the mid-1970s, social scientists predicted that premarital cohabitation would strengthen rather than weaken marriage (Trost

1975). Danzinger (1976) suggested that premarital cohabitation would serve as a screening device that would ensure the compatibility of prospective spouses. Along this same line of thinking, Peterman (1975) believed that cohabitants would gain experience in intimacy and therefore develop a greater degree of relational competence necessary for an enduring and fulfilling marriage.

Based on responses to questionnaires, Chatworthy and Scheid (1977) reported a less optimistic picture of the effect of cohabitation on later marital adjustment. They found that cohabiters were more disagreeable about issues of money, household duties and recreation; less likely to acquiesce in disagreements; and more likely to break up. The authors reasoned that because partners were less dependent on each other, their marriage was less intrinsic to their lives.

Newcomb and Bentler (1980) expressed a similar opinion about the effects of premarital cohabitation, stating that cohabitation allows "the circumvention of the requisite commitment and obligation necessary to build a relationship that is viable, meaningful and fulfilling" (p. 11).

DeMaris and Leslie (1984) surveyed couples who had cohabited two years before marriage and found them to be less satisfied in their marriage than couples who had not cohabited. Wives who had formerly cohabited reported a lower quality of communication when compared to wives of couples who had not cohabited prior to marriage. Watson (1983) also found a higher level of marital adjustment among those who had *not* cohabited prior to marriage when compared to those who had cohabited.

Looking at these studies from a methodological perspective, it is obvious that well-designed longitudinal studies are needed if one is to make future predictions about success in marriage. One four-year survey of sixty-eight couples by Newcomb and Bentler (1980) found that a higher proportion of cohabiters as compared to noncohabiters had divorced (36 percent versus 26 percent). For those who were still together after four years of marriage, noncohabiters reported a higher rate of marital adjustment. This study was partially replicated by Watson and DeMeo (1987). They found that noncohabiters reported slightly higher marital adjustment, but the difference was not statistically significant.

Most studies on cohabitation since 1986 have indicated that premarital cohabitation is correlated with increased marital instability and risk of future divorce (Booth and Johnson 1988, Bumpass and Sweet 1989, Newcomb 1986). A study based on responses from 13,000 adults found that the rate of separation or divorce within ten years after marriage was a third higher for those who cohabited when compared with those who did not cohabit (Sweet, Bumpass and Call 1988). In examining different types of cohabiting relationships, Demaris and Rao (1992) concluded that regardless of the nature of the cohabitation, persons who cohabited prior to marriage experienced higher rates of marital disruption than those who did not. A study of over 4,000 women in Sweden reported that women who cohabit premaritally have an 80 percent higher marital dissolution rate than those who do not (Bennett, Blanc and Bloom 1988). These authors suggest "a weaker commitment to the institution of marriage on the part of those who cohabit premaritally" (p. 127).

In a national random sample of telephone responses of 2,033 married persons, Booth and Johnson (1988) discovered that those who had cohabited, when compared to noncohabiting couples, had a lower level of marital success in the following four ways. First, they had less *marital interaction,* determined by spending time together eating meals, shopping, visiting friends, working on projects or going out on leisurely or recreational activities. Second, they had more frequent and more serious *marital disagreements,* including behaviors like slapping, hitting, punching, kicking or throwing things at each other. Third, they were more prone to *marital instability,* shown through actions like thinking the marriage was in trouble or considering the idea of getting a divorce; taking divorce action such as talking to friends or their spouse about the possibility of divorce, or consulting with clergy, counselor or attorney; or actually separating from the spouse or filing a petition for divorce. Fourth, these couples reported a higher incidence of *divorce* (Booth and Johnson 1988).

Research conducted in the 1990s found that having cohabited with someone other than one's spouse is predictive of lower marital adjustment. A study based on over 9,000 responses to a national survey made the following conclusion: "After controlling for other factors, results indicate that prior cohabiting relationships negatively influence current married and cohabiting relationships" (Stets

1993:236). Stets speculated that those who had cohabited with someone other than the intended spouse are predisposed to problems in relationships and carry over these problems to future relationships, including the experience of having been in a broken cohabiting relationship. Likewise, DeMaris and MacDonald (1993) also report that especially among serial cohabiters there is greater instability among first-married couples.

Is There a Selective Factor?

While research generated in the 1990s continued to find premarital cohabitation predictive of lower marital quality, part of this relationship is explained in terms of sample selection. A self-selection explanation would suggest that people who have personal characteristics that make them high risk for a divorce would also choose to enter a cohabiting relationship. Thus, the relationship between cohabiting and divorce is real, but one cannot say that cohabitation *alone* contributes to divorce. A study based on over 6,000 respondents in Germany concluded that the same "factors that increase divorce rates also increase premarital cohabitation rates" (Bruderl, Dickmann and Englehardt 1997:205). In a study of over 5,000 Canadian women, Hall (1996) concluded that the relationship between premarital cohabitation and divorce could be explained by the tendency to idealize that pure relationship in which one is self-actualized and which actually "contaminates" marriage (p. 1).

Thomson and Colella (1992) found that couples who cohabited before marriage were more dissatisfied with the quality of their marriages than couples who had not cohabited. However, these authors argued that the dissatisfaction in these marriages had more to do with the unconventional attitudes and lifestyles of these couples than with the decision to cohabit. Their more liberal tendencies gave them the freedom to express dissatisfaction and split when things did not go well. Nock (1994) found that cohabiters expressed lower levels of commitment to and happiness with their relationships and had poorer relationships with parents than did comparable married individuals.

Indirect support for a self-selection explanation is given by Clarkberg, Stolzenberg and Waite (1995) in their analysis of over 12,000 responses to a national survey. They concluded that "the choice between cohabitation and marriage is affected by attitudes and values toward work, family, use of leisure time, money, and sex roles, as well as toward marriage itself" (p. 609).

While selection factors may be at work in explaining part of the relationship between premarital cohabitation and lower marital adjustment, they do not explain it away completely. A comprehensive study done by DeMaris and MacDonald (1993) concluded that "controlling for unconventionality had only a minimal impact on the cohabitation effect" (p. 406). They also suggest, "Although family attitudes and beliefs tend to predict the attractiveness of a cohabiting lifestyle, they do not account for differences between cohabiters and non-cohabiters in instability" (p. 399).

Taking current findings into account, we can conclude that contrary to predictions made in the 1970s, one's participation in premarital cohabitation does not mean one adjusts better to marriage. Even more important, evidence points to the contrary of this initial optimistic prediction. This conclusion is consistent with McRae's (1997) review of the relevant literature. She states, "The results of research suggest that a strong negative association exists between premarital cohabitation and marital stability. " She finds that the link between premarital cohabitation and marriage dissolution is weaker among the younger generation, suggesting that "as cohabitation becomes the majority pattern before marriage, this link will become progressively weaker" (p. 159).

Is Cohabitation Good? A Social Scientific Response

Sociologists David Popenoe and Barbara Whitehead (1999) at Rutgers University have completed a comprehensive review of research on cohabitation before marriage. They have cautioned young adults to think twice about cohabiting prior to marriage, offering the following four principles. First, *consider not living together at all before marriage, since there is no evidence to support the view that cohabiting will result in a stronger marriage.* In fact, they warn that evidence suggests that if a couple lives together before marriage, there is an increased chance of divorcing after marriage. If a couple cohabits, it is probably least harmful (though not necessarily helpful) when it is prenuptial; that is, both partners plan to marry, formally announce their engagement and have already picked a wedding date.

The second principle is *not to make a habit of cohabiting.* They see the evidence as refuting the popular myth that persons "learn to have better relationships from multiple failed cohabiting relationships" (Popenoe and Whitehead 1999:10). Rather, multiple cohabitation is repeatedly found to be a strong predictor of the failure of future relationships.

The third principle is to *limit cohabitation to the shortest possible period of time.* While the Christian community might question the wisdom of this third principle, we should at least understand the intent and spirit with which it is given. It is based on Poponoe and Whitehead's (1999) conclusion: "The longer you live together with a partner, the more likely it is that the low-commitment ethic of cohabitation will take hold, the opposite of what is required for a successful marriage" (p. 10). Participation in a cohabiting relationship can have an eroding effect not only on the participants' view of the importance of commitment but also on societal ethics, which value unconditional commitment as a basis for marriage. From a purely functional standpoint, Popenoe and Whitehead realize that a high commitment ethic is necessary for marital stability.

The fourth principle is *don't cohabit when children are involved.* The spirit of this principle is based on the belief that "Children need and should have parents who are committed to staying together over the long term" (Poponoe and Whitehead 1999:10). Since cohabiting parents break up at a much higher rate than married parents, the impact of cohabiting on children can be devastating. In noting other ways in which cohabiting relationships are different from marriage, Poponoe and Whitehead (1999) point to evidence that "children living in cohabiting unions are at higher risk of sexual abuse and physical violence, including lethal violence" (p. 2).

Popenoe and Whitehead (1999) summarize: "These principles may not be the last words on the subject . . . [but] they are consistent with the available evidence and seem most likely to help never-married young adults avoid painful losses in their love lives and achieve satisfying and long-lasting relationships and marriage" (p. 1). Poponoe and Whitehead speak as social scientists, not as advocates for a Christian view of marriage. However, their view certainly comports well with the biblical wisdom that marriage is to be based on lifelong covenant commitments.

A Christian Response

A Christian response to cohabitation needs to be formulated at several different levels. We will organize our response around four questions: (1) What is the nature of commitment in cohabiting relationships? (2) When are two people married in the sight of God? (3) Does cohabitation pose a threat to the institution of marriage? and (4) How should the church respond to cohabiting couples?

Commitment in cohabiting relationships. The prominent reasons people enter cohabiting relationships include love, companionship, sexual exclusivity, economics, ambivalence toward marriage, loneliness and peer pressure. Whereas many of these are understandable reasons for living with a companion, the noticeable missing piece is covenant commitment. There is no understanding that two persons make a vow before God to commit themselves to each other throughout a lifetime. The biblical concept of a "mysterious one-flesh union" that is blessed by God is the essential missing piece in a cohabiting arrangement. Whereas an exclusive sexual union is an important aspect of cohabitation, just as it is in marriage, the mutual covenant provides an enduring, ongoing, faithful commitment through all aspects of marriage. It is *ḥesed* (the Hebrew root for "covenant") love that promises a faithful giving of oneself to the other and keeping that best interest of the partner in mind "for better or worse, richer or poorer, in sickness and health, 'til death do us part." Although humans cannot love unconditionally as God does, the model of unconditional commitment is a scriptural ideal for marriage.

The cohabiting couple may have a difficult time grasping the value of covenant love. The desired independence that frees one of such a commitment places a limit on the deepening maturity of the relationship. When partners are uncertain about permanent commitment, they will be prone to keep distance and protect themselves from the uncertainty of the future. A relationship of reluctance, a fear of becoming too involved or interdependent keeps emotional barriers up rather than breaking them down. Thus one of the biggest problems with cohabitation is that it can inhibit emotional intimacy and deeper levels of personal sharing and knowing. Holding oneself back limits growth in the relationship and inhibits partners from developing the deepest capacity for intimacy and loving.

It takes courage to know oneself and then reveal that self to a partner. When one has a clarified sense of self, one can take the risk to be vulnerable and surrender in self-giving ways. Covenant love gives freedom to express personal longings and fears and makes it possible to listen to the partner's thoughts, feelings, needs and desires, which are put on a par with one's own. Covenant love that is established in a grace-filled interdependence gives partners the courage to risk letting themselves be known. Being confident that a partner loves unconditionally, respects and accepts differences, and seeks mutual empowerment and intimacy is the backbone of mutuality and interdependence.

The "forever" covenant commitment gives a capacity to share without fear. Communicating covenant love through thought and action, regardless of obvious flaws and failures, means partners are able to be "naked and not ashamed." There is no need to hide because there is no need to protect oneself from a deeper attachment. The seal of this kind of covenant commitment is a profound one-flesh union, as one knows the other and is known in deeper ways.

When are two people married before God? Some might question what is meant by God's loving us unconditionally. The covenantal basis for Christian marriage is modeled after the covenant God made with Israel. God is pictured as trustworthy and forever faithful in expressing unconditional love to the people of God. The very foundation of covenant love is permanence, upon which sexual and emotional intimacy are built. Trustworthiness and faithfulness are the fruit of a forever love that establishes a solid foundation for secure connection. The deepening of love throughout the years develops a solid, rich love that expands into an even fuller and more complete covenant.

James Olthuis (1975) argues that Scripture calls for two main conditions to be present between two persons who want to join their lives together: (1) that the relationship be based upon a mutually shared covenantal commitment and (2) that it be consummated through sexual intercourse. This places the decision to marry squarely upon the two participants involved. If Olthuis's understanding of Scripture is correct, there might be a variety of ways a couple can cement their covenant commitment without fulfilling all of the societal expectations for marriage. This leads to several important questions.

First, does the couple need consent from parents or family before they can be considered to be married before God? While parental consent was part of Jewish marriage during biblical times, this was a cultural practice based on the mate-selection process. Whereas parental consent is certainly desirable, it would be difficult to find scriptural evidence that deems it a requirement for marriage.

Second, does a couple need to make their commitment before a community of believers before they are married in God's sight? One could argue that while it is wise to have support from a faith community, it is not a scriptural directive. Ray Tannahill (1980) points out that ecclesiastical consent to marry actually began in the twelfth century when the Roman Catholic Church decreed that marriage could commence only by consent of the Church.

Third, is the consent of civil authorities needed? Those who believe that persons should have the consent of the civil authorities point to health concerns, for example, blood tests for Rh negative factor or sexually transmitted disease, which have ramifications for each partner and their future children. Also, this gives the spouse certain legal, financial and property rights. While there are excellent reasons to seek the consent of civil authorities, it would be difficult to support this as a scriptural mandate.

Following a letter-of-the-law interpretation of Scripture, one could argue that none of the above conditions are required to be married in God's sight. At the same time, we think it is important to understand the spirit of the law, which recognizes family, community and civil structures that support marriage. Cohabiting couples who say they are married "before God" because they have a mutual covenant commitment, yet fail to make it public, miss out on a vital source of collective encouragement. The strength of a commitment is multiplied when it is made before a witness of believers who offer resources as well as a place of accountability. The wisdom of making commitments within a believing community is especially noticeable during times of trouble. A couple depends on others to keep them resilient when life stresses come their way.

Partners who fail to legalize their "marriage" lose out on the government's obligation to look out for the welfare of each partner, the couple and their children. This especially has ramifications for spouses and their children in regard to financial and property rights, benefits that occur when a relationship has the legal support of society. There is a sense in which a personal commitment is maintained through a supportive community and society.

Some do endorse a mutual covenant commitment made between an unmarried man and women before God and sealed through sexual intercourse as the minimal biblical standard; others believe there is a need for the commitment to be made in the presence of the Christian community and/or within the accepted formal structure of civil society. We believe the church needs to uphold the directive that sexual intercourse is reserved for marriage. The ceremony and the license are aspects that serve to integrate a couple into society. Evidence points to the fact that the individualistic ethic in our society keeps people from fully realizing the importance of personal commitments that are embedded in a community context.

Is cohabitation a threat to the institution of marriage? The church must make a distinction between how it responds to individuals who are in cohabiting relationships and how it responds to cohabitation as a practice. We advocate that Christians should offer grace over law. At the societal level we do believe that cohabitation poses a threat to marriage and family stability. In response, the church can offer an informed voice to support a societal practice that undergirds marriage and family life.

At present, marriage is institutionalized and cohabitation is not. This means that marriage in the United States is the accepted way of recognizing a social and legally binding relationship between a man and a woman. Attempts to deinstitutionalize marriage and institutionalize cohabitation undermine the institution of marriage and therefore pose a threat to marriage.

At stake is the unique institutionalized status granted to marriage by the founders of our country. Rather than being a passive agent, the church can be an active participant in the legal/political system. The move to give the same legal sanction to cohabitation as marriage is not an acceptable solution. The research indicates that cohabitation weakens rather than strengthens the marital bond. In Sweden, for example, thirty percent of all couples sharing a household are unmarried (Tomasson 1998). Since cohabitation there carries similar legal rights as marriage in regard to parenting and economic rights and responsibility, it becomes a disincentive to marry in Sweden. The legitimate concern is the further erosion of marriage as an institution in society due to shorter unions, a higher rate of breakups and an increase in the number of children growing up in single-parent homes.

The negative impact of cohabitation on children should be of especially grave concern to the church. Bumpass and Sweet (1989) compared children born to cohabiting couples who later married, to children born to couples who were married at the time that their child was born. They found that the children born to cohabiting couples were significantly more likely to spend a portion of their childhood in a single-parent home than were children born to married couples. And since there is ample evidence that the economic and emotional stresses of divorce have deleterious effects on children (Sandefur, McLanahan and Wojtkiewicz 1992; McLanahan and Bumpass 1988), we are concerned about the impact it has on the parent/child relationship.

How should the church respond to cohabiting couples? There are a variety of cohabiting situations, based upon a number of differing criteria for cohabitation, for example, degree of commitment, age of cohabiters, premarital versus postmarital cohabitation, the absence or presence of children, and the intent to have children or not. A detailed discussion of how the Christian community can wisely respond to each of these cohabiting situations is beyond the limits of this paper. We do offer some general guidelines, however, about how the Christian community might best respond to these different situations.

1. The Christian community should uphold the biblical standard that sexual intercourse is meant to be part of a permanent covenant commitment between two people before God and present that standard to couples in a compelling way.

2. When a couple engages in sexual intercourse without sharing a mutual covenant commitment, the church should lovingly help them understand how the biblical concept of covenant commitment can enhance and bring depth and stability to their relationship.

3. When a cohabiting couple is pregnant, the Christian community should be compassionate and offer a church home to them, thereby giving them a glimpse of the faithful presence of love and support of God's people. By experiencing this love, the couple will be more compelled to

consider the value of making a mutual covenant to each other and their children. The community should refrain from condemning or pressuring them to marry for the wrong reasons.

4. When a cohabiting couple makes a covenant commitment to each other, the church should offer a public ceremony within the community of faith to celebrate the covenant union. There should be no stigma placed on a couple who is pregnant or already have children from this union.

5. When a couple shares a mutual covenant commitment but still chooses a cohabiting arrangement, the Christian community should continue to show love and grace. Unconditional love expressed through the faith community offers the best model of God as the Christ who has his arms open and ready to receive and accept them when they are ready.

The Christian community must win trust by welcoming cohabiting couples into churches. The tragedy is that cohabiting couples who attend church usually stop coming because they feel condemned or unacceptable to the congregation. They turn away from the very body of believers who could surround them with loving support.

Cohabiting couples who have a mutual covenant commitment but fail to make it a public event miss out on the community celebration. Perhaps our society makes it more difficult for a couple to have a ceremony because of the elaborate and expensive weddings in our churches today. In the past, the wedding was a simple ceremony with local congregation and family members gathered to witness the couple taking covenant vows.

Judy's mother wore a simple gold dress for her wedding ceremony after the Sunday night church service. Her aunt and uncle stood with them, and the church provided cake and coffee for a small reception afterward. Jack's parents had a similar ceremony after the Sunday morning church service. They invited the family and a few special friends over to the house for a light Sunday brunch reception. A wedding was an occasion to support the couple's covenant commitment without all the fuss and flair of an expensive, elaborate wedding. Both our parents were married more than sixty years, a covenant commitment that lasted over their long lives.

The challenge to the Christian community is to be big enough to hold the tension of all seekers who come to church to consider the claims of Christ. The church needs to hold forth biblically based marriage and family norms, but at the same time show compassion and acceptance of persons who may not be living by these values. The discouraging truth is that living outside of biblically based norms can negatively affect one's attitudes towards those norms. Axinn and Barber (1997) found that "The more months of exposure to cohabitation that young people experienced, the less enthusiastic they were toward marriage and childbearing" and the more accepting of divorce (p. 608). Rather than reacting with anger or fear, the church should keep its doors wide open, welcoming all to come. We hope these couples will be drawn to such an embrace of grace.

In its stance toward the practice of cohabitation, we believe that the church can err in two ways: either by compromising the truth of Scripture and failing to uphold the sacred purpose of marriage, or by condemning and shutting the doors to those who cohabit. In upholding marriage as God's way with one hand, we should extend God's grace with the other. Our gospel must be full of *truth* and *grace*. The church needs to be the very place that reaches out to seekers, both those living outside biblical norms and those for whom biblical behavior has not yet become part of their lives. The church will have a minimal impact on the lives of those who are cohabiting until it clearly offers the hands of both truth and grace.

A couple may be on Christ's way without even knowing it. When a cohabiting couple establishes a covenant commitment, they have understood something essential about God's way. The Christian community can nurture a couple's natural inclination to continue to move in God's way through patience, respect and love that point them in that direction. Being compassionate rather than judgmental comes out of the assurance that God, who is the final judge, is the one who loves most fully. "Christ's love sees us with terrible clarity and sees us whole. Christ's love so wishes our joy that it is ruthless against everything in us that diminishes our joy" (Buechner 1992:58). The longing to help cohabiting couples find the joy of covenant love is a great privilege. So, let the Christian community show forth God's love in faithful, engaging ways that will draw those who cohabit closer to the way, the truth and the more abundant life.

Suggestions for Further Reading

Olthuis, J. 1975. *I pledge you my troth: A Christian view of marriage, family, friendship.* New York: Harper & Row.

Popenoe, D., and B. Whitehead. 1999. *Should we live together? What young adults need to know about cohabitation before marriage.* <http://marriage.rutgers.edu:80/shouldwe.htm>.

8

Marital Sexuality

Maximizing Sexual Fulfillment

Two are better than one, because they have a good reward for their toil.
For if they fall, one will lift up the other; but woe to one who is alone and falls
and does not have another to help. Again, if two lie together,
they keep each other warm; but how can one keep warm alone?
And though one might prevail against another, two will withstand one.
A threefold cord is not quickly broken. (Eccles 4:9-12 NRSV)

Marriage is a holy place in which profound personal, spiritual and
couple growth is possible. The partnership formed by husband and
wife is an entity that goes far beyond what each one can accomplish
alone. As two unique persons support and commit themselves to each
other throughout life's journey, they reap rewards of warmth, connection and strength. And with God at the center weaving these two lives
together into a threefold cord that is not easily broken, the potential for
a vital and fulfilling union is at its height.

Transforming oneself in relation to one's spouse is the ultimate
grindstone upon which marriage is sharpened. Each spouse is challenged to round off the rough edges and fill out the flat sides in order to

make a more complete whole. Marriage is full of wondrous possibilities but it can be a grueling process as well. Heartache and disappointment will be part of the refining process of living and loving in relationship. Hesitation about keeping covenant and fears about establishing closeness can hinder each spouse and the couple from reaching the possibilities described in the first paragraph. It takes courage to proceed in the direction of "two becoming one," for it takes determination to keep the best interest of one's spouse and the relationship in the forefront. The human tendency is to protect oneself from the vulnerability it takes to become emotionally and sexually interdependent. In fact, it is easy to get discouraged and hopeless about the marital relationship.

No More Luster in Our Love Life

Not long ago a married couple in their forties came to talk to us at the close of a marital sexuality workshop. They were rather hesitant at first, but then the wife blurted out their frustration, "Sex for us is like drinking day-old soda with the fizz gone out of it. Can you help us get the passion back into our marriage that we once had?" Unfortunately, this is a common complaint about the sex life of more than a few married couples. Ironically, when you ask married couples about their courting days, you often hear about the struggles they went through trying to control the fiery passion they felt for each other. But ten, twenty or thirty years later the fire seems to have fizzled away.

One of the comical scenes in the 1992 film *Fried Green Tomatoes* centered on the attempts of a bored, sexually frustrated housewife trying to rekindle passion in her marriage. After fixing a scrumptious meal, she sets a beautiful table with scented candles, their best china and crystal. She turns down the lights, anticipating her husband's delight with this romantic atmosphere after a long day at the office. As a final touch, she dresses herself up in a sexy outfit. When she opens the door to greet him, he takes one look at her, gasps in disbelief and screams, "For crying out loud, Kathy, have you gone mad? Get out of that silly outfit and let's eat." Her bubble is burst; she feels his rejection and wearily goes back to the complacency of the way things were.

Fortunately, marital sex doesn't have to be this way! We believe that it is not only possible for a couple to rediscover sexual passion but to increase the capacity for deeper levels of emotional and sexual fulfillment. The trouble is that many couples have accepted a comfortable blandness in their sex lives, thinking this is the way married sex is supposed to be. And, when they notice the sexual energy proudly displayed by young couples in public, they think to themselves, *Just wait a few years; it won't last.* Or, when they hear an older couple speak about sexual passion in their marriage, they roll their eyes in disbelief, doubting that it is possible.

God created humans with the capacity for intimate, passionate sex throughout their married life. However, only a "blessed few" reach a mature sexual experience, says David Schnarch in *The Sexual Crucible* (1991). Can one maintain passionate sex? The answer lies in recapturing, or perhaps capturing for the first time, the essence of a profoundly meaningful sexual relationship as God fully intended it to be. In fact, the recent survey conducted by researchers from the University of Chicago (Laumann et al. 1994) found that those in monogamous marriages not only had sex more often but enjoyed it more than any other group in their study. Nearly forty percent of the married couples had sex twice a week, and the great majority enjoyed orgasm as a part of their lovemaking experience. Marital commitment proved to be extremely important to these couples, and the vast majority had been faithful to their partner. This should not surprise us! Authentic sexual expression based on covenant, gracing and empowering principles is most likely to occur in a long-term committed relationship. Based on our model of sexual relationship presented in chapter three (covenant, grace, empowerment and intimacy), we look at the factors important in achieving a high level of marital sexual fulfillment.

Marital sexual fulfillment will be high when there is

☐ a high level of covenant commitment between spouses,
☐ a low level of conditional relating between spouses,
☐ a high level of mutual acceptance between spouses,
☐ a low level of shaming and blaming between spouses,
☐ a high level of differentiation between spouses,
☐ a low level of spousal fusion and overdependency,
☐ a high level of emotional intimacy between spouses, and
☐ a low level of emotional distance between spouses.

Covenant Establishes Trust

The permanence of lifelong covenant commitment establishes a solid foundation for a relationship as demanding as marriage. Each spouse brings unique strengths as well as human frailties as they pledge to put the priority on the relationship. In this holy crucible of marriage, spouses have the profound opportunity to know themselves more fully (identity) so they can share themselves more deeply (intimacy). In the vulnerability of the sexual relationship, there is an "I-Thou" interaction that puts spouses in tune with both themselves and their partner.

A sexual principle based on covenant is that the more secure a couple is in the relationship, the more complete and satisfying is the sexual response. In a survey done by Shere Hite (1976) women reported that they were most able to invest themselves sexually in a lifelong, monogamous relationship. When security is lacking, emotional restriction hampers their sexual responsiveness. Women who find their husband untrustworthy or fear being rejected or abandoned by him are less willing to give themselves sexually. This same survey also found that men benefit from a covenant commitment. They report feeling warm, secure and affirmed in their masculinity during sex with their spouse. These relationship themes of security and trust bring authenticity to the sexual act.

An Old Testament view of person-centered passion comes from the Song of Songs. The focus of the love is mutual: "I am my beloved's and my beloved is mine." This unreserved expression of love bursts forth out of confidence in the person and the relationship. The pleasuring principle in marital sex involves a mutual giving and receiving that takes place between two lovers. The greater the sensory pleasuring in a relationship, the greater the sexual adequacy. Person-centered sexual passion opens the lovers up to each other emotionally as well as bodily through expressions of touch and talk during the lovemaking. The lyrics of a popular country and western song express this principle in the vernacular: "I want a man with a slow hand, I want a lover with an easy touch." Authentic sexual expression is about the tender touching that communicates affection, desire, warmth and excitement. As evident in the great love scenes throughout the Song of Songs, the couple delights in the erotic passion they have for one another.

Grace Establishes Acceptance

While covenant provides security, grace establishes an atmosphere in which spouses can reach their full potential. Accepting a spouse just as he or she is means accepting his or her sexual value system. The personal value system determines the spouse's unique way of being a sexual person. Having deep regard and respect for a spouse's sexual value system is to have deep regard and respect for the spouse. A desire to know the spouse deeply includes a willingness to know about that person's hurts, failures and pains as well as successes, rewards and victories. Personal preferences about the sexual relationship must be understood in light of the beliefs, values and emotions that underlie them.

Sexual attitudes and values are developed through early childhood experiences and learned from the family, church and society. An important aspect of marital growth has to do with a couple's ability to attend to and grapple with differences. For instance, if either spouse is uncomfortable with some aspect of their sexual relationship, it is imperative that they can speak about their differences without being judged or feeling ashamed. Labels like "prudish" or "overly sexed" have no place in this discussion, for such responses only serve to undermine and condemn.

Acceptance allows the couple to determine what is right for each spouse as well as what is right for the relationship at any particular stage in the marriage. For example, after partners listen carefully to each other and honor their different value systems, sometimes a spouse will relinquish a sexual request for the sake of the other, while at other times a spouse will reevaluate and stretch beyond a comfort zone for the other's sake. The key is that both spouses are working for the good of the relationship toward a loving resolution. The gracing attitude helps the spouses see their differences as an opportunity for growth. Putting the priority on grace, differences become paths of deeper understanding that enhance sexual bonds.

Another aspect of grace is forgiveness. Rather than trying to persuade a spouse or hold grudges, mercy softens the sharp edges of differences. Misunderstandings and blunders that are part of every human relationship need to be forgiven so the couple can move on to better places. Undoubtedly, spouses will fail each other in a number of ways in the marriage, for no relationship is ever perfect! Each spouse will disappoint, offend and make mistakes in the sexual arena which will be hurtful. One spouse, for example, may feel rejected when the other fails to respond to a sexual invitation. Circumstances like busy schedules, young children, illness and work will sometimes inhibit or alter sexual interest. Grace is needed on a daily basis to bring restoration after disappointments occur. Those who have experienced traumatic sexual events in their past may struggle in various ways with the sexual relationship. Such situations require extraordinary understanding because of the seriousness of the violation. It takes time for sexual wholeness to be restored in such circumstances. Grace is the environment that helps heal those painful wounds.

Empowering Establishes Potential

The model of two becoming one flesh does not eradicate the individual. In fact, an individual spouse becomes even more defined through self-discovery in the context of the sexual relationship. Behind the "two are better than one" model is the idea that two independent persons have unique strengths to offer the relationship, which gives a potential that is not possible in isolation. A sufficient self gives each spouse an increased capacity to express and clarify sexual desires or values in a way that enhances the marriage. Without two separate identities, mutual interdependence is impossible. Some hold to the false notion that dependency or fusion is the ideal, for example, "I can't do it without you and I must lean on you to be strong." Two spouses who are hanging on to each other for dear life have no solid ground on which to stand. Strength is multiplied by two when each spouse stands on their own feet as they empower each other by working in tandem.

An empowering principle of marital sex is mutuality, rather than mutual dependency. This idea is conveyed in 1 Corinthians 7:4-5: "For the wife does not have authority over her own body, but the husband does; likewise the husband does not have authority over his own body, but the wife does. Do not deprive one another except perhaps by agreement for a set time, to devote yourselves to prayer; and then come together again, so that Satan may not tempt you because of your lack of self-control" (NRSV).

This passage acknowledges that each spouse has a separate body with separate sexual desires and differences and therefore they must be able to work out a mutually satisfying sexual relationship. Paul holds up full mutuality as the highest ideal in marital sexuality. Each spouse is encouraged to express personal preferences as well as acknowledge the desires of their spouse. It's not a matter of either spouse acting only out of their needs, but finding ways to incorporate the needs of their spouse as well. One does not simply act out of personal needs, but must recognize the need to find mutual resolve. The words "by agreement" are translated from the Greek word *symphōnia*, the same root word from which *symphony* is derived. The idea is to be of "one voice," out of reverence for Christ (Eph 5:21).

Authentic marital sexuality is best achieved when spouses engage each other out of mutual desire. There is no place for the misguided idea that the husband initiates while the wife acquiesces. Marital sexuality is to be characterized by mutual regard for the other, for oneself and for the relationship. Just as the orchestra makes harmonious music when each instrument contributes its own unique part, so the married couple reaches sexual harmony through personal expression of sexual interest and mutual agreement.

Some couples succumb to a give-to-get sexual exchange, striving to maximize personal gain. Each gives with the underlying expectation that he or she will get a return on what has been given. We believe this idea is contrary to a biblical view of marital empowerment. A give-to-get model focuses on power issues in a relationship. Spouses with less interest in sex can easily control the sexual relationship by withholding sex, just as the spouses with more interest in sex can be coercive in trying to get what they believe they deserve.

Control and sexual fulfillment are at basic odds with each other. Sexual fulfillment comes out of desiring and being desired. When one spouse freely expresses desire as an invitation rather than a demand, there is great joy when the partner responds. It is completely unacceptable for a spouse to respond out of obligation or duty, because this leaves the initiator emotionally bankrupt. There is little satisfaction if a spouse responds only because he or she cannot say no. The pleasure and emotional satisfaction comes when one knows the response is out of true desire and love. Here, spouses make room in themselves for the partner and join freely into a union of mutual exchange. Empowering love comes out of vulnerability and strength, rather than out of control and weakness. The empowering principle seeks the full potential of each spouse through a synchronous rhythm of interaction and interdependence.

Intimacy Establishes Connection

Finally, sexual intimacy deepens connection and understanding of one's personal sexuality. Sexual disclosure and vulnerability open spouses up to deeper self-knowledge. The ability to know and be known as spouses requires an emotional and sexual exposure in which intimacy flourishes.

"Men want sex! Women want intimacy!" The common notion that men experience intimacy through sex, while women experience intimacy through emotional closeness, is debatable. Certainly, many men enjoy emotional intimacy and many women enjoy sexual intimacy. However, while this may not be the whole truth, there seems to be a tendency in this direction. We believe that every couple must find a balance between these two dimensions of intimacy in order to blend them in mutually satisfying ways. Women may need to stretch themselves in sexual areas, whereas men need to challenge themselves in the emotional dimension.

When emotional security is lacking, the sexual appetite usually deteriorates, and when the sexual relationship is lacking, the emotional connection diminishes. An article by Duncombe and Marsden (1994) investigated attempts that partners make to sustain their sexual relationship. They noted that today's women refuse to fake orgasms to make their spouses feel good, which means it is more difficult to keep up the illusion that the marriage is fulfilling when it is not. The authors suggest that taking intentional steps to keep sexual and emotional intimacy alive in marriage increases the likelihood of mutual satisfaction. A couple can have the best of both worlds by attending to both aspects of intimacy. The erotic energy moves spouses toward deep emotional connection that enhances erotic expression. When women take greater responsibility for their sexual satisfaction and men make a stronger link between sexual and emotional intimacy, they say yes to couple intimacy.

Sexuality and spirituality are closely linked to couple intimacy. According to Paul Ricoeur, eros expressed with tenderness and fidelity leads to spiritual fulfillment (Ricoeur 1994:73). Eros has creative power for harmony in marriage, for it brings understanding and lessens the impact of differences. Ricoeur believes that many people fear the "yes" to their deepest sexual and emotional cravings. Yet, these cravings call people to accountability to bring their life into accordance with their desires. In acknowledging the cravings, a person is able to choose mutual gratification and enjoyment (Ricoeur 1994:80–84).

In the last thirty years the market has been flooded with material on how to enhance the sexual relationship. Perusing the many books on marital sexuality at any well-stocked bookstore will reveal the extent to which couples are interested in improving their sex lives. While the information for the most part is helpful, we have a nagging suspicion that most approaches focus far too much on the mechanics of sex. Pick up any one of these books and you will find an emphasis on technique. Based on our technologically oriented society, these books presume that the correct technique is the answer to most problems. To make an analogy, while we would all agree that the secret of maintaining a high-performance automobile is to keep it tuned up in accordance with the automobile manual, human beings are certainly much more complex than a machine.

Good marital sex, we believe, is much more an art than a science. We compare it to playing music or painting a work of art. The ability to complete a paint-by-number picture by matching the numbered paint colors with the numbered areas on the canvas may produce a multicolored landscape, but most of us would find it less than aesthetically pleasing. Unfortunately, instructing couples on strategies to improve the sexual relationship is often given with a sex-by-number mentality.

Some sex manuals present page after page of illustrations depicting different positions that are supposed to enhance sexual pleasure. Reducing sex to body maneuvers often leaves a couple puzzled about just how to get their bodies into those complex contortions. In addition, when disillusioned or dissatisfied with how things are going in the sexual relationship, it is now possible to blame a spouse for not getting the technique right. Imagine if you will, a couple in one of those incredibly challenging sexual positions. With sex manual in hand, the husband gazes intently at the illustration they are trying to manage. At the most inopportune time his wife makes an unnerving comment, "You'd better turn back a page, Sam. You must have missed something because this isn't doing a thing for me!"

Person-centered sex is so much more than technique! It involves the *meaning* of the sexual connection for the two individuals who are giving themselves to each other. Their sexual expression tells a story of their love for each other. It is about the mystery of these two unique persons who invited each other to participate in a mutually responsive union. This bold action of giving of self and receiving of other is an exciting interaction that maximizes emotional intimacy.

Common Sexual Struggles

A national sample of 6,029 married persons revealed that 16 percent of the married couples surveyed had been sexually inactive during a month prior to the interview. Factors that predicted the sexual inactivity in these couples were unhappiness with the marital relationship, lack of shared activity, increased age and poor health. The researcher concluded that the lack of sexual activity is often a danger signal for married couples (Donnelly 1993). The University of Chicago researchers (1994) found significant variation in spouses when it comes to sexual preferences, even though nearly 40 percent of married people said they had sex about twice a week and 75 percent of the married women said they usually reached orgasm during sex. Every couple has to work out various conflicts in their marital relationship, and sexual disagreements are part of that struggle. Resolving differences in the following common struggles in the sexual relationship will make a difference in the marriage.

Keeping the sexual relationship vital. The question of keeping vitality in the sexual relationship sometimes centers on the question of who initiates sex. This is a crucial point, not just about wanting to satisfy sexual desire, but about having feelings about being desired as a person. Some have said that the most important sex organ is the brain, since the mind has more to do with sexual response than the body. In order to become sexually aroused, the spouse must be in tune with and able to receive the signals that come into the brain so the body will respond. If the mind is saturated with worries, commitments and responsibilities, it easily can prohibit sexual thoughts from entering in. Sexual desire is not an automatic response but one that takes purposeful action. While all couples have periodic difficulty with sexual arousal due to external pressures, regular sexual activity is generally conducive to keeping this aspect of married life alive. Each spouse must be intentional in finding ways to get in touch with the sexual side and stay tuned into the sexual aspect of the marriage. Taking time out from a busy schedule to relax, having some moments of quiet conversation together as a couple or spending some time in each other's arms while listening to music or watching a movie is often enough to put the spouses in a responsive, receptive mood. Each spouse, as well as the couple together, is responsible for putting a priority on the emotional and physical connection, which enhances sexual readiness.

Unresolved conflicts. Some spouses have a problem being sexually intimate because of significant unresolved conflicts in the marriage. In a study of couples in their first years of marriage it was found that tension had a negative impact on sexual satisfaction (Henderson-King and Veroff 1994). Sex can become a power struggle in which one spouse refuses the other sexually or manipulates in order to gain an advantage over the other. For example, a wife who wants to have a baby may seduce her husband into having sex without using birth control. Or, the husband may withhold sexual intercourse because he does not want to risk a pregnancy. Whatever the conflicts, they can become a battle ground on the sex field. When sex is used as a bargaining tool or weapon to punish, express anger or gain power, intimacy is sabotaged. The point is, conflict and misuse of power are major barriers to intimate sex. In well-functioning marriages, spouses are able to work out conflicts without carrying them into the marriage bed.

Sexual desire ebb and flow. The mutual active enjoyment of being erotically attracted to and stimulated by a spouse is ego gratifying and empowering. There will, of course, be natural times of ebb and flow in sexual arousal and desire in any marriage. Jobs, combined with child-caring responsibilities, household tasks, and health problems, tend to diminish sexual responsiveness. The wife who works at an office all day, fixes the evening meal and cleans the house for three hours is not likely to have much sexual energy when she flops into bed dead-tired.

The husband who works long hours on a demanding job and spends the evening helping his son with homework and getting the laundry done while worrying about a report that's due the next day will also most likely have a diminished sexual desire. Dry spells require patience, restraint and support. Good sexual functioning takes time, energy and commitment. Couples who recognize these dry spells and adapt to the particular life circumstances will be better able to maintain their relationship through the ebb and flow. Then, when they've weathered the dry spell, they will avail themselves of the lush and fruitful season.

Feeling neglected as a spouse. In a study of couples in their first years of marriage, researchers found that affirmation was associated with sexual satisfaction (Henderson-King and Veroff 1994). A study of Korean-American couples found that higher levels of self-esteem, positive regard, communication and cohesion were all associated with sexual satisfaction (Song, Bergen and Schumm 1995). Both men and women need affirmation from their partner and complain when they feel neglected. In the busyness of life it's often the couple's relationship that gets neglected. Keeping alert to a spouse's needs, moods, emotions, thoughts and desires in nonsexual ways can combat some of this feeling of neglect. Planning creative ways to enhance the relationship through weekly dates, spontaneous lunch meetings or weekends at the beach or mountains will go a long way in helping a couple connect. Writing down small requests or desires that the partner can respond to each day will help spouses feel appreciated. These actions of care keep spouses in tune with each other's wishes. Taking time to communicate verbally and nonverbally through expressions of tenderness, affection, understanding, desire, warmth and comfort will go a long way in showing the person he or she is valued. Covenant vows include reaching out and staying in touch with the one you love.

Infertility. Approximately one out of five married couples have infertility problems at some point in their relationship. A study of twenty-two infertile couples reveals that most have unsatisfactory sex lives. The study found that infertility adversely affected sex for several reasons: intercourse had to be scheduled, it became a means to an end, privacy was invaded by medical professionals and the act of intercourse itself was a reminder of the couple's infertility (Greil, Porter and

Leitko 1987). These are painful issues for the couple to overcome.

Boredom. Talking together about the sexual relationship is one of the more difficult areas of communication for a couple. Yet, it's so important to make periodic evaluations about how each spouse feels about the sexual aspects of their marriage. Boredom with sex is a complaint that cannot be addressed unless a couple is able to talk about dissatisfactions and suggest needed change. Without taking positive steps to increase couple satisfaction, sexual routines quickly become ruts of dissatisfaction. Interacting and being accountable to each other as spouses keeps a relationship fresh and alive. Discussing sexual struggles will be the pathway to discovering new ways to contribute positively to the sexual relationship. To be naked and not ashamed includes honest, open communication.

Sexuality is enhanced by an element of playfulness. The sexual relationship benefits from enjoyable, uninhibited interaction. The ability to be spontaneous and unpremeditated indicates a certain comfort with sexual passion. A healthy view of oneself and one's body is vital to entering into an engaging sexual interaction. A gauge of one's sexual spontaneity is comfort with nudity and the sexual passion within self and partner. Embarrassment or self-consciousness inhibits just as contrived, ritualized structure stifles the interactive process of the lovers. Being authentically oneself means there is no need to put on pretenses or make too much of a production out of sex. Responsiveness, openness and invitation make each sexual experience something a little different.

Communication. Intimacy is communicated in a number of ways—through body language, overt physical behavior, symbolic gestures and oral and written language. Love can be expressed through a letter, poem or song. Judy cherishes the love poems Jack has written to her throughout their marriage, although they are disastrous as poetic art forms. However, there is also some truth to the idea that actions speak louder than words. Our eyes, lips, face, posture and general body movement do a great deal to express our sexual and emotional feelings. While many women find it easy to use words, men tend to express their feelings through actions. And some people are excellent at interpreting a spouse's nonverbal expressions, but a partner's body language can also give ambiguous messages that result in misinterpretation and misunderstanding. Spouses can also communicate a lack of interest by refusing to participate in an activity, turning silent or "forgetting" an important event.

A couple needs to be able to communicate sexual feelings and desires to one another verbally and nonverbally. Each spouse needs to let the other know what they desire sexually. There is no room for a guessing game. If a particular kind of touch inhibits rather than stimulates pleasure, one must indicate this to the spouse. Although sexual desire is often communicated in nonverbal ways, verbal communication ensures that partners do their best to attend to the sexual requests. Guiding each other through touch and short words of encouragement during lovemaking is a good way to care for the sexual relationship.

Spectatoring. A common problem for couples is taking on the role of "spectator" in the sexual event. This occurs when either partner removes themselves mentally during coitus in order to observe what's happening from the outside. Like being a spectator rather than a participant in a sports event, the spouse lacks personal involvement, which means something essential is missing. In a very real sense the partner gets lost in their head while focusing on the event rather than being part of it. Unfortunately, when the partner loses the lover, the love gets lost as well.

Spectatoring sometimes occurs because a spouse is overly concerned about her or his performance as a lover. Being self-conscious about how one is doing as a lover often places more anxiety on that person. Invariably it becomes a self-defeating activity because it reduces the interactional aspect to a minimum. In authentic sexual encounters the couple allows natural feelings, inclinations and actions to be part of the creative process between them. Seeing and sensing the partner gives important cues about how to move in harmony with one's partner. When spouses are passionately involved with each other in the act of coitus, there's no time to evaluate how they are doing because they're totally invested in the moment. Good marital sex requires active participation. In the presence of each other, the erotic dance of love happens between two people who are both acutely aware of and lost to each other in the mutual passion of giving and receiving. It is a fantastic and sacred adventure.

Summary

Monogamous, lifelong marriage has always been the ideal context for authentic sexuality. Just as covenant love permeates every aspect of life, it permeates marital sexuality as well. A study of forty-eight married couples found that having a shared purpose in life was associated with higher levels of sexual enjoyment (McCann and Biaggio 1989). Our common belief as Christians is that Christ gives us meaning beyond ourselves, and our lifelong goal is to serve him. Sex is a gift of God that reflects the meaning of God's self-giving grace.

In a lovely article entitled "Sleeping Like Spoons," John Milhaven explains how the familiar gesture of curling up next to his wife moves him so deeply. He writes, "The resistance goes out of me. The bed has my full weight on it. The nothingness of sleep has my full weight on it. All of me falls. Nothing holds back. . . . It is a blissful giving way by bodily self to itself. A sweetness of complete relaxing, of luxurious letting go of muscles, skins, nerves, and all. An effortless, sensuous shedding of all concerns, worries, even thoughts . . . as I slope down with Julie to sleep, thoughts float off. I don't think, I enjoy" (Nelson and Longfellow 1994:88).

Why is falling to sleep in the arms of a spouse such an appealing picture? It's the comfort of being known, accepted and loved by one who is committed to you. And when two lie together, they keep each other warm for two is better than one. In this place one can be in touch with the hidden parts of oneself. This safe haven is a place where fears do not penetrate. Two wrapped together in bodily trust is what intimacy is all about. The marital relationship is not just a refining crucible of growth but a comforting container of trust. Sleeping like spoons is what marital emotional and sexual intimacy is all about. Being part of a mysterious one-flesh union leaves a sense of well-being in one's soul.

Suggestions for Further Reading

Penner, C., and J. Penner. 1981. *A gift of sex: A guide to sexual fulfillment.* Waco: Word.

———. 1994. *Getting your sex life off to a great start.* Waco: Word.

Rousenau, D. 1994. *A celebration of sex: A Christian couple's manual.* Nashville: Thomas Nelson.

Schnarch, D. 1997. *The passionate marriage.* New York: W. W. Norton.

Thatcher, A., and E. Stuart. 1996. *Christian perspectives on sexuality and gender.* Grand Rapids, Mich.: Eerdmans. See section 4, "Sexuality and Marriage," pp. 169-209.

9

Extramarital Sex

Causes & Consequences

The Garden of Eden depicts the image of perfect freedom for intimacy between Adam and Eve. There were equality, similarity, diversity and union that God claimed were "very good." Adam's cry "bone of my bones and flesh of my flesh" indicates a deep longing to be with this one who was a suitable partner for deep communion and connection. But not all went well in paradise. This ideal union fell apart when Adam and Eve fell away from God. From this day on, intimacy would be hard to achieve. Domination and dependency would disrupt this idyllic scene. The propensity to follow their own way rather than God's way would wreak havoc on the one-flesh relationship.

The commandment "Thou shall not commit adultery" upholds the marital bond and encourages couples to work out their struggles in the context of a monogamous relationship. In fact, three of the ten commandments refer to sex outside the marriage covenant: "Do not commit adultery," "Do not covet your neighbor's spouse" and "Do not lie." These commands elevate the marital union as sacred and not to be broken. In other words, married persons should neither *seek* nor *have inter-*

course with anyone other than their spouse. Although these Old Testament laws were expressed in a patriarchal, polygamous culture where husbands had the right to take and divorce as many wives as they wished, these sexual options were to be within a legal marriage contract. These commandments protected women because they afforded them rights and privileges.

The warning against adultery sets the marriage bond up as a priority that must be guarded at all costs. The affirmative aspect of these commandments encourages married persons to work together toward an emotional and sexual union that keeps their relationship vital. Each spouse is responsible to keep the marriage covenant before the spouse and God.

The fifth commandment, "Thou shalt not lie," has implications for extramarital sex too. Lies and falsehoods are an inevitable part of an affair. Secrets come between the marital couple, for one cannot avoid the impact of lies that impinge on vows of fidelity.

Novelist Frederick Buechner declares, "I AM MY SECRETS!" Secrets indeed tell a story about who we are. The falsehoods told or lived out become part of and reveal truth about that person. When spouses discover they have been deceived, their often tremendous rage is due to betrayal of trust. When the covenant vow is broken, it pierces to the core of that promise. It's not only the adultery that is hurtful, but the secret that undermines the integrity of the relationship. The lie keeps the betrayed in the dark (and in a one-down position), giving them no choice in the matter. Lying compounds the destructive effect of adultery upon the marriage relationship. Truthfulness about the affair at least gives betrayed spouses an equal chance to protest, express opinions and feelings, and decide what to do about the particular situation. To rob them of choice leaves them at a profound disadvantage. We have a bias for disclosure versus cover-up, but caution is important: a decision to tell a spouse must be made out of a desire for reconciliation and healing. The confessor must weigh the potential hurt or harm that could come to the resolute spouse. It is wise to have a pastor or therapist help with these questions, the timing and the method of disclosure.

The Ten Commandments remind us that we are fallen creatures living in a fallen world. Although spouses may not always escape the temptation of wrongful desire, they can ask for forgiveness and seek the help of their spouse and God to keep the promises of the marital vows.

The seriousness of adultery is addressed in New Testament passages such as 1 Corinthians 6:18: "All other sins a man commits are outside his body, but he who sins sexually, sins against his own body. " Sexual intercourse is not only regarded as an external act but an internal offense that impacts self and spouse. One-flesh union symbolically joins a man and woman through memories, expectations, fantasies and secrets, so that even a casual affair has implication for the adulterer, adulteress, the spouse and all three relationships.

It is difficult to estimate the proportion of married persons who actually engage in extramarital sex. While husbands more than wives report a desire to be involved in extramarital affairs (Prins, Buunk and Van Yperen 1993), in studies conducted by Kinsey (1948, 1953) and *Cosmopolitan* (Wolfe 1981) and *Playboy* (Petersen et al. 1983) magazines, the rate of extramarital sex is assumed to be over 50 percent for women and over 75 percent for men. However, due to biased sampling, these rates are undoubtedly inflated. The most recent research, based upon a probability sample of over 3,000 adults, finds that 25 percent of men and 15 percent of women report having had sex with someone other than their spouse while married (Laumann et al. 1994). This lines up with people's attitudes towards extramarital sex, since roughly 75 percent of adults believe that extramarital sex is "always wrong" and another 15 percent believe it is "almost always wrong" (Laumann et al. 1994:22). But, given the sensitive nature of the question, the authors caution that subjects may underreport incidents of extramarital sexual involvement. Regardless of what persons morally believe about adultery, their behavior may not be congruent with those beliefs. The actual rate for extramarital sex is undoubtedly higher today than it has been in past generations.

The Decision to Have an Affair

Wiederman and Allgeier (1996) found in their study that young married couples presumed that the major source of extramarital sex is marital dissatisfaction. Although there may be as many reasons for adultery as there are adulterous affairs, affairs are known to follow certain patterns. We shall discuss these patterns in light of different types of affairs, then look at sociological and psychological explanations for why persons have affairs, and finally offer a moral explanation.

Based on hundreds of clinical cases of infidelity, Frank Pittman (1989) suggests four types of infidelity in *Private Lies: Infidelity and the Betrayal of Intimacy.* In the *accidental affair* there is no advanced planning; the affair "just happens." *Philandering* is the practice of seeking many partners for the precise purpose of engaging in affairs as if it were a sport. *Romantic affairs* are usually the culmination of a developing relationship between two people who feel they love each other. *Marital arrangements* constitute a type of affair in which a couple agrees to stay married (sometimes without living together) but allows for long-term sexual relationships with persons outside of the marriage. Each of these types of affairs involves different reasons for adultery. There is a mixture of sociological, psychological, relational and moral reasons behind the choice to indulge in extramarital sex.

The most comprehensive attempt to identify sociological reasons for extramarital sex is based on responses from 833 adults to four National Opinion Research Center General Social Surveys. Using a sophisticated statistical technique known as path analysis, Reiss, Anderson and Sponaugle (1980) identify key factors predictive of extramarital sex. These factors include low religiosity, attitudes of gender inequality, liberal political attitudes, premarital sexual involvement, marital unhappiness and marital sexual dissatisfaction. In addition, the study found that the spouse who had more power and control in the marriage was also the one more likely to engage in extramarital sex. Prins, Buunk and Van Yperen (1993) found that females who felt a lack of equality in their marital relationship were more likely to desire and actually engage in extramarital sexual behavior.

These findings are consistent with equity theory, which predicts higher rates of extramarital sex in marriages where there is *unequal* power. The basic idea of this theory is that people need to feel they are getting as much out of the relationship as they are putting into it. Most people keep mental tabulations to figure out whether the benefits outweigh the sacrifices they put forth. Elaine Hatfield et al. (1978) predicted that people who felt "underbenefited" in their marriages would be the ones to engage in extramarital sex. Indeed, that is what she found. Underbenefited subjects engaged in extramarital sex earlier in their marriage and with more partners than those who felt equitably treated or "overbenefited." More recently, Prins, Buunk and Van Yperen (1993) found that women who felt they were not getting all that they deserved in their marriage were more likely to consider extramarital sexual involvement as an acceptable behavior.

Beyond sociological explanations, extramarital sexual involvement can also be understood in light of individual psychological needs and how these needs are met or not met in the marriage relationship. Based on clinical research David Schnarch (1991, 1997) has developed an explanation of extramarital sexual involvement based on one's level of differentiation. He suggests that spouses with low levels of differentiation tend to be fused (overly dependent) at one extreme or emotionally cut off (overly distant) at the other.

Differentiation is described as the human process of integrating the needs for connection and self-regulation in the marital relationship. Key aspects of differentiation are: (1) the ability to maintain a clear sense of self in close proximity to one's spouse, (2) the ability to soothe personal fears and anxieties from within the self, (3) the ability to be nonreactive to the anxiety of the spouse, and (4) the ability to tolerate the natural struggle and discomfort of marital discord in order to grow as an individual and as a couple.

Schnarch comments, "Marriage is where you find out who you really are. . . . The struggle in marriage is to find out who you are while maintaining your boundaries with a partner who is all too eager and ready to tell you" (1993:1). Herein lies the "marriage crucible," a refining place where every married couple must grapple with differences and various relationship struggles in order to develop a clear sense of self. By developing a "self-in-relation," the spouse is able to hold on to himself or herself while resisting the partner's attempt to define him or her. Through these marital dynamics, each spouse is challenged to develop an internal awareness of self in relation to the other, which increases that person's level of differentiation. One becomes more highly differentiated in the context of the relationship by taking risks (expressing wants, needs, desires, passion) and being vulnerable (expressing hurts, pains, weakness, hopes, fears) with one's spouse. True intimacy is possible when spouses are secure enough to let themselves be known and desire to know and be responsive (not reactive) to their partners. Through open communication and relationship struggle, highly differentiated spouses develop an interdependency in which they clearly express themselves, yet put the best interest of the spouse and the relationship as a priority as well.

People who lack a healthy degree of differentiation are ripe for extramarital affairs, according to Schnarch (1993). There is a tendency to confuse fusion with emotional closeness. Undifferentiated spouses are "overly" dependent on each other for validation and self-definition, which gives them an inordinate power over each other. When a person lacks a clearly defined self, it is extremely disconcerting to face the inadequacy felt when one is unable to meet the demands of the partner. In light of these dynamics, an extramarital affair becomes an attractive alternative. The affair saves the spouse from having to face his or her inadequacy and serves as an escape route. Idealization of the new relationship (affair) flames a fantasy about oneself. The thinking goes something like this: *I must be really attractive for this person to take such an interest in me. Therefore I'm perfectly adequate and don't need to change anything.*

Hopefully, marital intimacy develops through a solid commitment that lasts throughout the various stages of marriage and family life. Living in the real world, spouses face marital and life struggles, disappointments, desires, failures, meaning and purpose that can bring about mutual respect and relational interdependence. In a vital marriage, the two spouses are in it together and accountable to each other, so there are no illusions about self or the other. Honest communication, self-awareness, vulnerable reflection and open sharing lead to deeper levels of intimacy. In fact, differentiation brings wholeness and deeper connection, because highly differentiated spouses do not fear losing themselves in the emotional closeness. The solid sense of self gives freedom to love in more expressive and more vulnerable ways. The bottom line, according to Schnarch (1993), is that affairs occur more frequently among those who fear intimacy rather than those who desire to become more intimately acquainted with oneself or one's spouse.

Booth and Dabbs (1993) considered biological evidence that may affect one's tendency to have affairs. They found that men who produce high levels of testosterone were less likely to marry, and when they did marry were more likely to have troubled marital relations, extramarital sex violations, violence toward spouses and a lower quality of marital interaction.

While one must consider the complex social, psychological, relational or even hormonal factors that influence the decision to have an extramarital affair, we must not forget that the person makes a moral choice. Although some may follow a spur-of-the-moment impulse, the extramarital affair is more often a premeditated act. Based on her research, Lynn Atwater (1982) found extramarital affairs usually move through the following five stages:

1. a tolerant attitude toward the possibility of the affair
2. the opportunity for the affair
3. the presence of extramarital models (in novels, movies or television dramas)
4. a time of mental rehearsing about how the affair will take place
5. the consummation of the affair

The progression from thought to action suggested in these stages is consistent with the social psychological literature that indicates how human attitudes and behaviors are related. Just as behavior can affect our attitudes, so can our thoughts affect our behavior if we allow them to germinate in the desires of our mind.

This understanding of why affairs occur is consistent with the biblical view of sin, holiness and temptation. Sin is not only a matter of the external—our behavior. It is also a matter of the heart—our attitudes and desires. Jesus spoke of "adultery of the heart" in Matthew 5:28. The thrust of this teaching is that adulterous thoughts can be the beginning of adulterous affairs. Jesus shows how thoughts, as well as actions, keep a person from reaching the deepest possible communion with their spouse. Coveting or lusting after someone outside the marriage harms those involved. The one who commits adultery shapes his or her character through the deceitful and unfaithful action; the abandoned spouse feels betrayed, angry, neglected and confused about what's happening; the children are insecure as they sense the distance and disruption between their parents; and the other person involved in the affair remains uncertain about his or her place and future in the adulterer's life.

Thoughts and action go together, says Jesus; adultery (even of the heart) is against God's way. We must not merely do the right things, we must desire the right things. When desire goes astray in thought, action is soon to follow. To live responsible lives in contemporary society means we must cope with temptations in a culture saturated with sexual messages. We must keep our conscience clear, drawing appropriate lines so we will make responsible choices about what we desire and toward whom our desire is directed. When we read Atwater's findings in the light of Scripture, we realize that movement from each stage to the next involves a conscious choice. And everyone is responsible for their choices and the consequences of their action.

Consequences of Broken Covenant

Affairs can have very serious consequences on marriage. In writing about the crises of infidelity, Pittman and Wagers (1995) contrast seven myths with seven truths about infidelity. The *first* myth is that since everybody is unfaithful, affairs are to be expected as a normal part of marriage. In truth, infidelity is not normal behavior but a symptom of some problem, usually having to do with the person or the marriage relationship. The *second* myth is that affairs are good for a marriage. In truth, while affairs can bring about a crisis in which an enduring marital problem can be solved, affairs are dangerous and often inadvertently end marriages. While the *third* myth states that affairs prove that spouses no longer love each other, the truth is that prior to the affair the marriage may be seen as quite good and many spouses still claim to love each other. The *fourth* myth asserts that the unfaithful partners are the sexier spouses since they are seeking more sex than what is available in the marriage. The truth is that, although affairs involve sex, sex is usually not the primary reason to have an affair. The motivation is usually to bolster a lack of ego or sexual confidence. Myth number *five* is that the affair is the fault of the resolute (faithful) spouse. The truth is that no one can drive someone else to have an affair. While the *sixth* myth states that there is protection through ignorance of a spouse's affair, the truth is that affairs are fueled by secrecy and threatened by exposure. Finally, the *seventh* myth is that after an affair, divorce is inevitable. The truth is that marriages can, with effort, survive affairs if the affairs are exposed and relational trust is rebuilt.

Based on their clinical experience, Pittman and Wagers (1995) believe that this last truth is a crucial point. Couples need to know it is important to rebuild trust by dealing openly with the two key factors—dishonesty and jealousy—if the marriage is to survive.

Another consequence of an affair is that it affects the balance of power in the marriage. For example, the resolute (faithful) spouse may take a morally superior attitude and blame or shame the unfaithful spouse. The offended spouse may hold the affair over the other by pointing out the moral weakness in the other. This shift in power can be especially noticeable when marriage partners hold to faithfulness in marriage as a standard.

Although we might assume that the resolute spouse has the upper hand and gains the power in the marriage, the reverse can sometimes be true. Resolute spouses can be peppered with questions of self-doubt and inadequacy, asking themselves what's wrong with them and wondering whether they are attractive or adequate as a sex partner. The emotional fusion that is common in many couples leaves them with the unspoken belief that the affair is a negative reflection on their competence. Even language that is used, such as "dumpee" and "dumper," puts the power in the hands of the one who has had the affair.

In a strange way, the spouse who strays is somehow validated because he or she has found acceptance by somebody else. Now it's two against one, and the offending spouse may actually have more status than the resolute spouse. In a certain sense, spouses who are having the affairs are powerful because they have been able to diminish or betray the resolute spouses through their actions. Especially if the resolute spouse is overly dependent, it is easy for the offending spouse to insinuate that the resolute spouse is blameworthy or inadequate. In this case, they use the affair to their advantage and can be defiant and seemingly gratified by depriving, hurting or being "one up" on the resolute spouse.

In cases where there is unequal power, the resolute spouses often succumb to the defeating self-doubts and spousal-inflicted doubts, failing to rightly protest the broken covenant. This lets the offending spouses off the hook, fails to keep them accountable and continues to let them escape with little consequence. The lack of confrontation not only avoids the issue of the affair, but fails to deal directly with important differentiation issues in the marital relationship. Therefore the inability to deal effectively with the affair leaves the problem unresolved, maintains the emotional fusion (dependency) in the couple, continues the lack of self-determination in each spouse, keeps the power hierarchy one-sided and allows a lack of intimacy to continue permeating the marriage. In other words, things stay the same rather than the situation being an impetus of growth and change.

Is Healing Possible?

As pointed out in the previous section, adultery does take a serious toll on the marriage at a number of levels. However, we now want to focus on how the couple can survive an affair, how healing can take place after the broken trust and how a couple can be transformed by facing the affair head-on. Also, this section will give family members, friends, counselors and ministers some helpful guidelines about how they can be part of the healing process.

A ministerial response to an affair is to walk with the couple at a slow enough pace so they can deal with what's happened rather than rush into a quick solution. Staying with the anxiety and tension is essential so the wronged spouse can express the myriad of feelings, thoughts and reactions about what has happened. Whether this is done alone or as a couple takes discernment. Acknowledging the consequences of disobedience means we take God's commandments seriously, repent and recognize the implications of our actions.

The intervention process for working with infidelity devised by Frank Pittman (1987) may be helpful here.

1. Emergency response—defuse the crisis with the hope that your marriage can survive it.

2. Calm down and come together—talk about the crisis in a face-to-face encounter.

3. Define the problem—come to an understanding about the circumstances of the affair.

4. Identify a solution—decide on a course of action that will overcome the crisis.

5. Negotiate differences—find mutually satisfying ways to deal with differences.

6. Relationship recovery—continue on a path of healing.

From a psychological point of view, it is important to help spouses grapple with their internal as well as external responses. There is a likelihood that unequal power or dependency are common themes. The affair may be the very thing that brings up important issues about fusion and fear of intimacy in a relationship, as discussed in the section on differentiation. It is especially challenging to find and hold on to oneself in the midst of pain. As the couple is able to tolerate the tough examination of themselves and their marriage, they will need to find the strength to eventually relinquish their pain and/or desire to punish. When underlying anger, dependency and insecurity themes are dealt with, the couple has hope for recovery. Now they will be open to questions like, "What do I want to do?" "What would God have me do?" "What kind of relationship can we develop and do we want to create?" During this period of redefinition, a couple usually is able to grow as they humbly stand before God to ask a blessing on their renewed covenant.

If the spouses happen to be particularly young in their faith or lack maturity in the Lord, we can gently offer Christ as the solid place to stand. It is God rather than the spouse who ultimately determines one's ability to be differentiated. Spouses may be able to understand how the concept of being "differentiated in Christ" gives freedom to make choices out of spiritual strength rather than in reaction to each other. This development of self can be an unexpected but valuable area of growth.

The nature of marriage changes when people raise their "level of differentiation" in Christ. It means a spouse chooses to be faithful out of a personal, moral conviction, not because it's demanded by spouse or society. Actions are *not* out of desire to control or hurt a partner or because one is afraid to challenge a spouse. The decision to be monogamous comes out of a clear conviction that this is God's best plan. A covenant is not a social exchange that says faithfulness begets faithfulness, but one makes a covenant commitment because it is honoring to God. "Identity in Christ" gives a *real* sense of knowing who and Whose we are. While is it certainly good to be validated by others, and our spouse in particular, our true validation is in Christ Jesus.

So, it is Christ's validation we seek, and no one else can take our identity in Christ away from us. This spiritual perspective means the resolute spouse does not have to spend an inordinate amount of time focusing on the wrong that has been done, for this only continues to fuel the fusion. Demanding penance and placing guilt on the unfaithful spouse may make the resolute spouse feel powerful, but the obsessive thoughts and angry desires to punish actually control the person. True repentance and accountable action through the power of the Holy Spirit ultimately bring about long-term change.

The move toward reconciliation does not excuse or make light of the seriousness of the wrongdoing or the breaking of God's command. Neither does it minimize the grievous consequences of broken trust. Both spouses are encouraged to find their true place of belonging in Christ as they respond to what has happened between them. Dealing honestly with hurt, pain and betrayal is part of the personal healing process that eventually clarifies one's identity and self-worth in relationship to God. Indeed, genuine repentance and forgiveness lead to the needed restoration.

The resolute spouse can draw strength from the book of Hosea, considering the anguish and anger God expressed to Israel, who had gone "whoring" after other gods. Israel's choice was a reflection on them, not on God. Yet, their unfaithfulness broke God's heart, so he reminds them how much he loved them from the beginning, how he held them close to his chest and guided them by the hand of loving kindness. Rejection is especially heartbreaking when one has experienced such deep connection.

The unfaithful spouse can also be encouraged by the Parable of the Prodigal Son (Lk 15:11-32). Knowing that even when one strays away from the Father, God is waiting with open arms to offer grace and forgiveness. God's loving arms are wide open, ready for the one who has strayed to turn around and come back home to the Father—a beautiful picture of restoration. When the unfaithful spouse repents and changes through action and attitude, recovery is well on its way.

The Healing Hand of God

Frederick Buechner (1992) offers the following reflection about the ramifications of keeping secrets in a covenant relationship and how healing is necessary to restore that breach of trust. He opens up the scene with God strolling through the Garden of Eden the day after

Adam and Eve have eaten the forbidden fruit. They did what was forbidden and in the process broke their covenant with their creator. God
quickly lays bare the present situation by asking them, "Where are
you?" They must admit that they are hiding themselves from God.
Buechner wonders, "What is it they want to hide? From whom do they
want to hide it? and what does it cost them to hide it?"

Then to lay bare the past, God asks them what they have done. Once
again, Buechner ponders, "What did they hope would happen by
doing it? What did they fear would happen? What was it that made
them so ashamed?" They must face the consequences of what they
have done. These questions offer them a way to reveal the truth so they
then have the opportunity to heal what has been broken between them.

But this is not all! The most moving part of the story comes next, as
God makes garments of skins and clothes them with his own hands.
Buechner writes, "They can't go back, but they can go forward clothed
in a new way—clothed, that is, not in the sense of having their old
defenses again behind which to hide who they are and what they have
done but in the sense of having a new understanding of who they are
and a new strength to draw on for what lies before them to do now"
(p. 70). Healing is possible and a couple is able to find new ways to
reestablish their covenant commitment.

Affair Prevention: Three Types of Friendship Intimacy

Sexuality is an integral part of ourselves as we interact with opposite-
gender persons outside the marriage. Sharing different sides of ourselves with others in close friendship is a wonderful part of being created in relationship. In modern society men and women work and
socialize together in close proximity, have meaningful friendships and
develop significant relationships with others. We have much to gain
from these interactions, but we have much to lose if we don't learn
how to integrate them into our lives as married persons.

One answer to preventing extramarital affairs is to avoid close contact with those of the opposite sex. But such an extreme reaction con-
tradicts the biblical ideal of living in community and being members of
the body of Christ. It also assumes that we are incapable of being morally responsible in our relationships. Also, the idea that a spouse must
meet all our needs gives an unrealistic picture of marriage. God brings

people into our lives to deepen our experiences and help us become what God wants us to be. The key is not to pull away from others, but to establish guidelines about the relationships we have outside the marriage. We might ask ourselves, "Does the friendship enhance or threaten our marriage?" Following are descriptions of three types of friendship intimacy and discussions of the implications of each in terms of marital fidelity.

Similar interest and intellectual intimacy. Common interests and similar intellectual pursuits bring people together in engaging interactions. Colleagues in any field of interest love to debate and dialogue with one another about their specialties. Just go to any party and notice how people gravitate to each other according to their interests. The discussions are often invigorating whether it be the latest theory about something or a classical debate about an issue. Discussions like this are stimulating, for they help us define our ideas, beliefs and values. Dialogue with others brings us fresh ways of thinking and expands our horizons.

Intellectual intimacy is seldom threatening to a spouse, so there is usually no need to restrict connections on this plane. In fact, it often relieves a spouse from feeling obligated to be interested in everything one's partner is invested in. One example is those who love talking sports as opposed to those who have no interest whatever in that topic. There certainly are times, however, when for one reason or another a spouse may be threatened by such a relationship; these situations must be discussed and attended to with care.

Emotional intimacy. Sharing with friends about our life's journey is a special way of coming to know them at a personal level. In particular, having someone share disappointments, joys, feelings, doubts, hopes and dreams can bring about a level of emotional connection. This may include talking to each other about the friendship itself, disclosing how we feel about events going on in our lives or opening up in other vulnerable ways that let this person know us better. Often, we look for someone to talk to about our problems when we're down or facing particular struggles in our lives. Being listened to, cared for and understood deepens our emotional connection with this special person in our life.

You may rightly suspect that this kind of intimacy has more potential for misunderstanding. Your spouse may understandably be uncomfortable with the depth of emotional sharing and personal disclosure between you and another person. It may be that a spouse is jealous of the closeness and tenderness shared between you and another person. Other spouses are quite relieved that their partner has someone else to share with, because they may feel overly responsible or unable to interact on this emotional level.

In most cases, emotional sharing with a same-gender friend is no threat to a spouse. However, when spouses are inattentive, they will lose out on these deeper levels of personal disclosure. When spouses abdicate this position, spousal intimacy is inhibited; this increases distance between spouses.

Emotional sharing with someone of the opposite gender is more likely to lead to jealousy and anger. Such spousal concerns, when openly discussed and negotiated, can lead to clear and reasonable boundaries and appropriate guidelines in opposite-gender emotional sharing. One obvious guideline is to take time and effort for spousal communication. A couple must make concerted efforts to share what's going on in their lives. While some spouses are better at sharing than others, interacting about personal things needs to be practiced throughout the marriage. When emotional sharing needs go unmet, the desire for emotional connection with someone outside the marriage increases the potential for an affair.

Physical intimacy. All people need to be touched in caring ways by caring friends. Some people are skin hungry because they've received so little physical affirmation in childhood and have an enormous need for concrete evidence of love expressed through touch. We call some friends "teddy bears" because they give such wonderful, warm hugs to let us know we are loved. Some people are great at giving us that pat on the back, a shoulder to cry on or a comforting touch when we need encouragement. This is physical touch with no sexual connotation. It is genuine friendship freely given no matter who is around to see. Even when such touch is offered in private, it is free of sexual overtones.

However, although physical touch can bring warmth, comfort and closeness, it can also be misunderstood. Sometimes even a comforting touch can unknowingly bring out a sexual response. One person may feel it and the other be totally unaware or deny anything sexual. Sometimes both persons sense the sexual vibes and pull away in order to set more appropriate boundaries. However, it may happen that one or both will not only sense the sexual feelings but follow through on them.

How does one deal with physical intimacy? How is the touch you give received by the other person? Are boundaries unclear or being violated in any way? Is there ever discomfort or confusion about the touch? What about kisses—are they okay? What kind, how long and in what context? What is the meaning of the kiss—is it simply a greeting of fond expression or is there a romantic or sexual meaning? For instance, in our couples' group, we greet one another with a "holy kiss." It is an agreed-on way we show our affection for one another.

Once again, in the area of physical expression, spouses need to discuss how they feel about the giving and receiving of touch in relationships outside the marriage. Perhaps one simple guideline is to always touch in a public setting. Some spouses are quite free to make personal choices in this matter because there is a solid trust. Yet, it behooves spouses to openly share experiences they have with others outside the marriage. Couple integrity is increased by discussing implications of these relationships and faithfully following through on mutual decisions about touch.

Affair Prevention: Guidelines for Couple Integrity

Affair prevention begins with an awareness of the type of relational needs discussed above. Beyond this, we must realize that we will have attractions for others, and we need to think ahead of time what to do about it. We offer the following guidelines for couples.

Be aware of feelings. A first principle is to be alert and aware of thoughts and feelings you have about your friendships. This is best accomplished by openly communicating with your spouse about your interactions with same- and opposite-sex friends. Denial and defensiveness are the first signs that indicate a questionable intention or motive. Deceit is tempting when you want something bad enough, writes Lewis Smedes in *Sex for Christians* (1976). It's not lust that gets most people into trouble but their lack of awareness of, or denial of, attractions, temptations and their tendency to make exceptions for themselves. Honesty with self and partner is the only policy.

We believe it is important to talk openly with your spouse about anything that comes up for you in any particular friendship. Discuss the extent of the intellectual, emotional and physical interaction; mutually set limitations in terms of the kinds of activities or amount of time you spend with friends; and establish appropriate boundaries in each unique situation. For the best interest of your marriage, come to a united decision about any matter of concern and mutually commit to it.

No secrets please. Keeping secrets about a friendship is an automatic red flag that must be addressed immediately. If there are sexual feelings, you must admit this to your spouse so the two of you can decide how to appropriately proceed with that situation. If as a spouse you are uncomfortable for any reason, you are obliged to bring this up for discussion. The integrity of the marriage is of foremost importance. Bringing out all feelings and questions is absolutely the right thing to do. Sometimes your spouse is the best judge of things you don't notice in a social interaction. For example, listen when a spouse says, "I notice you being especially flirtatious around so-and-so. Are you aware of how much she/he seems to seek you out?" Your willingness to hear what your spouse says is a sign you are completely open in these areas. In an attitude of love, keeping as the top priorities a spouse's best interest and the integrity of the marriage will safeguard your relationship.

The current state of the marriage. When a marriage is at its peak strength, there are more possibilities for a spouse to be close to others at all levels of friendship. When a marriage is at its weakest, there is greater vulnerability, and special caution must be taken to keep the integrity of the marriage the priority. Questions to ask yourself and your spouse center on how each spouse's personal needs are being met in the marriage and what might be lacking at this particular time in married life. Until you address your marital issues, friendship intimacy may have to be put on hold because it takes away from working on what's wrong in the marital relationship. When the marriage is at a vulnerable place, this is exactly when the spouse is most tempted to look for attention outside the marriage. The new relationship becomes a distraction or substitute for what is missing in the marriage, and the marital troubles are sidetracked or avoided altogether.

Marriage always has priority. Couples who are newly married have strong expectations that they will be faithful to each other. Marriage is your primary commitment and friendship is always secondary. When your intimate friendships support and strengthen the marital dyad, you will feel safe and content with those intimate connections. But when they take away or undermine the marriage in any way, it jeopardizes your marriage covenant.

Unfaithfulness is a serious offense because it breaks the marital vows made to each other in the presence of God. However, lest we be smug, we must remember that one can commit adultery of the heart, as Jesus reminded us. This is a sin that easily besets us. Every spouse must take an honest look at their positive contributions to the marriage rather than act pious because they have never technically committed adultery. Lewis Smedes (1976) helps us take an honest look at ourselves by asking how we have failed to keep our marriage covenant.

> A man or woman can be just too busy, too tired, too timid, too prudent, or too hemmed in with fear to be seriously tempted by an adulterous affair. But this same person can be a bore at home, callous to the delicate needs of the partner. He or she may be too prudish to be an adventuresome lover, and too cowardly to be in honest communication and too busy to put oneself out for anything more than a routine ritual of personal commitment. One may be able to claim to have never cheated . . . but may never have tried to grow along with their partner into a deep personal relationship of respect and regard within marriage. Their brand of negative fidelity may be an excuse for letting the marriage fall by neglect into dreary conformity to habit and, with that, into a dull routine of depersonalized sex. I am not minimizing the importance of sexual fidelity, but anyone who thinks that morality in marriage is fulfilled by avoiding an affair has short-circuited the personal dynamics of fidelity. (pp. 168-69)

Suggestions for Further Reading

Grenz, S. 1997. *Sexual ethics: An evangelical perspective.* Louisville, Ky.: Westminster John Knox. See chapter 5.

Harley, W., and J. H. Chalmers. 1998. *Surviving an affair.* Grand Rapids, Mich.: Revell.

Pittman, F. 1989. *Private lies: Infidelity and the betrayal of intimacy.* New York: W. W. Norton.

Part III
Inauthentic Sexuality

10

Sexual Harassment

The Uninvited Eroticizing
of a Relationship

Sexual harassment is any form of unsolicited language or touching containing sexual overtones. It includes sexual jokes, suggestive talk and unsolicited physical advances. Other forms of sexual harassment include giving compliments that are uncomfortable for the receiver and denying a person the choice to avoid listening to sexual conversations or sexually oriented jokes. Whether implicit or explicit, conversation or behavior may not continue if someone objects.

Since allegations of sexual harassment occur primarily within the context of the workplace, a workplace definition is helpful. The Equal Employment Opportunity Commission (EEOC) defines sexual harassment as "unwelcome sexual advances, requests for sexual favors, and other verbal or physical conduct of a sexual nature" (1980:74676). The EEOC suggests three defining features regarding sexual harassment: (1) submission to sexual misconduct is either explicitly or implicitly a term or condition of employment; (2) submission to or rejection of such conduct by the employee is used as the basis for employment decisions regarding the employee; and (3) sexual misconduct unreasonably interferes with an employee's work performance due to an intimidating, hostile or offensive work environment.

Although it may be tempting to limit concerns about sexual harassment to the workplace, a Christian perspective must go beyond that to widen the awareness of all forms of sexual harassment as equally wrong, no matter what the circumstances or where it happens.

Explanatory Models

After summarizing the research on sexual harassment in 1982, Tangri, Burt and Johnson offered three explanatory models about harassment—the organizational, sociocultural and biological. Fitzgerald and Shullman (1993) organized the research findings in terms of the incidence, context and consequences of sexual harassment. Most recently, Tangri and Hayes (1997) use the metaphor of an onion to suggest explanatory models.

Using a sociobiological evolutionary process model, Tangri and Hayes (1997) begin with the "deep structure," or innermost layer, of their theoretical onion in identifying *natural/biological* explanations of harassment. For example, *hormonal* factors intrinsic to the genetic male system contribute to the tendency for men to be promiscuous in their pursuit of women. Another influence is the *evolutionary adaptation process,* which explains sexual harassment in terms of adaptation to reproductive cost-benefit ratios. The idea here is that reproduction entails different costs and benefits for men and women. Since women have only a few eggs, their investment in the reproductive process is great, so they have learned to be "choosy shoppers"; but because men have unlimited amounts of sperm, they seek to diversify their "investment" and thus maximize the possibility that their genes are passed on. Tangri and Hayes (1997) conclude that the *natural/biological model* is insufficient in itself as complete explanation, but it is a good place to start (pp. 114-16).

The next layers of the onion comprise *organizational models* that focus on structural arrangements that make it more likely for sexual harassment to occur in the workplace. One example is *sex-role spillover theory,* which sees sexual harassment as a carryover of normal, day-to-day gender-based societal attitudes and behaviors that are brought into the workplace. While flirtation would be viewed as legitimate in a certain social situation, this kind of behavior could qualify as sexual harassment in a work situation. A limitation of this theory is that it doesn't explain why there is a disproportionate number of men who engage in sexual harassment. Ultimately this theory also relies on sociocultural explanations of sexual harassment.

Organizational power theory is another model that identifies social structures that maintain power differentials that perpetuate sexual harassment by enabling the more powerful to manipulate the less powerful. As a result, sexual harassment is more likely to occur in hierarchical organizations that promote and perpetuate power differentials. Rogers and Henson (1997) show how asymmetrical power relationships explain the high incidence of sexual harassment with temporary workers. A study investigating the prevalence of sexual harassment among 916 female family practice residents indicates that 32 percent reported unwanted sexual advances, 48 percent encountered sexist teaching material, 66 percent experienced favoritism based on gender, 36 percent were given a poor evaluation based on gender, 37 percent were targets of malicious gossip, 5.3 percent were punished punitively based on gender and 2.2 percent were sexually assaulted during residency (Vukovich 1996). As a result almost one-third of these female residents experienced low self-esteem and depression. In some cases the effects were so severe that the residents required therapy or requested a program transfer. Power differential in the workplace sets up potential sexual harassment that can lead to serious emotional trauma and professional liability.

Sexual harassment of males is also reported in the context of power differentials. It is interesting to note that men report being most threatened by coercive behavior that challenges their male dominance (Berdahl, Magley and Waldo 1996). It may be that because males tend to organize relationships around hierarchy, a distorted sexualizing of power and control is especially intimidating by men who are in one-down positions.

The next layers of the onion are the *sociocultural models,* which consider sexual harassment to be part of the larger cultural system. Sexual harassment is viewed as a fulfillment of culturally prescribed behavior rooted in sociocultural norms, values and institutions. Lee et al. (1996), for instance, expose what they call a "culture of sexual harassment" in their study of secondary schools, where they found that 50 percent of students report that they sexually harass or are sexually harassed. These authors believe sociocultural structures are at the root of harassment.

Thus, when a social structure includes both a power differential and exploitative cultural attitudes toward females, sexual harassment is more pronounced. Examples of this are restaurants that require waitresses to wear skimpy, tantalizing outfits with sexually suggestive slogans on the back. In studying the relational dynamics between the waitresses, the customers and management, Loe (1996) concludes that female employees "commodify" their sexuality as a means of earning a living. Unfortunately, the active participation of female employees in an exploitative workplace minimizes the offense in the minds of many. In this case the frequent occurrence of sexual harassment fueled by these two factors leads to a normalization of commodification in the workplace, and a cyclical reinforcement that sexual harassment is to be expected.

Whereas sociocultural models provide an explanation of why sexual harassment happens, they nevertheless fail to answer the questions of why all men or all powerful people don't harass and why the same behaviors are perceived and experienced differently by men and women. For an answer to this we must turn to the outer layer of the onion—*individual differences*.

Questions about individual differences center on how those who sexually harass are different from those who do not, and how those who are harassed differ from those who are not harassed. Among other things, when compared to nonharassers, male sexual harassers have difficulty taking the perspective of another, are more authoritarian, have negative feelings about sexuality and have a low view of their masculine self. In comparison to nonvictims, victims of sexual harassment depart more from conventional sex-role scripts and are less traditional in sex-role attitudes (Tangri and Hayes 1997).

In conclusion, Tangri and Hayes see a consensus emerging across all of the theories of sexual harassment. "When it comes to heterosexual interactions, women experience a narrower range of male behavior that is acceptably sexual. . . . The *system* of heterosexual relations is adversarial and coercive" (p. 125).

Whereas Tangri and Hayes give a helpful explanatory model of sexual harassment, there is a need to move beyond the value-free stance they take. The best example of how this might be done is detailed in the chapter "A Critical Theory of Gender Relations" in *After Eden: Facing The Challenge of Gender Reconciliation,* edited by Van Leeuwen et al. (1993). As applied to an understanding of sexual harassment, critical theory would not only focus on the power differentials between sexual harassers and those who are harassed, but also challenge the legitimacy of organizations and systems in which it is perpetuated. Critical theory also assumes that persons who are harassed, regardless of their circumstance, are not stripped of the abilities to think critically and to act as agents of change and transformation of systems tolerant of sexual harassment. Our strategy in the next section is to utilize a critical-theory approach anchored in the biblical text as a basis for understanding sexual harassment and determining what can and should be done about it on the individual and structure levels.

A Biblically Based Integrative Process Model
Based on this social-scientific explanation of sexual harassment, we are ready to suggest a biblically based process model of sexual harassment and an appropriate grievance process in response to this behavior. We begin by suggesting that sexual harassment can best be understood as a complex process of interaction involving individual behavior within the context of power-based sociocultural systems. To this we add a biblically based understanding of sexual harassment that includes three elements: (1) a definition of sexual harassment that considers both the motive of the initiator (harasser) and the experience of the one offended (harassed); (2) a distinction between affirmation and harassment; and (3) a comprehensive grievance process.

(Note: Although sexual harassment applies to both men and women, for the sake of simplification and because it represents the most common pattern, most of our illustrations will portray the male as the harasser.)

Defining Sexual Harassment: Balancing Motive and Act
Attempts to objectively define sexual harassment are based typically on a narrow individualistic view, which fails to take into account the

motive of the initiator and the experience of the offended. Sexual harassment has both an objective (the act of harassment) and subjective (the perception of harassment) dimension. In considering any alleged offense the Bible points to the importance of considering both the motive of the accused and the effect of the act upon the accuser. This is perhaps most clearly stated in Exodus 21:12-14, "Anyone who strikes a man and kills him shall surely be put to death. However, if he does not do it intentionally, but God lets it happen, he is to flee to a place [God] will designate. But if a man schemes and kills another man deliberately, take him away from my altar and put him to death." A right understanding of the Ten Commandments also involves God's intent for a moral law that takes into account both the act and intent. Whereas the first nine commandments refer to acts, the intent is implied within each (Kaiser 1983). That the act includes the intent is most explicitly seen in the Tenth Commandment, Do not *covet* your neighbor's house or your neighbor's wife.

Determining the appropriate response to a charge of sexual harassment requires considering the act and the intent. For example, one man might embrace a woman and she receives it as a genuine expression of emotional support. Another man may embrace the same woman, and she feels a sexual overtone. The two acts of embracing are not the same, because of differences in how they were intended or how they were received. The intent of the man and the woman's interpretation of the act determine whether it was sexual harassment, and both must be taken into account in the grievance process.

If a woman responds to the first hug with discomfort, the man acting from pure intent is still accountable for his behavior. At the very least, he may be guilty of a lack of good judgment in how he expressed support. Upon sensing her reaction he should respond accordingly— by acknowledging her discomfort and apologizing if necessary. Generally, it is best to ask before embracing.

At the personal level, individuals will vary greatly in what they report to be incidences of sexual harassment. Much of the variation reflects differing social background and life experiences. For example, factors such as having an overly protective mother, observing fewer positive behaviors between parents and experiencing unwanted sexual contact during childhood are all associated with experiencing a greater number of objective incidents of sexual harassment (Houston and Hwang 1996). Beneath the experience of sexual harassment is the woman's perception of the event. However, there is evidence that some background factors can desensitize one to sexual harassment. Strouse, Goodwin and Roscoe (1994) found that exposure to high levels of pop music videos as well as dysfunctional family dynamics increase tolerance of sexual harassment among adolescent girls.

Figure 10.1 depicts an attempt to balance the motive of the initiator with the experience of the offended.

Sexual harassment as the motive of the initiator is represented on a continuum ranging from *High* at the top to *Low* at the bottom. Sexual

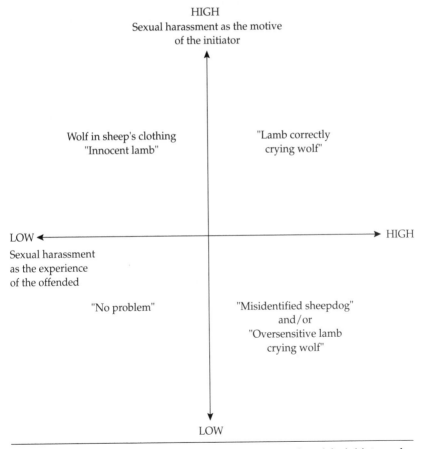

Figure 10.1. **Defining sexual harassment: Balancing the motive of the initiator and the experience of the offended**

harassment as the experience of the offended is represented on a continuum ranging from *Low* at the left to *High* at the right of the table. A given social encounter may be anywhere within the bounds of the figure. At the lower left corner is a social encounter that is clearly not sexual harassment. There is no motive to harass on the part of the initiator, nor is harassment experienced by the recipient. At the upper right corner we have the exact opposite. Here the initiator is the sexual aggressor and the encounter is clearly perceived as harassment by the recipient. This is clearly an offense; the "wolf" has been identified, and both parties know it.

The difficulty in identifying sexual harassment occurs when there is a lack of congruency between the motive of the initiator and the experience of the offended. The upper left corner of the figure represents an encounter in which the initiator is sexually harassing the person, but that person does not perceive it as harassment. This might be a case of a "wolf appearing in sheep's clothing," or a woman being so used to this treatment that she rationalizes that "men will be men" and doesn't even judge this behavior as harassment. In the lower right corner we represent an incident in which the initiator does not intend sexual harassment, but the action is perceived as sexual harassment by the receiver. The incongruence can stem from two types of situations. First, this might be a case of the overfriendly protector who is misidentified as an aggressor. Without meaning to convey sexual innuendoes, some men (and women) might relate in a way that is perceived by the other as sexual harassment. For example, a man who offers a woman a ride home out of genuine concern for her safety might be guilty of bad judgment but not of sexual harassment. Second, some women may be overly sensitive to a male's initiation in a social exchange. The innocent question or statement offered is perceived by the woman as having connotations that the man did not intend. She may have misread this situation because of previous experiences of sexual harassment or exploitation.

We have given some examples to illustrate the four extremes, but in reality, sexual harassment comes in different degrees and shades. Thus, at the very center of the chart are incidences in which compliments are given where the intent of the initiator and the experience of the receiver vary greatly depending on a variety of social contexts, for example, differences in age, status and power; the degree that two people know each other; and the social situation. The "dance" between men and women is fraught with multiple layers of possible mixed motives and multiple interpretations.

Distinguishing Between Harassment and Affirmation

This leads us to a related issue, namely that a statement that might be given and taken as affirmation in one social context may come across as sexual innuendo, a put-down or even a sexual threat in another. Spoken words or behavior might be considered affirmation or sexual harassment depending upon the intent of the initiator and how it is experienced by the receiver. For instance, upon meeting for the first time, a man may say to a woman, "Your red hair is astonishing!" Is this affirmation or sexual harassment?

Figure 10.2 illustrates the relationship between sexual harassment and affirmation during a social encounter.

The vertical continuum represents the verbal content, from a statement of affirmation at the top to a sexual threat or put-down at the

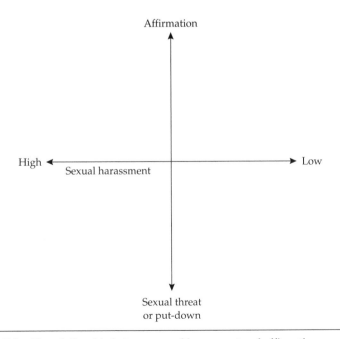

Figure 10.2. The relationship between sexual harassment and affirmation

bottom. The horizontal continuum represents the degree of sexual harassment from *High* at the left to *Low* at the right.

As a way of gaining a functional understanding of the issue, examine the following statements and try to place each comment within the figure: (1) "I admire your creativity and style," (2) "You have an illogical mind," (3) "I could open up a sexually uptight person like you," (4) "You have a beautiful body," and (5) "Your work reflects a feminine [or masculine] sensitivity." We suggest that the first statement most clearly fits in the upper right quadrant, the second statement in the lower right quadrant, the third statement in the lower left quadrant, and the fourth statement in the upper left quadrant. The last statement might be the most problematic, for some might argue that behavior can't be both affirming *and* involve sexual harassment. However, the recipient of such a comment can at one level feel affirmed, but at another harassed.

Our point is that we must think in both dimensions when assessing a given behavior. Sexual harassment applies to both men and women. Although it is less common, women do sexually harass men, and certainly sexual harassment within the same gender occurs as well. Reversing the gender of the initiator and victim can affect the way sexual harassment is defined. Often the traditional view of men as the sexual aggressor shades our interpretation of behavior. Most people perceive behavior differently based on the gender of the initiator. For example, a study of secondary-school students found that 31 percent of the girls and 18 percent of the boys experienced some form of sexual harassment at school (Timmerman and Bajema 1996). Another study of over 1,200 secondary-school students revealed that 83 percent of girls and 60 percent of boys received unwanted sexual attention in school (Lee et al. 1996), and a sample of 927 workers in Taiwan revealed that 35 percent of the women and 13 percent of the men experienced sexual harassment in the workplace (Loe 1996). Sexual harassment of males is almost always in the context of power differentials. It is interesting to note that men report being most threatened by coercive behavior challenging their male dominance (Berdahl, Magley and Waldo 1996). Possibly males tend to organize relationships around hierarchy, resulting in a distorted sexualization of power and control, which is especially felt by men in power-down positions.

Cultural context is another factor important in determining sexual harassment. Objective definition and subjective experience of sexual harassment are embedded in a wider cultural context. Persons from different cultural backgrounds differ in their interpretations of what constitutes sexual harassment. Studies of sexual harassment in formerly all-male institutions, such as the armed services, illustrates how subcultural contexts must also be taken into account in understanding sexual harassment. Miller (1997) found that men who believe and resent that women in the military have unfair advantages (for example, exemption from combat roles and less stringent requirements) also admit to harassing their female counterparts. The study suggests that harassment may be strongest from men who feel passed over or stuck in the Army's system of rank. Other studies support the influence of resentment as a motivation for sexual harassment. For example, interviews of 22 African-American female firefighters indicated a climate of resentment among male firefighters that was expressed in passive-aggressive ways (Yoder and Aniakudo 1996). The study found that a climate of initiation rites and pranks among male firefighters fueled resentment by excluding female firefighters.

Although the sociocultural context of sexual harassment is vast, these studies illustrate the complex factors involved in sexual harassment. A comprehensive understanding of sexual harassment includes individual, social and cultural factors, which shade our response to sexual harassment on individual and structural levels.

Grievance Process

Grievance is the process of addressing the wrong of sexual harassment. Recent notorious legal cases are responsible for the increased public attention surrounding sexual harassment. Virtually all moderate- to large-size organizations use a grievance process for handing sexual harassment charges. A Christian perspective on sexual harassment must develop a grievance process that is based on such major biblical themes as justice, mercy, retribution, restoration and reconciliation. Figure 10.3 illustrates a biblically based model for handling sexual harassment.

Justice versus mercy. Besides the tension between act and motive discussed in a previous section, Scripture holds justice and mercy in balance. A biblical perspective of grievance encompasses concern for the

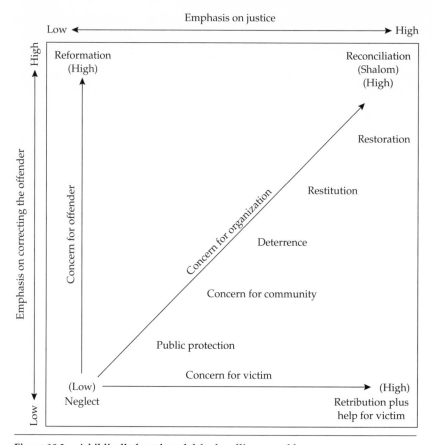

Figure 10.3.   A biblically based model for handling sexual harassment

victim and the community (justice) and concern for the offender (mercy). In figure 10.3 an emphasis on justice is represented horizontally from *Low* at the left to *High* at the right. An emphasis on mercy and correcting the offender is represented vertically from *Low* at the bottom to *High* at the top. This dual concern is part of the larger biblical teaching about law and grace.

Our understanding of the relationship between law and grace is clearly addressed by Paul in his statement, "Christ is the end of the law so that there may be righteousness for everyone who believes" (Rom 10:4). As Paul elaborates on this text, we learn that there is nothing wrong with the law itself, for it points the way to live according to

God's intention. The problem with the law is that because no one is perfect, the law can't be fulfilled. In his excellent book on New Testament ethics, Richard Hays (1996) proclaims, "Christ is the *telos* of the Law" (p. 414). Thus, Christ is the "end of the law" in the sense that he is the perfect fulfillment of the law. Because of Christ's perfection and righteousness, our righteousness is not dependent upon our keeping the law, but upon our faith in Christ.

Understanding our relationship between law and faith in Christ gives clarity to the relationship between justice and mercy. God's holiness demands his justice, but Christ's incarnation and resurrection provide mercy. The following is an example of how both principles need to be part of a grievance process.

In a general sense *justice* involves *concern for the victim* (represented by the horizontal arrow at the bottom of figure 10.3), while *mercy* shows *concern for the offender* (represented by the vertical arrow at the left of the figure). The Old Testament emphasizes concern for the victim above the offender. However, a rationale of grievance based on Old Testament teachings alone is one-sided, showing little concern for the offender. The life and teaching of Christ temper justice with mercy toward the offender.

Under God's justice, we are accused and found guilty. But God shows mercy to us through Christ. Jesus illustrates the balance of justice and mercy in Matthew 5:38-39: "You have heard that it was said, 'Eye for eye, and tooth for tooth.' But I tell you, do not resist an evil person. If someone strikes you on the right cheek, turn to him the other also."

When the Pharisees brought a woman caught in the act of adultery to Jesus, they were right in asking whether she should be stoned according to the law of Moses. (Actually, according to the letter of the law, *both* she and the man with whom she committed adultery were to be stoned [Deut 22:22-24].) Jesus, however, showed mercy when he challenged, "If any one of you is without sin, let him be the first to throw a stone at her." After her accusers had left, Jesus turned to the woman and said, "Then neither do I condemn you. . . . Go now and leave your life of sin" (Jn 8:7, 11). Mercy is not simply letting the offender off without consequences, but rather mercy demands repentance and rehabilitation. The mercy Jesus teaches is a call for change.

Jesus' call for mercy is contingent upon balancing two elements: the act of the offense and the intent of the offender. As noted in a previous section, the Bible teaches that redress for an offense must take into account both the act and the motive.

Grievance within the Christian community. A biblical model for handling grievance equips us to address the question of sexual harassment in a church or Christian organization. First, Christian organizations handling cases of sexual harassment incorporate a respectful balance of concern for the victim, for the offender and for the organization. By working toward healing and restoration, persons demonstrate accountability for their actions.

Figure 10.3 represents a balance between concern for the victim, the offender and the organization. Unfortunately, denial is a common response within the Christian community regarding the existence of sexual harassment. Neglect is represented in the lower left corner. Failure to implement a grievance process in the face of a sexual harassment charge is neglect of the victim, the offender and the organization.

However, there may be good reasons why a victim fails to pursue grievance. Serious matters that need to be taken into account include feelings of powerlessness, shame, fear of job loss or other retaliation and need for taking time to process the offense before making it public.

The victimized individual is the first concern in any sexual harassment grievance process. A primary concern for the victim is thematic in the Old Testament and in Jesus' teachings. In the Parable of the Sheep and the Goats, Jesus taught, "Whatever you did for one of the least of these brothers of mine, you did for me. . . . Whatever you did not do for one of the least of these, you did not do for me" (Mt 25:40, 45). However, a church or religious organization that shows high concern for the victim, but none for the health of the offender or the organization in which the offense took place, narrowly limits its response to a *retribution* model.

The purpose of retribution is revenge for the victim by having the offender "pay" for the offense. The law of revenge was enforced by the ancient Hebrews, often providing a punishment similar in nature to the offense, but specifying the maximum limit the punishment could take (Ex 21:23-36). Retribution not only attempts to equal the score between the offender and the victim, but it might also serve to have a unifying effect upon society. When a societal norm has been violated, retribution draws attention to the legitimacy and need of the norm for the preservation of society. The practice of secrecy within the church and parachurch organizations regarding sexual offenses sabotages healing at the community level.

The opposite view emphasizes the belief that *rehabilitation* is the only consideration for deciding appropriate punishment. Such extreme thinking promotes a victim society, excusing offenders as victims of dysfunctional families or hostile, uncaring communities. According to this view, punishment is replaced by treatment (Hughes 1983). This view is problematic in that it fails to show concern for the victim, and fails to treat the offender as a responsible human being. Failure to hold people responsible for their behavior minimizes their humanity as creatures of God who are divinely given self-will.

Concern for the community is another reason given for advocating punishment of the offender. Punishing offenders for the good of the community is usually referred to as *deterrence*. The theory of deterrence proposes that punishing by example will discourage others from committing the same offense. Obversely, lack of accountablility for the offense will diminish the community's resistance to the same offense (Nathanson 1987). Theoretically, concern for the community might be thought to correspond to the use of deterrence. When there is low concern for the community (represented in the lower left corner of figure 10.3), the motivational force of deterrence is low. As concern for the community increases (represented in the figure as a movement diagonally toward the upper right corner), there is an increase in deterrence. However, concern for the good of the community can be motivationally expressed at several different levels.

At a basic level, community protection from sexual harassment stems from a motivation for community safety. Merely removing the harasser protects the community; however, this does not deal with the offense within the context of the community, as deterrence does— holding the offender up as an example. For this reason public protection (such as removal of the offender) is lower than deterrence on the "concern for community" continuum. Although the Bible advocates deterrence as a response to an offense in social relationships, it has more to say about *restitution* and *restoration*.

Restitution uses punishment to compensate for the harm done to the victim. Exodus 21 contains a number of examples of punishment as restitution:

> If men quarrel and one hits the other with a stone or with his fist . . . he must pay the injured man for the loss of his time and see that he is completely healed. (21:18–19)

> If a man hits a manservant or maidservant in the eye and destroys it, he must let the servant go free to compensate for the eye. (21:26)

> If a man uncovers a pit or digs one and fails to cover it and an ox or a donkey falls into it, the owner of the pit must pay for the loss; he must pay its owner, and the dead animal will be his. (21:33-34)

Exodus 22:1 teaches that in certain cases restitution needs to be more than the loss inflicted on another: "If a man steals an ox or a sheep and slaughters it or sells it, he must pay back five head of cattle for the ox and four sheep for the sheep." So strong was the Old Testament emphasis upon restitution that inability to pay back a loss to the victim could result in the offender being "sold to pay for his theft" (Exodus 22:3). The rest of Exodus 22 continues to detail the types of punishment to be carried out based on the principle of restitution.

The absence of restitution in society today may reflect the hyperindividualistic emphasis that pervades contemporary society. The exception to this, or perhaps its consequence, is the increasing number of exorbitant civil suits, including those for sexual harassment. The legal system seeks punishments that are equivalent to the harm done to the victim. However, rarely does the offender make recompense to the victim directly. Only restitution offers the victim the hope of recompensation for the real loss incurred at the hands of the offender. The absence of restitution may be one of the reasons why victims in our society cry out so harshly for revenge. Our grievance systems rarely provide for any other way in which the victim can feel that his or her loss is being "paid for." Restitution is especially appropriate when society at large is victimized. An example of this took place a few years ago when a highway contracting company in Nebraska pleaded guilty to bribery. Instead of sending the guilty to prison, the judge ordered them to endow a $1,475,000 chair of ethics at the University of Nebraska (Bennett 1987). A similar approach in cases of sexual harassment might order the offender to distribute literature and educate others on the issue of sexual harassment. Restitution may also prove more effective in rehabilitating the offender.

The upper right corner of figure 10.3 represents an ideal concern for the victim, the offender and the community. The practice of these three motivations by the community (public protection, deterrence and restitution) constitutes *restoration*. At the interpersonal level the process of restoration repairs or reestablishes unity. Restitution begins the process of restoration at the interpersonal level. Restitution reestablishes equity in the relationship between the harasser and the victim. There are some interpersonal changes necessary in order to foster restoration. The harasser must go through a process of sorrow, confession, true repentance and asking forgiveness for the wrong committed. In response to true repentance, the victims must be open to dealing with feelings of anger, rage and hurt so they can ultimately be willing to forgive.

The Christian basis for interpersonal restoration is the biblical model of reconciliation. In the Old Testament reconciliation was made possible when a sacrificial atonement (the Hebrew verb *kāpar* meant "to cover") was offered for sin (Lev 6:30; 16:20-22). Jesus elaborated the meaning of reconciliation by tying it to reconciliation from an offending brother: "Therefore, if you are offering your gift at the altar and there remember that your brother has something against you, leave your gift there in front of the altar. First go and be reconciled to your brother; then come and offer your gift" (Mt 5:23-24). The Greek word for being reconciled is *diallassomai,* which means "to be changed entirely." Reconciliation or interpersonal restoration is for the benefit of the offended as well as the offender. God desires that all broken relationships be restored.

Jesus taught his followers to take the initiative in seeking reconciliation. The basis of this teaching on reconciliation is powerfully illustrated by Christ's atoning death: "Be reconciled to God. God made him who had no sin to be sin for us, so that in him we might become the righteousness of God" (2 Cor 5:20-21). The theology of the cross provides a basis for Christians to pursue and achieve reconciliation with an offending person.

Reconciliation or the attempt at restoration in the harasser-harassed relationship must not be prematurely rushed, however. Individuals must be given time to admit to and experience deep feelings of betrayal, grieving, anger, rage and desire for revenge. Each individual process in moving toward reconciliation is unique and different. The last thing victims need is pressure to forgive the harasser. Only after the offended have been able to let go and disarm the emotional power that the offense has in their life, is forgiveness possible. However, forgiveness never means condoning or excusing the offense. It is the conscious choice of the one offended to let go and extend forgiveness by the empowering of God's grace. True reconciliation requires penitence of the harassers for their offense. When there is true repentance from the harasser and forgiveness from the harassed, restoration transforms into interpersonal reconciliation. Jesus illustrates the process of interpersonal restoration in the Parable of the Good Neighbor, in which two enemies become as neighbors to one another.

Sexual Harassment as a Social Justice Issue

A biblical view of reconciliation also calls for restoration at the *social structural* level. Communities have the potential to create environments in which sexual harassment is likely to be the accepted norm, most notably in all-male institutions. An example of this situation is the Tailhook scandal. Naval officers had a tradition of celebrating their graduation at a place called Tailhook. In former times, when no female officers were a part of the festivities, sexist jokes and skits were an acceptable part of the rite of passage. However, the addition of female Naval officers added a new dimension to this sexist subculture. The situation got out of control as the male officers began grabbing, fondling and attempting to disrobe the female officers. After an initial denial, the Navy commander minimized the situation by suggesting that "boys will be boys." Marginalized and insulted, a number of the female officers filed official complaints of sexual harassment. This not only ended in the forced resignation of the commanding officer, but in a self-examination and restructuring within the Navy.

There is a logical relationship between sexual harassment and sexual discrimination. Communities practicing sexual discrimination, including churches and parachurch organizations, by their very nature provide a social environment conducive to sexual harassment. Furthermore, it is unlikely that a community promoting sexual harassment will be challenged by anyone within the community, and so it is likely that the community will continue the practice. In a community allowing racial discrimination, certain members deny equal rights to others because of their race. When a conflict develops between a member of the majority group and the minority group, an opportunity is created for the system to be challenged. Any minority member refusing to accept a place of subordination will encounter organizationally sanctioned harassment. One need only to examine the response of racially discriminatory social orders for more insight into this type of social structure. In fact, inappropriate sexual behavior is not defined as "harassment" but rather as "just rewards" to persons who don't know their place.

Sexual discrimination, like racial or any other form of discrimination, needs to be thought of as a social justice issue. An excellent model on how justice in biblical perspective might be applied to gender relationships is given in *After Eden: Facing the Challenge of Gender Reconciliation* (Van Leeuwen et al. 1993). These authors find that "nowhere in the Bible is there any suggestion that 'justice' is limited to the marketplace and other 'public' arenas of activity. . . . Those who would be members of God's kingdom, *whatever* their race, nationality, class, or gender, are called to weave a seamless web of justice *and* righteousness *and* peace throughout all areas of their personal and corporate lives" (pp. 426-27).

Christians need to regard social structures that are prone to sexual harassment as a social justice issue. Biblical justice is oriented towards *re-creating* communities so that each gender participates fully and equally in society. As Mott (1982) states: "The difference between scriptural and classical justice lies in the understanding of what is to be the normal situation of society. The Scriptures do not allow the presupposition of a condition in which groups or individuals are denied the ability to participate fully and equally in the life of the society. For this reason, justice is primarily spoken of by the biblical writers as activity on behalf of the disadvantaged" (p. 65).

When women are not free to live in their full femininity because they fear being sexually harassed, there is no *shalom* (see upper right corner of figure 10.3). Shalom is "the human being dwelling at peace in all his or her relationships: with God, with self, with fellows, with nature" (Wolterstorff 1983:69). A characteristic of groups, communities or organizations embodying shalom is *just peace*. If peace and order are present, but sexual harassment is the norm, there is no shalom. Punishing those committing sexual harassment without addressing the problem of harassment-friendly social structures falls short of a full view of biblical justice. The principle of *redress* is foundational to biblical justice, and stands as an obligation to correct an unjust social structure (Lev 25:25-28; Ps 107:39-41).

Conclusion

In response to the question of which is the greatest commandment, Jesus replied, "Love the Lord your God with all your heart and with all your soul and with all your mind . . . and . . . love your neighbor as yourself" (Mt 22:37, 39). Sexual harassment violates Christ's commandment to love our neighbor as ourselves. The Bible further teaches that both male and female are made in the image of God (Gen 1:27), in Christ there is neither male nor female (Gal 3:28), and followers of Christ are to be in mutual submission to one another (Eph 5:21) instead of lording it over one another (Mt 20:25-27). Sexual harassment denies the image of God in the other, negates our oneness in Christ and usually involves an abuse of power; therefore, the Christian community must actively combat it, for when one member suffers, all suffer together (1 Cor 12:26).

We have suggested that a biblical response to sexual harassment will incorporate high concern for the harassed, the harasser and the community in which the harassment takes place. Failing to be concerned for the harasser not only ignores the humanity of the perpetrator, but will also result in the perpetrator repeating the harassment in the future. The evidence suggests that those who sexually harass are likely to be repeat offenders. Sexual offenders first need to be stopped, but second, need to be helped to develop healthier, more human ways of relating.

A biblical response to sexual harassment involves redress and restoration at both the interpersonal and community level. A concerned response is incomplete if it focuses *only* on the victim and the offender; it must seek the restoration of a just peace at all social structural levels.

Such a situation is poignantly described in Isaiah 11:6-8: "The wolf shall live with the lamb, the leopard shall lie down with the kid . . . and a little child shall lead them" (NRSV). Without losing concern for the victim and the offender, a biblical view of restoration following sexual harassment will also encompass the holistic connotation of shalom as community well-being.

Suggestions for Further Reading

Conway, J., and S. Conway. 1993. *Sexual harassment no more.* Downers Grove, Ill.: InterVarsity Press.

O'Donahue, W., ed. 1997. *Sexual harassment: Theory, research, and treatment.* Boston: Allyn & Bacon.

Ruther, P. 1996. *Understanding and preventing sexual harassment.* New York: Bantam Books.

11

Sexual Abuse

A Violation Deep Within the Soul

Sexual abuse leaves a gashing wound deep within the heart and soul of a child. It's a "hushed-up secret that's too big for seventy-times-seven forgiveness," according to one survivor. We must face sexual abuse for what it is, a spiritual violation that has a profound impact on the child, the family and society at large.

Celie, a fourteen-year-old girl, tries to put words to her experience of being sexually abused by her stepfather in *The Color Purple* by Alice Walker (1982). She writes to God in her private diary since her stepfather has warned her to "never tell nobody" about what he has done. Here are a few excerpts to help us understand her pain.

> Dear God,
> I am fourteen years old. I am [crossed out] I have always been a good girl. Maybe you can give me a sign letting me know what is happening to me. (p. 11)

> Dear God [written after she told her friend Shug about the abuse],
> It hurt me, you know, I say. I was fourteen. I never even thought bout men having nothing down there so big. It scare me just to see it. And the

way it poke itself and grow. . . . I start to cry. I cry and cry and cry. Seem like it all come back to me, laying there in Shug arms. How it hurt and how much I was surprise. How it stung while I finish trimming his hair. How the blood drip down my leg and mess up my stocking. How he don't never look at me straight after that. (pp. 108-9)

Celie's world got turned upside down, leaving her in utter disarray about what went wrong. This young girl was not only shattered by the basic trust that was broken between herself and her stepfather, but by the long-term effects of the incestuous intrusion later in her life. It was a pain too deep for words, yet when she finally shared the unspeakable secret with her trusted friend, Shug, it was this woman's accepting love that helped bring healing to Celie's soul.

Defining Sexual Abuse

Sexual abuse is broadly defined as a sexual act imposed on a child or person who lacks emotional, maturational and/or cognitive development. Being in a dominant position (because of age, physical strength or a parental or older sibling role) perpetrators invite, lure or force a child to have sexual contact with them. This may include such behaviors as showing pornographic material, telling explicit sexual stories, disrobing inappropriately, sexual touching, intercourse, oral or anal sex, or penetration of genital or anal openings with an object. Using their more powerful position, perpetrators take advantage of a child's normal curiosity, innocence, and physical and mental vulnerability.

Sexual abusers come from all walks of life and economic and cultural groups. Whether blue collar or professional, rich or poor, male or female, adult or minor, religious or nonreligious, Caucasian or non-Caucasian, perpetrators commit serious crimes against children. Sex offenders are usually known (relative, friend, professional or family acquaintance) to the child who is abused. It is less common that a child is sexually abused by a complete stranger.

Pedophiles are sex offenders whose preferred or exclusive method of achieving sexual excitement is through engaging in sexual activity with children. These adults have a conscious interest in using prepubescent children for sexual gratification. Pedophiles are high-risk offenders who often begin offending at a young age and have a record of prior offenses and multiple victims.

Incest is more specifically defined as a sexual violation between persons related by blood or marriage, including step-parents, caretakers or live-in partners who assume a parental role. The powerful parental position leaves the child especially vulnerable to their requests or demands. Instead of protecting and providing for children dependent on them, the offender misuses authority to coerce them into sexual compliance. It is a shattering blow of betrayal when the sacred parent-child trust bond is broken. No child is ever prepared for such a twisted reversal of relationships.

After reviewing the major studies on familial sex offenses, David Finkelhor (1980) found sibling incest to be one of the most common forms of sexual abuse. In a study done by Johnson (1988), it was found that 47 percent of child and adolescent perpetrators had abused a younger sibling (Durocher 1992). The two dominant patterns of sibling incest are power-oriented/aggressive acts and enticing/erotic acts. The power position of an older sibling is an important factor in sibling abuse. Wasserman and Kappel (1985) discovered that verbal coercion was reported in 57 percent of the cases of 161 adolescent sex offenders, and O'Brien (1989) found that younger brothers and sisters are usually forced to engage in sexual intercourse against their will. Sometimes sibling sexual abuse is motivated by anger or jealousy toward a sibling who is perceived to be favored by the parents. In other cases siblings who cling together for comfort in physically abusive or neglectful homes may find the overly close relationship becomes sexual.

Many families minimize sibling sexual abuse because they define sexual contact between siblings as normal sexual curiosity. Maddock and Larson (1995) point out how attitudes about normal sex play between siblings vary across cultures and even within cultural groups. Some groups are very casual about sibling sexual contact while others impose strict sanctions. In most cases, however, concern is rightly expressed when sexual activity takes place under any kind of coercion or force. Age differences between the siblings, duration of contact and motivation of participants are other factors to take into account when assessing sexual sibling abuse. Of course, it is always a serious offense when specific acts like vaginal or anal penetration, oral-genital contact or intercourse occur. The family must never close their eyes but remain appropriately alert to any sexual activity that occurs between siblings.

Family involvement in the treatment of sibling abuse plays a significant role because it shores up the leadership role of parents in terms of providing proper supervision and guidance. Family therapy can be a resource in helping family members learn appropriate ways of caring, connecting and upholding the sacred bonds of family trust.

Prevalence of Sexual Abuse

It is difficult to obtain reliable statistics on the actual number of sexual abuse cases in any culture due to the shame and stigma felt by victims, offenders and their families. Reports of sexual abuse from studies of women in general populations have ranged from 7 percent to 50 percent (Roosa et al. 1997) depending on how abuse is defined. David Finkelhor (1994), a well-known researcher in the area of sexual violence, substantiated 150,000 childhood sexual abuse cases in the United States in 1993. Jehu (1990) estimated that 27 percent to 54 percent of all females have experienced some form of childhood sexual abuse, which means there may be as many as 34 million adult women who have been molested as children (Hudson 1996:71). Some estimate that one out of every three children under the age of eighteen has been sexually abused (Fortune 1983:326).

The actual number of sexual abuse incidents is most likely to be higher than studies indicate, especially among boys. Males are more reluctant to report sexual abuse experiences with other males, due to stigmas about masculinity and implications of homosexuality. Other factors that contribute to underreporting in both males and females include shame, a feeling of responsibility in some way for the abuse, blocked memories and confusion about what constitutes sexual abuse.

Of children who are sexually abused, females are at a higher risk (83 percent) than males (17 percent). Preadolescence, a time when sexual development is pronounced, is the time of greatest risk for sexual abuse. Social isolation is another factor that places a young person at risk for sexual abuse. It's unclear, however, whether loneliness and isolation from peers come prior to the abuse or if the isolation is a way to cope with abuse that has already occurred (Finkelhor 1997).

Living in a home with a nonbiological father also places a child at greater risk for sexual abuse in that home. Trepper and Barrett (1989) found stepfathers to be five times more likely than natural fathers to abuse children, and the abuse is of a more serious nature. The explanation for this finding may be that the strong incest taboo observed throughout most cultures of the world is what keeps biological fathers from sexually abusing their daughters. Especially when the biological father is sufficiently bonded with his children, he is less likely to treat them as objects of his sexual desires. Some surmise that the presence and participation of a father during the birth of his children increases his emotional attachment, dissuading him from incestuous thoughts and behaviors toward his own children.

The Incestuous Family

The incestuous family may look normal on the outside, but inside the home, relationships are seriously disrupted. In many of these homes, a closed boundary around the family keeps others out, while rigid roles within the family promote male dominance, female subservience and authoritarian parenting. These dynamics set up a conspiracy of silence. No one dares tell an outsider what goes on inside the family, for this would be considered a profound act of disloyalty. Power and fear are tactics used to undermine weaker family members, who are not allowed to question authority or expose the truth. Family members learn to walk on eggshells, be extremely cautious and tentative and keep their feelings to themselves.

While rigid family dynamics, as mentioned above, can lead to an extremely harsh reaction to sexuality, the chaotic home is also problematic. For example, when there are no clear boundaries or respect for personal space, a child's privacy can be invaded physically, sexually and emotionally in a variety of ways. Whether it's a case of sleeping in a crowded room or in the same bed, or having an open-door policy that gives free access at anytime to any member, a child's personal privacy is being invaded. Practices in the home such as vulgar sex talk, erotic suggestions and sexual suggestions cause discomfort and confusion. Substance abuse is also often part of the chaos, breaking down normal inhibitions and opening up unacceptable sexual possibilities that otherwise would be contained. Laxness in boundaries as well as hostile rigid interactions leave children fearful, vulnerable and unprotected.

A study conducted in Dunedin, New Zealand, found the postabuse adjustment of 138 women to be especially poor when there was a negative relationship with parents. One way these children escaped a difficult home situation was to participate in sports or achieve in academics (Romans et al. 1995).

Father-daughter breach. A characteristic of incestuous families is emotional disconnection and inability to empathize with others. The father who sexually abuses his children sees them as property, is emotionally immature and is unable to fulfill his needs in nonsexual ways. He has little capacity to take their feelings or wishes into account and resorts to controlling, coercing and seducing children under his control.

In a large sample surveying 775 women survivors of childhood sexual abuse (ages twenty-five to forty-four), 80 percent of the subjects also reported emotional and physical intrafamilial abuse (Ussher and Dewberry 1995). Family dynamics included frequent verbal coercion, blaming, making threats and being exposed to various acts of physical and sexual violence. Onset of puberty at a young age, suffering abuse from one's father or stepfather, repeated sexual intercourse and prolonged abuse are factors that contribute to the extensive negative impact on the victim.

Mother-daughter breach. When a daughter is sexually abused by her father, she often feels angry at her mother for not having prevented the abuse. Whether a mother was in denial, neglectful, self-engrossed or in a powerless position, she nevertheless failed to protect her daughter.

An overly dependent, passive wife may find it easier to pretend abuse is not happening than to confront her perpetrator husband or boyfriend. She may choose to keep quiet because she fears the ramifications of exposing what she knows. Sometimes mothers are willing to sacrifice their daughters in order to appease their husbands. A mother may blame her daughter for what happened, calling her a "slut," "the other woman" or "home-wrecker." This mother may be resentful, jealous or hostile toward her daughter after the abuse is revealed. Such reactions drive an enormous wedge between mother and daughter. And, in a small percentage of cases, the mother is an active participant in the abuse, leaving the daughter with a double dose of betrayal.

Intergenerational abuse. The Bible speaks of intergenerational sin in Exodus 20:5 and Deuteronomy 5:9. The fact that the sins of forefathers are passed from generation to generation can be seen through studies that show how sexual abuse tends to repeat itself over generations. Romano and DeLuca (1996) found a higher prevalence and more severe childhood sexual abuse reported by sexual perpetrators when compared to nonsexual offending criminals. An investigation of forty convicted child sexual offenders had a similar result. The researchers found that the twenty men who had been sexually abused as children reported almost three times as many victims as the twenty who had not been sexually abused (Renshaw 1994). In a study of eleven female sexual offenders, compared with female offenders incarcerated for nonsexual crimes, the eleven sexual offenders reported a higher incidence of childhood sexual abuse and physical abuse within their families. They indicated that the victimization played a role in sexual dissatisfaction as adults (Kaplan and Green 1995).

A sexual abuse victim needs an enormous amount of energy to cope with the pain. Some withdraw by burying their heads in books, some are compliant by trying to make everything all right in the family, some use distraction to numb the pain, and some act out in self-destructive ways.

Some time ago I (Judy) counseled Jennifer, a young mother, and her eight-year-old daughter, Katey. I noticed how Jennifer distanced herself and was unresponsive as Katey desperately tried to make connection. Something seemed drastically wrong, but it wasn't until I learned about the generational abuse history that the pieces of the puzzle came together. During one session Jennifer revealed the physical and sexual abuse she had endured as a child by her mother, who had been sexually and physically abused as a girl by her father and grandfather. It dawned on me that she was keeping distance from her children so she wouldn't repeat abusive behavior; staying disconnected was the best way she knew to protect her children. Her mother's twin sister, Aunt Mae, finally assured her niece that one does not have to continue the generational abuse patterns. Aunt Mae proudly announced, "The buck stops here!" She had never laid a hand on her children and she promised to spend time in Jennifer's home to show her how to be close to her children without repeating the abusive patterns. That day Jennifer broke through the fear and replaced it with a new picture of family interaction.

Creating a safe environment. Having considered the various ways parents abuse or fail to protect their children from abuse, let's explore what parents can do to create a protective home environment.

Setting and keeping appropriate boundaries is a good place to begin. When personal boundaries are identified and respected, each family member is awarded a sense of personal worth and power. Being alert to discomfort between family members and disruptions in relationships gives the family an opportunity to talk openly about what's happening to cause that reaction. When communication paths are open, children can share their concerns about any sexual indiscretions that occur. So often the reason a son or daughter does not disclose sexual information to parents is out of fear that they will not be believed or that parents will be unable or unwilling to do anything about it. A parent who takes immediate, appropriate action when sexual issues are disclosed gives children assurance that such matters will be effectively dealt with and not tolerated in the home.

Developing connection through careful listening and appropriate response to children's requests for change assures them that parents put the best interest of their children as a priority. Actions that ensure privacy, deal with discomforts expressed and make needed changes give family members a sense of security that their needs will be met.

Profound Damage

Sexual abuse, whether done by a family member or a stranger, whether a single act or ongoing pattern, cuts to the very core of a child's soul. Survivors of sexual abuse suffer from a wide variety of disorders such as major depression, dissociation, eating disorders, anxiety disorders, body pain, addictions, acting out behaviors, and self-esteem issues (Briere and Elliott 1994; Heise 1993; Kendall-Tackett, Williams and Finkelhor 1993; Pecikonis 1996; Romans, Martin and Mullen 1996).

The power differential automatically places the child in an out-of-control situation. Robbed of personal power, the child is at the mercy of the abuser. Hays and Stanley (1996) discovered that women who were sexually abused as children, for example, experience extreme stress in keeping dental appointments due to similar feelings of being out of control and in close proximity with the dentist. Peters and Range (1995) found that subjects who had been abused were more likely to be suicidal as adults than those who were not abused.

Mental disorders. Research indicates that prolonged, severe childhood abuse plays a significant role in the development of serious mental illness. "Numerous well-documented studies done since 1987 indicate that 50-60 percent of psychiatric inpatients, 40-60 percent of outpatients and 70 percent of all psychiatric emergency room patients report childhood physical and sexual abuse or both" (Wylie 1993:29). Bessel Van Der Kolk, a professor at Harvard Medical School, and a team of researchers conducted a comprehensive study of trauma patients, finding that nearly half of the psychiatric patients had experienced extreme distress as a result of childhood sexual abuse. The symptoms included inability to regulate emotions, intense suicidal ideation, somatic disorders, negative self-perception, poor relationships, chronic feelings of isolation, despair and hopelessness (Wylie 1993:70). It's astonishing to think that the prevention of child abuse and neglect could drastically reduce the number of patients needing psychiatric treatment.

The physical and emotional experiences of childhood sexual abuse leave many victims wanting to erase themselves from life. They avoid situations in which intimacy is required and stay away from others (men in particular) in order to protect themselves from further abuse. Like most defenses, such strategies may provide temporary relief, but they also keep a person frozen in the pain and loneliness.

Ava said she just wanted to cuddle up in her afghan, lock all the doors and windows, pull down the shades and rock herself for hours in her rocking chair every day after work. To be by herself in her controlled world was all that mattered to her. When someone knocked on the door, it sent a streak of fear through her heart that she couldn't explain. All she knew was that she didn't want to open the door and face the person on the other side. She felt safe in her cocoon, worlds away from people she believed could harm her. Although she managed to drag herself to work each day, she was always relieved to return to the security of her apartment. In her extreme difficulty in trusting others, she surrounded herself with animals who felt safe to her and brought her comfort.

Ava hid from the world because interacting with others made her feel extremely fragile. Beneath the external mask she wore in public dwelt a confused, fearful, lonely person. She pretended to be cool, calm and collected so no one would discover the truth about her sexual molestation. She was desperate to find ways to soothe the trembling injured child within.

Her desire to protect herself is understandable. Basic survival needs supersede any thought of connecting with others. In her own protective cocoon she could at least prevent another betrayal from ever happening again. The enduring pain of her childhood has robbed her of vitality.

Living with the scars of sexual abuse. A myriad of feelings (rage, horror, terror, regret, anguish) flood a survivor after she is abused. If pregnancy occurs, there are further excruciating decisions about whether to keep, abort or adopt out the child. It seems impossible that a young girl could go back to being a "normal" teenager after going through sexual experiences far beyond her age. Some abuse survivors describe themselves as "damaged goods," recalling that's how they felt after enduring the sexual abuse. While no one should ever be labeled as damaged goods, it is understandable why she feels this way. Her innocence and virginity have been taken from her against her will and she has subsequently suffered a significant loss of self.

Survivors of sexual abuse often judge themselves harshly, in addition to feeling condemned by others for what happened. What a sexual abuse survivor needs more than anything is a trustworthy, supportive person to listen to her story. She needs a safe place to let her defenses and pretenses down. She needs a Christlike presence so she can share her deep hurts.

By facing the hurts of the past it is possible to heal from the crippling effect of the abuse. While it takes a solemn commitment to confront the painful experiences of sexual abuse, the process of remembering eventually helps a person release the destructive impact of the abuse. Revealing the truth is difficult work, for it brings up primitive, intense emotions, but naming the abuse means the person is no longer fighting an invisible enemy. Venting bottled-up feelings helps release the rage, which eventually opens up a space to feel and grieve the deeper pain. Now that the enemy has been brought into the open, the sexual abuse is no longer a secret; the victim can place the blame where it belongs and enter into recovery as a survivor.

Survivors of sexual abuse must be able to define themselves in terms of the whole of who they are, rather than this one aspect of their life. The suffering is not to be denied or forgotten, but talking about the pain can become an eventual pathway to healing and restoration. When released from the crippling effects of the sexual abuse, a person is then free to construct a new identity. This old story has a new ending because it no longer haunts like a ghost from the past. Victory often comes through the help of a professional therapist, a supportive friend, a small group and a faith community. The following story is an example of this kind of healing.

Cindy was sexually abused as a child and desperately sought love and affection from others. Unfortunately, she became stuck in a continuous pattern of chaotic and destructive relationships. As a result, her self-esteem plummeted to an all-time low and she believed she would be better off dead. At this point of desperation she entered therapy.

The first thing Cindy asked was, "Will I ever be normal?" She certainly had not lived a normal childhood when compared to her peers and she began to tell her painful story in bits and pieces to her therapist, Gretchen. Gretchen listened with compassion and acceptance. Little by little Cindy began to trust and felt hopeful for the first time in years. She could reveal her painful experiences in the context of an unconditional committed therapeutic relationship. After much exploration, self-disclosure and empowerment, she experienced a healing of her heart and soul.

A year later Cindy met a wonderful man named Geoffrey. Over time, she was able to share her story with him. Although they were romantically attracted, it was the solid friendship that brought them into a step-by-step growing intimacy. The sexual aspect of their relationship was "on hold," as Geoff wisely put the priority on Cindy as a person. Time in therapy together gave him a deeper understanding of the dynamics of Cindy's sexual abuse. His patient, gentle approach is what mattered most to her and it was not surprising that their friendship blossomed into a satisfying, deeply committed love.

Research indicates how important it is to work with the partners of sexual abuse survivors in a common therapy modality (Reid, Wampler and Taylor 1996). An important component of sexual abuse recovery is receiving support from a partner who is educated about the implications of childhood sexual abuse. The partner's needs and issues about the abuse must not be overlooked (Firth 1997). The therapist can pace the therapy in ways that are best for the survivor and the partner to ensure a successful outcome for the relationship.

The Issue of Remembering
Some children may block out memories of being sexually abused in order to remove themselves from the terror of the experience. This response is understood as a defense mechanism that allows children to survive what they cannot comprehend at the time it is happening.

The therapeutic community has recently been under scrutiny for taking early childhood memories of sexual abuse as fact. Elizabeth Loftus, a professor of psychology at the University of Washington, is outspoken in her efforts to dispel the myth that human memory is infallible. She believes that memory can be inaccurate, fabricated, distorted, confused, altered and indistinguishable from fact. Since current research shows that memory is marginal before age two, she questions whether a young child has the mental structure to form coherent long-term memories. Along with others, she cautions that people (therapists included) are naive about the mind's capacity to remember and retrieve details. Memory can be particularly unreliable because it is a complex process that involves a selective perception of past events (Wylie 1993). It is important to acknowledge that not all accusations are true and that false accusations (some of them malicious) can have devastating effects on the falsely accused.

Those who have admitted to making false accusations against family members later say their therapist planted the idea in their heads. The False Memory Syndrome Foundation (FMSF) advocates for parents who they believe are innocent victims of a collusion of revenge that occurs between a therapist and their adult clients. They say the therapist gets the clients to make an accusation as a way of cutting the "umbilical cord" so they can differentiate from their family. Psychiatry professor George Ganaway believes that in a "delayed adolescent rebellion," the daughter blames her parents, displacing her dependency needs on the "all-accepting" therapist, who becomes a substitute parent figure (Wylie 1993).

Professional sexual abuse therapists consider this explanation as an unlikely scenario since the primary goal of therapy is to work toward independence, not dependence on the therapist. While it's certainly possible for some clients to be motivated and persuaded by their therapist, most sexual abuse victims minimize the trauma of what happened. In fact, they are quite willing to accept blame rather than place blame on those who did the abuse. In addition, memories bring up such deep feelings of shame that survivors do anything to avoid the intense pain that comes up when remembering.

It is more likely that therapists find it very difficult to hear the details of the sexual abuse horror and the excruciating memories it brings up for clients. It is exhausting work for both client and therapist. An ethical therapist listens with an open mind in order to help the client discern the truth and would not try to convince, persuade or draw conclusions for clients. The main role of the therapist is to create a safe sanctuary in which clients can ultimately tell their story while seeking wisdom and discernment, which brings healing to their soul.

A Spiritual Matter

Family therapist Cloe Madanes (1995) addresses the impact of sexual abuse on the family system. She sees sexual abuse as a "spiritual pain" in the heart of the child and believes it is necessary to explore the spiritual implications of this offense. She believes the first step for the offender is to recognize that he has inflicted a serious spiritual wound on his victim. Second, he must confess, with sincere and deep remorse, and be able to convincingly explain *why* what he did was wrong. Restoration, she writes, is a total package of making confession, seeking forgiveness and making amends.

In the case of sibling incest, a brother's rightful role as protector of his sister has been broken and must be restored. The violation of the sibling covenant requires specific steps to bring about a necessary healing to that broken relationship. The offender must recognize the deep distortion of his actions so he can sincerely ask forgiveness of his sister and confess that he has caused her great suffering. When he is able to acknowledge the impact of his abusive actions, he can then ask for forgiveness and make reparations. Madanes (1995) works with the entire family so they can eliminate the destructive patterns of intrusion, domination and violation and replace them with constructive patterns of love, protection and empowerment.

The secret of the abuse must be entirely out in the open so that all family members can recognize what went wrong and how they can join together to make things right. They are challenged to make the home environment a safe place where abuse will never happen again. One aspect of becoming responsible and caring is for the offender to make concrete restitution for what he has done. In a proper protective role, he needs to give sacrificially out of his care for the victim. For example, he may start a savings account for her future education to which he contributes money each month. When the perpetrator sees himself in a new light, he gains the self-esteem needed to be in rightful relationships with others. We agree with Madanes that it is critical to reach offenders at an early age if the cycle of abuse is to be broken. Changes in the family environment and relationship patterns offer hope for a new way of living.

Facing the Pain of the Past

Here are some steps to take in dealing with past sexual abuse. In the role of friend, counselor or minister, be kind, take your time, be patient, allow the survivor to take her time, and let God be very present throughout the process.

Make an assessment. This step involves a courageous self-examination of feelings, thoughts and behavior. Effective self-assessment requires observation of one's functioning in the world and the impact of one's behavior on others (spouse, family, friends and coworkers). Developing and sharpening these observations and asking honest, reflective questions will be the beginning point.

Grieve past hurts. It's not enough to understand how the past is tangled up with the present. One must acknowledge and then grieve the wrongs done during one's childhood. This is a crucial step because it names the concrete events so a person can rightly feel the pain, rage and sadness of what happened. Grieving the past hurt will take time and may be done in private or in the presence of a trusted person or group of persons. Private reflection and candid sharing of thoughts and feelings with a trusted confidant bring a helpful balance. It is also beneficial if other family members can validate and share experiences about growing up in an abusive home. Appropriate expressions of anger and sorrow give the family the opportunity to support each other in a communal way. Sometimes doing a simple healing ritual together with caring friends and relatives can put the abuse in perspective and be an important part of the process of getting beyond it.

Take responsibility. Something interesting begins to happen when survivors examine how the past informs the present. Understanding present behavior in terms of old roles and patterns helps them make sense of current relationship dynamics. Insight gained establishes new ways of relating.

Forgive. Forgiving those who have caused the pain is the most difficult action ever asked of a person. It's difficult to imagine forgiving someone who has caused such extreme harm, especially if the offender is unwilling to admit the wrong committed and shows no remorse. Coming to a place of forgiveness does not condone the actions of the offender. What was done is never acceptable! And forgiving does not mean one forgets or ignores the impact of being wronged, nor does it release that person from accountability for their actions. In fact, forgiveness does not even require extending reconciliation, for this may not be possible. Forgiveness means you have the capacity to let go of the destructive impact the experience has had on you so you can be free of the destructive impact of the abuse.

Survivors must remember that forgiveness is not a single action, but an ongoing process that continues throughout life. People recover by fully understanding the depth and meaning of what they are forgiving. Every step is a courageous step that moves a person in the direction of change from the inside out. Irreparable damage has been done and the relationship itself may be irreparable, but a person's inner journey of healing is what brings a peace that passes even human understanding. It is God's way of freeing survivors from the brutal spiritual wounds that have left a bitter stain. Forgiveness releases survivors from the bondage of self-destruction.

Self-forgiveness is another part of the healing process. God is waiting and eager to forgive. Those who receive God's forgiveness will experience the life-changing power of God's grace. When the Holy Spirit empowers a person to bury what's behind, one becomes a new creature and all things can become new.

Summary
In this chapter we have concentrated on restoring authentic sexuality where harmful sexual acts have left serious injury. Once again, referring to the four biblical principles of authentic sexuality, we see how possessive love is the exact opposite of covenant love. An unconditional love always has the best interest of others in mind; people practicing this faithfully protect and take responsibility for children in their care. Exposing children to shameful sexual acts is the exact opposite of accepting and nourishing them. The gracing principle makes repentance, forgiveness and restoration a daily process of living in broken relationships. Sexual control, coercion and manipulation crush rather than build up and are the exact opposite of empowerment. The empowerment principle helps family members feel competent and self-sufficient through high regard for personal rights, boundaries and mutual respect. Finally, secrets and denial distort and distance family members, while the intimacy principle ensures open communication and close connection. These biblical principles promote hopeful, healthy sexual relating and prohibit abusive family environments.

We must be a faithful presence as a community of prayer and support to abuse survivors by pointing them to the all-knowing, all-loving God who is capable of restoring wholeness. These verses from Psalm 6 bring comfort, understanding and hope in this journey:

> I flood my bed with tears; I drench my couch with my weeping. My eyes waste away because of grief; I grow weak because of all my foes. Depart from me, all you workers of evil, for the Lord has heard the sound of my weeping. The Lord has heard my supplication; The Lord accepts my prayer. All my enemies shall be ashamed and struck with terror; they shall turn back, and in a moment be put to shame. (vv. 6-10 NRSV)

Suggestions for Further Reading
Deblinger, A., and A. Heflin. 1996. *Treating sexually abused children and their nonoffending parents: A cognitive behavioral approach.* Thousand Oaks, Calif.: Sage Publications.

Fergusson, D. 1999. *Childhood sexual abuse: An evidence-based perspective.* Thousand Oaks, Calif.: Sage Publications.

Maddock, J., and N. Larson. 1995. *Incestuous families: An ecological approach to understanding and treatment.* New York: W. W. Norton.

Reid, K., and M. Fortune. 1994. *Preventing child sexual abuse: A curriculum for children ages five through eight.* Cleveland, Ohio: United Church Press.

12

Rape & Sexual Violence

Destructive Sexualized Power

Sexual violence of any kind is an extreme form of inauthentic sexuality. Sexual force against the will or without the understanding of another person is a problem that most find difficult to comprehend. Sexual assault continues to be the most rapidly growing violent crime in America (Dupre et al. 1993). According to the U.S. Department of Justice, a woman is raped (a form of sexual violence that involves vaginal penetration) every two minutes somewhere in America.

While 354,670 women reported being victims of rape or sexual assault in 1995 (National Crime Victimization Survey 1996), one of the most startling aspects of this survey is the number of rape crimes that are unreported. The FBI and the U.S. Justice Department estimate that only 36 percent and 26 percent, respectively, of all rapes are reported to the police (National Crime Victimization Survey 1996). The most common reasons for not reporting these crimes are the belief that the experience is a private or personal matter and the fear of the assailant's reprisal.

The U.S. Department of Justice report *Violence Against Women* (1994) exposes the social circumstances contributing to rape. One of every four rapes took place in a public area, with 68 percent occurring at night, between the hours of 6 p.m. and 6 a.m. In 31 percent of rapes the offender was a stranger, in 29 percent a weapon was used, and in 45 percent the rapist was under the influence of alcohol or drugs. In 47 percent of rapes the victim sustained injuries other than sexual injuries, and in 75 percent of cases the rape victims needed medical care. About 81 percent of rape victims are white, 18 percent are black and 1 percent represent other races. About half of all rape victims are in the lowest third of income distribution and the other half in the upper two-thirds.

This chapter will focus on individual, familial and sociocultural aspects of rape crimes. We will consider the dynamics surrounding those who commit violent crimes as well as the impact sexual violence has on victims/survivors, their families and the community. We urge the church to be involved in the recovery process so that substantial healing and transformation can be experienced at all levels. This includes actions like consciousness-raising education about gender inequality and power patterns; promotion of positive, authentic sexuality values; reconstruction of beliefs and attitudes in the broader community; and social-political endeavors that will reduce sexual violence in our world.

The Cultural Context

By surveying anthropological data on the prevalence of rape in 156 cultures over 4,000 years of human history, Sanday (1981) identified the cultural context of rape. The survey identified 47 percent of these cultures as *rape-free societies,* where rape was either infrequent or did not occur, and 18 percent as *rape-prone societies,* where rape was either culturally allowable or largely overlooked. Rape-prone societies embrace a social ideology of male dominance and are characterized by a high level of interpersonal and intergroup violence.

It is disturbing that the United States today ranks as one of the more rape-prone cultures. The U.S. Federal Bureau of Investigation (1990) estimates that 20 percent of women living in the United States will at some time in their life suffer the trauma of an attempted rape. The high incidence of rape in our culture seems to correlate to three main factors: (1) masculinity that is defined by aggressiveness rather than gentleness; (2) commonly held myths suggesting that women frequently mean yes when they say no, and that men can't control their sexuality once it is aroused; and (3) dating patterns that sanction privacy and time alone between a man and a women who barely know each other (Holzman 1994).

At one extreme, *rape* is defined as an act of uncontrolled passion due to a lack of female partners (Posner 1992), and at the other, a biological drive that impels men to maximize the number of women with whom they procreate (Gelles and Wolfner 1994). In an effort to synthesize the extremes, Ellis (1991) offers a bio-psycho-social theory of rape. He states that "rape is sexually motivated, not only by the sex drive, per se, but by the drive to possess and control others to whom one is sexually attracted. . . . Natural selection has favored a stronger sex drive in men than in women" (p. 638). Although Ellis believes that these sexual motivations are innate, he thinks the violence is learned. We believe these explanations are vastly inadequate.

Accumulated clinical evidence seems to indicate that rape is less an expression of sex than it is of violence and represents an extreme expression of male power (Brownmiller 1975). Out of this suggestion, a sociocultural theory of rape has developed which finds that cultural constructions of gender and sexuality serve to shape men's beliefs and attitudes about their masculinity, about women and femininity and about relational expectations in a sexual encounter. Research supports a correlation between men's beliefs about rape myths and the sexual aggression in their behavior (Lisak and Roth 1990, Malamuth 1996).

Lisak and Ivan (1995) suggest that men lacking the capacity for relational intimacy and empathy are more likely to be sexually aggressive. Rape is viewed as an unnatural, pseudosexual act. It is an irrational, nonsexual desire used to meet unfulfilled power needs. Rapists use sexual behavior to act out their anger, aggression and hostility toward women and rarely mention sexual satisfaction or pleasure as a reason for the assault.

The erroneous belief that any act that employs sexual organs must be sexual is what has confused theories of motivation for this crime. Rape is primarily about violence, not sex. It is an act in which sexual organs are the tools of aggression and dominance. On a broader level, rape can be understood as reflecting societal attitudes that people have a right to impose their sexuality on others regardless of the other's wishes. This societal attitude perpetuates the idea that dominant-subordinate relationships between two people are all right. When coercive sex is sanctioned, violence is a logical end. When sex is viewed as a mutual choice between equals, intimacy is a logical end.

In part, the myth of manhood is a reflection of our "seductive society." The playboy image defines a real man as one who is successful in seducing women. As reflected in the philosophy of his namesake, *Playboy* magazine, a playboy is a skilled manipulator of women, knowing when to turn the lights down, what music to play on the stereo, which drinks to serve and what topics of conversation to engage in. The playboy reduces sexuality to a packaged consumption item demanding no responsibility. The successful encounter is when the bed is shared, but the playboy emerges free of any emotional attachment or commitment. When playtime is over, the "plaything" can be discarded in a manner befitting our consumer, disposable-oriented society.

The playboy is admired for being able to entice, persuade or coerce a woman into what he wants from her, namely sex. Granted, the ideal playboy is so irresistible that resorting to physical force as a means of obtaining sex is a strike against him. Nevertheless, the playboy models two characteristics that are common to a cross-section of men who attempt acquaintance rape. First, they reduce a woman to a sexual object instead of developing a total caring relationship with her; second, they lack respect for women and for their rightful boundaries.

Profile of a Rapist

A little more is known about men who attempt stranger rape than acquaintance rape. The majority of these men come from disturbed family backgrounds in which their parents neglected, deprived or harshly punished them as children. Home life is characterized by low income, marginal employment and inadequate supervision. Many were raised by only one parent or by a relative or foster parents.

On the personal level, rapists have an aggressive attitude toward women. These men are motivated by feelings of hatred, rage and contempt for women. They desire to control and humiliate their victim. Rapists have very low self-esteem and special insecurities about their manhood. Most feel weak and ineffective in relating to women. The greater their insecurity, the greater the desire to attack, subjugate and subdue the victim. They treat women as objects and have little or no capacity to view them as human beings. Far from being oversexed, rapists are usually sexually inadequate. In fact, a majority of rapists who are married have problems with erection and orgasmic functioning. In addition, many report that they frequently cannot function sexually with their victims (Janssen 1995).

In a comprehensive study of 800 convicted rapists, Goleman (1985) classifies rapists into four types. Fifty percent are *exploiters,* those who find a victim in a vulnerable situation and decide to rape without premeditation. These men are the least violent and stand the best chance of being rehabilitated. Twenty-five percent are *compensatory* rapists. Feeling themselves to be severely inadequate sexually and totally unattractive to women, they believe that force is necessary and even deserved because women reject them. *Enraged* rapists make up 20 percent of the rapists studied. These men are seldom motivated sexually, but want to humiliate and dominate women. For these men, rape is usually an act of hate. Five percent are *sadistic* rapists who attempt to inflict as much pain as they can upon their victims. The bizarre fantasies of these men can result in a fatal injury to the victim.

Date Rape
Up until fifty years ago rape was rarely reported or even openly discussed. It was assumed that all rape happened between strangers. As rape has become an issue of public concern, the increase in reported numbers of acquaintance rapes does not come as a surprise. A study by Storaska (1975) reported that 35 percent of all rapes occurred on dates, and in an additional 35 percent of the cases the rapist was an acquaintance (a friend, neighbor, relative or coworker). These results were verified by the U.S. Department of Justice (1984) study, which found that one-third of all rapes were acquaintance rapes. A four-year study of 315 adolescent girls from a rural area found that 23 percent reported unwanted sexual activity on dates and 15 percent said they had experienced date rape (Vicary, Klingaman and Harkness 1995).

In a study of 332 female Christian college students, 51 percent indicated that they had experienced an unwanted sexual incident in their past, of which 15 percent were described as stranger assault and 11 percent as date rape (Neal and Mangis 1995). There is evidence that date rape may be even more frequent than reported, as one study found that few women who had been date raped actually reported it (Finkelson and Oswalt 1995).

Three major perspectives have been used to explain date rape (Humphrey and Herold 1996). *Socialization theory* emphasizes gender socialization processes promoting a culture that supports date rape. Normalization of sexual coercion as an acceptable masculine behavior is the foundational core element of this process. Truman, Tokar and Fischer (1996) have found more date-rape-supportive attitudes and beliefs among men who endorse rigid traditional gender roles, express negative attitudes towards feminism and evidence homophobic attitudes. *Feminist theory* points to patriarchy, with its corresponding norms of unequal power distribution between females and males, as the cause of date rape. *Psychopathology theory* tends to treat rapists as psychologically maladjusted individuals who have had unusual childhood experiences. Sexual aggression is understood as developing primarily within the individual rather than explained by external factors.

Much evidence indicates that males resort to deception as a means of gaining sexual favors from a date. In reviewing studies on premarital sexual conflict, Long et al. (1996) state: "Males are more likely than females to use strategies that encourage coitus to the point of lying about their motivation for intimacy, whereas females are more likely to use strategies that avoid intercourse" (p. 302). A study of 673 college males found that one in four admitted to having lied to have sex, with most lies centered on the theme of caring for or being committed to the person. This researcher also found that alcohol is commonly used as part of attempted sexual aggression by males (Fischer 1996). In a study of college students, Kanin (1985) found that date rapists were more than three times as likely as nonrapists to try to get their dates intoxicated.

For many men the line between friendly sexual persuasion and coercion is often a boundary they have trouble defining for themselves. They act on the myth that woman engage in token resistance, which is to believe that when a woman says no to a sexual advance, she really means yes. She only says no to show she's not a "pushover" or to play a game of resistance when she really wants sex. They assume she is really inviting the advances through subtle verbal and nonverbal cues such as the way she dresses. High-school seniors, for example, were more likely to view a date rape victim dressed in provocative clothing as more responsible for her assailant's behavior and therefore determine that the rape was justified (Cassidy and Hurrell 1995).

A study of 112 adolescent girls revealed that victims of unwanted sexual activity tend to have more sexually active same-sex friends, poor peer relationships, low emotional status among peers, an earlier age of menarche and early sexual involvement (Vicary, Klingaman and Harkness 1995). The authors concluded that adolescent females who date at an early age could be more at risk for unwanted sexual advances.

Studies comparing male and female attitudes about sexually aggressive behavior show that males are more prone to blame the female for aggressive sexual behavior (Johnson et al. 1995; Grant, Folger and Hornak 1995; Bell, Kuriloff and Lottes 1994) and view sexual aggression as more excusable when alcohol is used (Fischer 1996), when it's part of a long-term relationship (Sheldon-Keller et al. 1994) or when a woman is provocatively dressed (Workman and Orr 1966). In general, males are more accepting of sexually aggressive behavior and less demanding that an aggressor be punished for such behavior. These studies indicate that males both underrate the seriousness of this crime and undermine efforts to control it.

Rape Prevention

Undoubtedly the first and primary concern after a sexual assault has been committed is the victim. However, if essential change is to occur, the beliefs, myths and attitudes of the rapist and the rape-prone society must be addressed. All too often a convicted rapist commits another sexual crime soon after he is released from jail. Our immediate response is to lock up sexual offenders and throw away the key. Our motive to protect ourselves and to make society safe from sexual predators is certainly appropriate. However, by itself this response is short-sighted because it fails to address the need for radical, long-term behavioral change in the offender, nor does it focus on the familial, communal and sociocultural levels.

We find it extremely troubling that the United States, ostensibly a Christian society, is classified as a rape-prone society (Sanday 1981).

We must examine the sociocultural elements in our society that qualify it for such a dishonorable status.

At the familial level, sexual offenders usually come from inadequate, neglectful and abusive home environments that are lacking in nurture and solid guidance. At the community level, the absence of positive models of manhood makes it difficult to develop a secure and adequate self that can engage in satisfying adult relationships. At the societal level, self-interest and lack of regard for others lead to dehumanizing, marginalizing and violating practices. Digging even deeper into the cultural layers of society, power and control are dominant themes of masculinity that are harmful to women.

What can be done to change the rapists who commit sexually violent acts? This is a difficult question to answer! Some research has been done on the sexual arousal patterns of sexually violent men in an effort to come up with solutions. According to Blader and Marshall (1989), rapists and nonrapists have different sexual arousal response patterns. While rapists have the ability to perform the responses of hostile aggression and sexual arousal at the same time, normal males find these two responses quite incompatible. Related research focusing on stimulus control discovered that rapists were more aroused by descriptions of forced sex than were nonrapists (Quinsey and Chaplin 1984). In an insightful article Janssen (1995) described a pattern in which rapists were motivated by hostility (emotions of rage, hatred, contempt) and the desire to humiliate the victim. Through physical dominance and control, the rapists express hatred toward women.

A variety of treatment programs are offered to offenders, although the effectiveness of these programs is inconclusive. Most community programs, like the Sexual Violence Northwest Treatment Center in Seattle, use a combination of treatment intervention strategies. In individual and group therapy, both cognitive and behavioral modification approaches are used to help offenders practice impulse control as well as to reformulate internal patterns of sexual desire. Men with less robust cases of sexual violence may make good progress with treatment, but like the alcoholic, may be a few steps away from reoffending unless they stay in treatment or in twelve-step groups that keep them accountable. Success is defined as the ability to control one's behavior by not acting out inappropriate sexual impulses when they occur.

Violent sex offenders are less likely to change. Many have socio-pathic tendencies and express little or no empathy for their victims. Some prison treatment programs make use of group sessions in which rape survivors confront rapists as a way of getting them to feel remorse and take responsibility for their crime. The success of such programs is mixed, depending on the severity of the offense and the response to the treatment.

Most date-rape offenders don't have the psychological aberrations of stranger rapists. These men are more likely to deny the intent of their behavior and excuse themselves for failing to respond appropriately to the protests of their date. In this case, treatment focuses more on educational interventions. Based on results of college campus consciousness-raising programs about rape, these preventive programs are effective. One such program targeted the commonly held false beliefs that promote or condone coercive sexual behavior. Its cognitive-based intervention treatment was successful in significantly changing the date-rape beliefs of college males. Another model focused on men who had little ability to show empathy toward their victims. This model was also successful in increasing empathy skills and awareness among college men (Schewe and O'Donohue 1996). In another case, a mixed-gender intervention program reported favorable change in attitudes of college males toward date rape (Holcomb et al. 1993).

It is encouraging to learn that consciousness-raising workshops have proven effective in changing attitudes and beliefs about rape. The church can use similar methods to heighten awareness. Christian singles need to be aware of destructive sexual beliefs, attitudes and behaviors. Marie Fortune (1996) has developed a workshop for church youth groups and Sunday school classes titled "Sexual Abuse Prevention: A Study for Teenagers." This five-session workshop addresses the topic of date rape with sessions entitled: (1) "Rape Is Violence, Not Sex"; (2) "The Good, the Bad, and the Confusing"; (3) "All in the Family"; (4) "Expectations of Ourselves and Others"; and (5) "Truth In Advertising." Fortune uses a variety of role-play and case situations to help youth recognize red flags when they occur so they will be able to assert and protect themselves from such unwanted encounters. It is a great service to offer educational programs that help singles establish and maintain authenticity in dating relationships.

Ministering to Rape Survivors

(Note: *Since there are negative ramifications of labeling someone a rape "victim," from this point on we will use the term* survivor. *And since the majority of survivors are female, we will use the female pronoun for the remainder of this chapter.*)

Rape survivors all share an overwhelming experience of having been physically and emotionally violated by the rapist. In addition, they report a number of intense feelings like fear, powerlessness, shame, guilt, anger and hate (Resick 1993). At the appropriate time, the survivor needs a safe place to deal with each of these primal feelings. Discerning how, when and who will come alongside to help her work through the loss, grief, rage, denial, helplessness, depression and fear is of crucial importance. The survivor not only needs a safe place, but a trusted person and the right pacing for her unique process.

Research on posttraumatic stress disorder has been informative in describing the various emotional phases a survivor is likely to experience. Initially, she is overwhelmed by the shock and disbelief of what's happened. The survivor wonders, "Did this really happen to me?" Later, when awareness is acute, she asks, "How could this happen to me?" There can be extreme feelings of fear and anger, which may get expressed through uncontrolled crying or total withdrawal from others. This is a time when the survivor is acutely preoccupied with the offense, and these responses can last from a few days to a few months, depending on the seriousness of the abuse trauma. Physical reactions such as loss of sleep, eating disturbances, vaginal irritation or bleeding are common complaints. The emotional reactions include mood swings, extreme expression of feelings, and distrust or cautious attitudes toward others.

After the violation has occurred, she is acutely aware of what it means to live in a threatening and dangerous world. She realizes that bad things do happen to good people. Her lifestyle choices are now made in light of what has happened to her. This reorganization phase can last from weeks to even years. Adjustments may involve changing one's routine, such as driving rather than walking to and from work, changing one's job or even moving to a new location. There might be dreams or nightmares in which the survivor plays back the rape, sometimes imagining different endings, such as being killed by the rapist. The trauma may express itself in a phobic reaction, a hatred or extreme fear of men, especially those who possess characteristics similar to the rapist. Phobias may also be centered on places similar to where the rape took place or certain activities that were part of the rape experience.

Survivors need to be assured that it is normal to experience this vast array of feelings. In addition to pastoral care and personal counseling, many rape survivors benefit from being part of a support group of other rape survivors. Discussions with those who have been through a similar experience can help normalize the traumatic feelings, ongoing anxiety and unexplained reactions. It helps to see one's progress over time and to be supported by those who can truly understand what a victim is going through.

Counseling for the survivor's family is another area of ministry. Each member is affected by the offense and each person needs a place to work out the implications of what has happened. The mother of the victim may cry, "How could this happen to my child [or our family]?" Although the crisis belongs to the victim, family members feel a similar helplessness and have strong emotional reactions as well. The father or brother of the victim, for example, may react in a fit of rage and seek revenge.

Whereas these responses are understandable, more than anything else the survivor needs the family's support. She should not be put in a situation where she has to take care of others at this point. Sometimes the survivor is so concerned with the reactions of family members, she will try to hurry her own process to prove to everyone that she's all right. This keeps her from proceeding in her own time so that a complete process of healing can take place. A false sense of renewed health won't last long if not all the feelings have been addressed. She needs her family to be by her side responding in supportive, trustworthy ways that affirm her process.

The husband or boyfriend of the survivor will also have a range of feelings and human reactions about what happened. This deeply affects their relationship, and he must be part of the counseling as well. However, these husbands or boyfriends may be reluctant to participate in counseling, as found in a study by Brookings, McEvoy and Reed (1994). They reported that 85 percent of crisis counseling centers surveyed indicated that males did not use the services. These authors believe that the presence of male counselors at these crisis counseling centers would give men the message that counseling is important for them as well.

A wise counselor will honor the differences in how God is uniquely at work in each survivor as well as in the lives of those who love them. Some work through feelings and issues rapidly, while others take more time; some talk a lot, others very little; some find creative ways to express emotions while others need to write things down in a factual manner. The survivor is the only one who can decide about how fast to travel through the path of recovery.

Sexual violence may become a crisis of faith for the survivor. When this happens, the survivor needs to be able to know that such doubts are acceptable. The counselor, friend or family member can encourage the survivor to express feelings and think through doubts because God is big enough to embrace these anguishing questions. Rather than admonish, "You don't really believe that!" one must give reassurance, "God knows about your deep hurt and loves you deeply. "

A spiritual issue may center on the survivor trying to make sense out of her experience. Here it is important to focus on the details of what happened to her. This is a way she regains a sense of control over the situation, a way of coming to grips with the actual event. Simplistic formulas that minimize the experience of the survivor are not helpful.

The offense against the survivor may raise the question, "Why did I have to suffer this heinous crime?" It is important to affirm that this violence is a grave offense to God. In struggling with her involuntary suffering, the survivor may ask, "Is there any meaning in this experience for me?" Here it is vital to be aware of the cultural and religious beliefs that the survivor holds. One study found that in their struggle to bring meaning to the experience of being raped, women were negatively influenced by unhealthy cultural beliefs, myths and stereotypes about women and sexuality. For example, making reference to the survivor being "soiled" or "ruined" as a result of the rape brings up negative and shaming connotations (Lebowitz and Roth 1994). The belief that the violation has ruined one for life has spiritual implications. This might be especially true of the unmarried victim who was saving herself sexually for a life partner in marriage. She may be tempted to think of herself as "tainted goods," similar to a victim of child abuse.

We must assure the survivor that virginity is no more affected by this assault than a person's first gynecological exam, which may rupture the hymen. A woman's virginity symbolizes her integrated sense of self-worth. The victim must be able to hold on to her sexual worth as a function of her personhood rather than her physical status as a result of the rape.

The survivor can often grasp the idea that God is present in her pain and cares deeply about what she has suffered. Out of the pain and suffering, she can be sustained by a deep connection with her personal Savior. When she is tempted to feel that God has abandoned her, she can cry out with the psalmist, "My God, my God, why have you forsaken me? Why are you so far from saving me, so far from the words of my groaning?" (Ps 22:1-2). Faithful Christians throughout history and Christ himself have felt such abandonment. The fact that she is able to shout out her anguish to God means she believes God is there to hear her cry. God hears, understands and does not turn away. When we act as God's representatives, our presence and acceptance of her anger can mediate God's faithful presence during recovery.

When anger comes, it must not be judged as bad or good, but as appropriate. Anger on the part of one who has been sexually assaulted is a healthy response. The survivor should be able to vent her anger, for she has been wronged. When anger is turned inward it can lead to depression, loss of self-esteem and helplessness and can be expressed through self-destructive behaviors such as substance abuse or suicide. Awareness and expression of the anger energize the survivor to take appropriate action that can restore her sense of power and self-worth. Justice requires an accountability through actions that will ensure future protection from these crimes.

The last step is a conscious decision the survivor makes that the rape experience will no longer have a disarming power over her life. This is a vital aspect of healing, for it allows the survivor to move on with her life. It does not mean the offense is minimized, but the negative impact no longer has the intensity it once did. She is empowered through the resources of faith, family, friends and community who have shown the love of God to her in her time of crisis.

Conclusion

A holistic response to sexual violence includes concern for the victim, for the behavior of the offender and for the community or society in which the offense occurs. In chapter ten we presented a model detailing an adequate response to sexual harassment that balances these three concerns (see figure 10.3). Although sexual violence is a more serious offense, the responses are applicable. Brokenness caused by sexual violence requires a repair that encompasses every aspect of this crime.

Suggestions for Further Reading

Beblinger, E., and A. Heflin. 1996. *Treating sexually abused children and their nonoffending parents: A cognitive behavioral approach.* Thousand Oaks, Calif.: Sage Publications.

Fortune, M. 1995. *Keeping the faith: Guidance for Christian women facing abuse.* San Francisco: Harper & Row.

Fortune, M. 1983. *Sexual violence: The unmentionable sin.* New York: Pilgrim Press.

Thatcher, A., and E. Stuart. 1996. *Christian perspectives on sexuality and gender.* Grand Rapids, Mich.: Eerdmans. See section 9, "Sexuality and violence," pp. 377-409.

13

Pornography & Erotica

The Greek root for pornography is *pornē,* **meaning "female cap-**tives." Under its original meaning pornography is the use of sex for subjugation, aggression, degradation, abuse, coercion, violence, dominance, control, sadism or rape. Today's contemporary use of the term *pornography* has a much broader meaning, including sexually explicit art, literature and film. Pornography's expansion of meaning into the arts has led to relativism in determining and defining it. As a result some would argue that pornography is in the eye of the beholder. While we think this is going too far, labeling anything that is sexually stimulating as pornography is also inaccurate. In deciphering the difference, a distinction must be made between pornography and erotica (erotic material).

Both erotic and pornographic material can be sexually stimulating; however, pornography is used to degrade others, while erotica celebrates human sexual experience. Although erotica is sexually arousing material, it is not meant to degrade women, men or children. Pornography, on the other hand, uses subjugation themes for the explicit purpose of sexual arousal. Pornography *always* dehumanizes, and we believe dehumanization is a violation of the value God places on human life and sexuality. Therefore we believe pornography is offensive and unacceptable.

Distinguishing Between Erotica and Pornography

Although it would be helpful to have a sharp distinction between pornographic and erotic sexual materials, this is often more difficult than one thinks. It is important to consider both the objective *content* of sexual material and the subjective *effect* the content has upon any particular person. Recognizing that the impact of sexual material can be as different as the persons consuming it, we focus first on the content dimension.

In figure 13.1 we suggest that the portrayal of sexual content ranges along a continuum from *degrading sex* at one end, to *dehumanizing sex* at the left of the middle, to *affectionate sex* at the right of the middle and to *committed sex* at the opposite end.

The important criterion in attempting to distinguish between pornography and erotica is the *value* or *meaning* (or lack of it) given to sex, not necessarily the degree of sexual explicitness. For example, a film containing sexually explicit scenes of tender, passionate lovemaking between a married couple may be described as erotic but not pornographic. On the other hand, a film glorifying degrading or dehumanizing sex but with less sexually explicit material is still pornographic. The shading from dark to light in figure 13.1 represents the murky distinction between erotica and pornography.

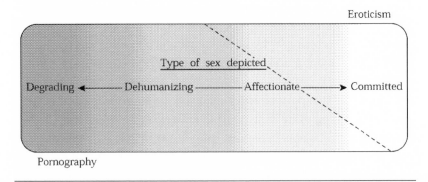

Figure 13.1. **Pornography and eroticism**

Distinguishing whether sexual *content* is pornographic or erotic is even more problematic when the purpose of the artist or filmmaker may be to communicate destructive aspects of pornography. Recent films such as *Pulp Fiction, Leaving Las Vegas, Boogie Nights* or those of screenwriter and director Paul Schrader, such as *Taxi Driver, American Gigolo* and *The Pornographer,* powerfully illustrate the destructiveness of pornography. Some Christians consider Schrader's films pornographic because of the explicit sexual material. Actually, these films are among the strongest and most effective antipornographic messages produced in popular culture. In his films Schrader exposes the tragic effects of the dehumanization process involving objectification for sexual stimulation. Films depicting a distortion of sexuality may be stimulating, even though the purpose of the work is not for sexual stimulation or glorification of dehumanization. An educational documentary condemning sexual abuse may contain material that is sexually stimulating. Many things people see or read can be a source of sexual stimulation. Therefore it is appropriate to guard our thoughts and emotions with careful discernment. Recognizing distortions and identifying dehumanizing sexual messages within our society do not eliminate but certainly can minimize the effects of the material on us.

Exposure to pornographic material can be both educational and tantalizing. It is important to recognize, normalize and monitor the conflicting motivations that exposure to pornography can produce. For example, a made-for-television movie on rape can educate the audience about the extreme emotional and psychological damage of rape to survivors. However, the same material can also be used to tantalize a large audience and produce a higher rating.

Schrader is candid about the need for commercial success in the entertainment business. He explains that a screenwriter must find "a rip in the social fabric and create a film metaphor which deals with the tear. That is as good a way as any to be commercial. . . . Sex and violence are all-encompassing fantasies that permeate every possible market. Screenwriting appeals to these needs more than the other forms of media because the numbers have to be bigger" (cited in Schultz et al. 1991:97-8). One cannot label all works exposing the dehumanizing effects of inauthentic sex as pornography. However, it is important to question the motives and presentation of these works.

Sexually graphic material can both expose sexual depravity in a nonerotic way and arouse the sexual appetite. There is a place for depicting the harmful, degrading effect of pornography, but the usefulness of graphic, realistic depictions of pornography can become lost in the titillation of the content depicted. When this happens, the content of a work depicting pornography may itself be seen as pornographic. The graphic material depends on its immediate context and on the content of the film as a whole to give the work meaning.

Regardless of the work's motive or the truthfulness of the content, it is difficult to predict the *effect* of explicit material on a particular viewer. What one viewer experiences as erotic, another may experience as disdainful and disgusting. Unquestionably, sexually explicit material, regardless of the context and content, should be restricted to mature viewers, although age is no guarantee of psychological or sexual maturity. In order to recognize sexual degradation, one needs a certain degree of sexual health and moral discernment. The absence of these two factors increases the likelihood that one will concentrate on the sexual stimulus, missing the deeper meaning of the work.

The Effect of Viewing Pornography

In 1971 the Commission on Obscenity and Pornography came to the controversial conclusion that there was not enough evidence to support the "antisocial effects" of pornography. The stimulus material in the study did not include rape or coercive behavior.

Some argue that the effect of viewing pornography is positive. Those advocating this view emphasize the cathartic effect of pornography, relieving feelings and desires that can lead to harmful effects if acted out. A parallel view maintains that vicarious viewing of violent behavior releases pent-up violent impulses rather than encouraging violence. The application of this reasoning to pornography normalizes aggressive sexual urges, arguing that pornography contributes to the release of aggressive feelings, thus preventing inappropriate sexual behavior. This view assumes an evolutionary process depicting men as more sexually aggressive than women. Pornography is seen as serving society by reducing sexual aggression in men that may harm women.

Recent findings do not support the cathartic view. Evidence actually points in the exact opposite direction, suggesting pornography *increases* sexually aggressive urges and attitudes of men toward women. Allen, D'Alessio and Brezgel (1995) analyzed thirty laboratory studies on the effect of exposure to pornography on aggressive behavior. They concluded that sexually aggressive behavior was induced by pictorial nudity, material depicting nonviolent sexual activity and media depictions of violent sexual activity.

Figure 13.2 represents our attempt to summarize the effects of pornography on the viewer. Most notably the figure traces the procedural effect of viewing pornography on individuals with sexually aggressive attitudes and behavior.

This summary is based on an experimental research design that tested attitudes and beliefs before and after the viewing of pornographic material. In general the research concludes that after viewing pornographic material subjects have a *more* callous attitude about sexual violence toward women and rape victims. Furthermore, they are more likely to *commit* a sexually violent act if they would not be caught!

Priming effect. The arrow leading from the bottom left side of figure 13.2 to "viewing pornography" represents the priming effect. This priming effect suggests that the impact of communication is greater when the viewers' beliefs are consistent with the information in the communication. Beliefs of viewers who oppose the messages in pornographic material are less likely to be influenced or changed as a result of viewing pornography. However, pornography is more likely to reinforce attitudes of those having beliefs similar to pornographic material, because these individual beliefs are primed to accept the information.

Arousal and desensitization. Figure 13.2 shows two major ways pornography directly affects the viewer. First, pornography influences sexual

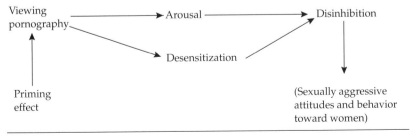

Figure 13.2. The effect of viewing pornography

arousal. Those with a healthy psychosexual self find the dehumanizing aspects of pornography unappealing. However, consistent viewing of pornography initiates a conditioning process associating sexual aggression with sexual arousal. Behavior is influenced and acquired by modeling. Watching women become sexually aroused while being raped can become sexually arousing to a viewer. The modeling of sexual aggression therefore influences behavior, in this case, sexual arousal. In its most aberrant form, a constant diet of pornography creates a distorted sense of sexuality. As a result of this distortion, normal eroticism becomes insufficient for sexual arousal. Arousal becomes a function of increasingly dehumanizing and sexually degrading stimuli. Since most of the material cannot be acted out, the viewer must personalize the content in order to achieve arousal. By inserting themselves into the content, viewers take on a psychosexual persona that is both dehumanizing and dehumanized.

Second, pornography *desensitizes* the viewer to attitudes about dehumanizing human psychosexuality. The psychological process of desensitization decreases the emotional effect of a dehumanizing event. For example, the repetition of the Rodney King beating in the media was responsible for *desensitizing* members of the jury to the brutality of the beating. After viewing the tape for the first time, some jurors were horrified. The same jurors also admitted that repeatedly viewing the tape increased desensitization to the material. The application of this process to pornography suggests that repetitive exposure to sexually aggressive material against women leads to a desensitizing effect on the viewer. One study reports that some men began to believe that women enjoy being raped (Malamuth 1984). It is significant that these men had been shown pornography depicting a woman becoming sexually aroused while being raped.

This desensitization process initiates a rationalization process minimizing the protests of women against sexual aggression of men. These rationalizations create the belief that, despite their protests, women desire sexual aggression (Allen et al. 1995). This myth is a familiar and consistent message promoted in pornographic material. Ultimately, viewers internalize this message, become less emotionally affected by the content and objectify the victimized female.

Disinhibition. Disinhibition is a result of the conditioning effects and desensitization of sexual aggression in pornographic material. The disinhibiting effect increases the viewer's sexually aggressive attitudes and behavior toward women. Currently there is little information *directly* linking exposure to pornography with illegal sexual behavior, although research shows compelling correlational evidence that persons who engage in illegal sexual behavior have been high consumers of pornography (Schneider 1996). However, there is ample evidence suggesting that aggressive and coercive sexual material depicting women in submissive roles are salient disinhibitors. It is safe to conclude that viewing pornography may not *cause* sexual aggression toward women, but it is a significant factor in attitudes of sexual aggression and behavior.

In his research on the effects of pornography on college males, Malamuth (1984) reports that 41 percent *might* rape if they were certain of not being caught. Malamuth concludes that the aggressive content of pornography is the major contributor to subsequent aggression toward women. Because subjects showed an increased lack of inhibition after viewing the pornographic material, Malamuth concludes that viewing pornography makes a significant impact in reinforcing a cultural climate that accepts, and in some cases promotes, sexual aggression toward women.

Is Erotica Harmful?

The 1986 Commission on Obscenity and Pornography reversed the decision of the 1971 commission, concluding that evidence *does* link pornography to sexually aggressive attitudes toward women. Like pornography, erotica arouses one's sexual feelings and desires, but unlike pornography, it does not necessarily reinforce sexual aggression or coercion (Pallard 1995). Aggressive content that occurs within an erotic context is the *key* contributor to aggression against women (Pallard 1995). Based on the differential effect of erotic and pornographic film content upon subjects in their study, Saunders and Naus (1993) conclude that their results "provide empirical support for the conceptual distinctions between 'erotica' and 'pornography' " (p. 117).

However, the commission's conclusions about sexual aggression do not exonerate eroticism as unharmful. In their review of relevant research, Allen, D'Alessio and Brezgel (1995) concluded that "consumption of material depicting nonviolent sexual activity increases aggressive behavior." Although pornography depicts sexual aggression towards women, erotica can depict *dehumanizing* sex. From a biblical point of view, dehumanizing sexual material is pornographic rather than erotic, promoting self-gratification void of intimacy or intimate affection. Erotica that elevates dehumanizing sex creates a cultural climate that depersonalizes sex. Within this context, sex is merely a primal and mechanistic physiological need, like scratching an itch. Therefore depersonalized sexually explicit material is pornographic because it elevates the sex act above sexuality, dehumanizing both the individual and the relationship.

Depersonalized sex is not central to all erotica, and some erotic material can be a helpful context for developing sexuality. Avoidance of all erotic material would rule out exposure to much of what is accepted as fine artistic expression. There is a significant amount of erotic material in classic novels, plays and films, especially when depicting sex within the context of a caring, loving and even committed relationship. Painting, sculpture, literature, theater and film are powerful mediums for eliciting erotic responses. In addition sexually explicit material is not a necessary component of erotica. A glance, a slight touch or even the unbuttoning of a glove can elicit a strong erotic response. The questions then become, When is exposure to erotica good, and when is it harmful? Following are four guidelines.

First, unlike pornography, *erotic material is often subjective*. A significant component in defining erotica is explained in the principle of diminishing return. This principle suggests that the more familiar something becomes, the less effect it seems to have. What is wildly erotic to one individual may lack any stimulus for another. A gothic romance novel may be erotic to a fourteen-year-old girl but dull and uninteresting to a thirty-four-year-old woman. Since a kiss between a man and a woman is forbidden in some countries, depicting a kiss in a film could be a powerful erotic stimulus in those cultures. Although the principle of diminishing return applies to all cultures, its application is subjective and depends on the context of the culture.

Second, *it is important to respect our Christian liberties when viewing erotica*. Although we've referred to the apostle Paul's words in 1 Corinthians 6:12 before, his instructions are applicable to respecting Christian liberties: "I can do anything I want to if Christ has not said no"

(LB). Although this principle may feel uncomfortable, it is important not to judge another's actions where Scripture's teachings are not absolute. In addition, honest discernment is helpful in discriminating between the things that direct us in God's way and those that do not.

Third, *the effects of erotica are dependent on the context of one's situation.* Paul continues in 6:12, "But some of these things aren't good for me. Even if I am allowed to do them, I'll refuse to if I think they might get such a grip on me that I can't easily stop when I want to" (LB). Paul's use of *but* qualifies freedom in Christ. The qualification addresses the degree of influence and the range of negative effect that something other than God may have on us. The third principle does not negate the second. Paul isn't saying that "these things" aren't good, but that they aren't good for him.

For the Christian, "these things" may include erotic material. It is a strong possibility that Paul was specifically addressing the issue of erotica. In the following verse Paul writes, "But it is not true that the body is for *lust.*" According to Paul, certain types of erotica may not be wrong in and of themselves. However, the context of the erotica can determine whether erotic material is healthy or unhealthy. Paul warns that things such as lust "might get such a grip on me that I can't easily stop when I want to." A second issue Paul addresses is control. Scripture clearly teaches that the Christian should only be under the control of the Holy Spirit. When erotica becomes part of a personal compulsion, it has an inappropriate degree of control or influence on us, and it is outside of God's desire for our lives. Paul hints at the addictive danger of eroticism in its strongest sense. An addiction to erotica works in a similar way to a drug addict needing a fix. Like the physiological need for a drug, the psychological need for erotic material controls the viewer or reader.

Fourth, *erotic content can be seared into the memory.* The images of graphic erotica can be difficult to erase from memory. An erotic memory can flash into one's mind at the most inappropriate moments, similar to videotape suddenly playing back in the mind's eye. A recent client of ours, Brad, told us of the toll that past exposure to pornographic films was taking on his sex life with his bride of just two years. He regrets his decision to watch X-rated videos with high-school friends. Some of the images from those videos haunt him when he is having sex with his wife. Pornographic images replay in Brad's mind, tarnishing his attempts to engage in a person-centered sexual experience with his wife. He admits these images are difficult to erase from his mind.

Erotic material seems to be especially tempting and influential to men. Many men empathize with Brad and share his struggle (Hart 1995). Maintaining purity, amidst a deluge of mass media seeking control of our minds, is a constant battle. It is important to admit the problem, resist further exposure to dehumanizing material and try to take captive images that are incongruent with God's design for our sexuality. Confession and accountability are important aspects of change and growth toward purity. We may not be able to keep images from entering our mind, but we can decide how long these thoughts remain and what we do with them. Since we create and reinforce our fantasy life, it is possible for us to choose to eliminate dehumanizing fantasies from our minds. Reminding Brad that he had a choice gave him hope and a renewed vision for loving his wife with his whole heart and mind.

It is important to monitor fantasy processes for dehumanizing elements or aspects. Scrutinizing our fantasy life helps us to discern when we are disregarding God's commandment to love and instead focusing on personal pleasure. Mature people must take responsibility for their fantasy life by assessing the effects of fantasy on themselves and relationships with others. They are also discriminating about what they expose to their mind, heart and soul.

Masturbation

Since fantasy and the use of erotic and pornographic material often accompany the act of masturbation, there is much confusion surrounding this form of sexual release. Historically, society has fabricated myths in an attempt to discourage people from masturbating. Folk wisdom has associated masturbation with hair loss, warts, pimples, skin disease, blindness, impotence and mental illness. As a result many who were raised under these myths have attached an intense amount of guilt to masturbation. Laumann et al. (1994) found that 54 percent of men and 47 percent of women report feeling guilty after masturbating.

From an early age boys typically engage in self-stimulation more than girls, possibly because their genitals are external. Unfortunately society often sends a message to girls very early in life that they are not to touch themselves below the waist. Self-discovery through masturbation can help boys and girls learn about their bodies and affirm themselves as sexual beings. Masturbation can allow one to explore the pleasures of the body without guilt or shame.

Kinsey (1948) found that 95 percent of adult males and 60 percent of adult females had masturbated to orgasm prior to marriage; however, his findings are suspect because of the nature of his sample. The most common reasons given for masturbating are, in descending order of frequency, relief of sexual tension, physical pleasure, unavailable partners, relaxation and aid in falling asleep. The best available study, based on a cross-section of over 3,000 persons ages eighteen to sixty, found that 37 percent of men and 58 percent of women report they did not masturbate during the past year (Laumann et al. 1994). These figures differ by individual circumstance; most noticeably, masturbation is less frequent among those in a stable sexual relationship. About 80 percent of men and 60 percent of women report that they usually or always experienced orgasm when masturbating.

Christian perspectives. How are Christians to view masturbation? First, we must realize that children's self-exploration of their body is natural and a necessary process for developing an awareness of their anatomy. They need to form good feelings and attitudes about every part of their body, including the sexual zones. This will help children understand that these parts of their body are good parts of themselves.

Next, we must recognize that the Bible is silent on the topic of masturbation. Therefore any case built either for or against it is based on inferences made from biblical passages that do not directly address it.

There are three major Christian views on masturbation. The *restrictive* view maintains that masturbation, under any circumstance, is sinful. In contrast, the *permissive* view assigns a healthy and moral value to masturbation under any circumstance. This view considers masturbation to be a harmless and positive method for increasing awareness and responsiveness in our sexual identity. The *moderate* view maintains that masturbation can be both healthy and morally appropriate, but also suggests that it has the potential to be unhealthy and morally inappropriate.

The *moderate* view seems to be the most reasonable. Masturbation can be a healthy, enjoyable way for a person without a marital partner to experience sexual gratification. Since God has created humans as sexual beings, masturbation provides a way for individuals to experience their sexuality and meet their sexual needs. Many Christians battle feelings of guilt associated with masturbation and sexual repression. Freedom from sexual guilt and repression allows one to find more compatible methods to accept and affirm our God-given sexuality.

However, masturbation is not always psychologically and morally healthy. Compulsive masturbation, like compulsive eating or even compulsive sleeping, can be harmful. Compulsive sexual behavior can lead to destructive and devastating sexual addictions spiraling out of control. Yet, it is important not to automatically equate harmful and disruptive activity with sinful activity.

Masturbation can be a method for releasing frustration or an escape from threatening interactions or responsibilities. During periods of stress, masturbation can be used to reduce anxiety or provide an emotional escape from an unpleasant task (Laumann et al. 1994). When used as a mechanism for coping with feelings of fear or inferiority, masturbation can be an anesthetic that keeps us from dealing with unhealthy patterns controlling us.

Within marriage masturbation can be a negative factor if it deprives the other spouse of sexual fulfillment. Similarly, if a partner is using masturbation to avoid sexual problems in the marriage relationship, both the relationship and the partner can be affected negatively. On the other hand, when married partners have different desires regarding the frequency of intercourse, masturbation can be a helpful and loving way for dealing with differing needs. The relationship is always the priority. Couples need to confront sexual problems hindering intimacy in the relationship rather than escaping problems through masturbation.

Masturbation, lust and fantasy. Masturbation is often associated with lust. Jesus addresses the issue of lust in Matthew 5:27-28: "You have heard that it was said, 'You shall not commit adultery.' But I tell you that anyone who looks at a woman lustfully has already committed adultery with her in his heart." This passage addresses lust for a specific woman in thought or deed, which violates the boundaries set by God. Jesus warns that lust leads to adultery, and adultery is sin. However, lusting is not the same as fantasizing.

Fantasies about future possibilities are usually benign, and masturbating with one's spouse or future spouse in mind can be a way of creating a more personal context for an otherwise solitary act. Desiring a specific person, and dwelling on ways to fulfill that desire, is a form of lust. Fantasy, on the other hand, is more general and does not include attempts at achieving that exact fantasy. Usually one can tell the difference between patterns of fantasy and lust.

Fantasy can develop into lust. For example, pedophiles may masturbate and fantasize about sexual interactions with young children. Over time, boundaries between fantasy and lust can become blurry, and pedophiles may seek out a young victim to act out their fantasy. Obviously, engaging in sexual activity with a child is a sinful act that can stem from a fantasy life that lacks boundaries. Monitoring and regulating our fantasy life help us remain within God's intended context for ourselves as sexual beings.

Destructive fantasies often stem from a need for power. Increasing awareness about needs met through fantasy clarifies any discrepancies between our motives and God's intended purpose. For example, a destructive fantasy disregards God's commandments to love others, to not covet and to not harm others. Similarly, viewing erotic pictures while masturbating incorporates an element of dehumanizing sexual exploitation that is outside God's intention for humanity. The major concern is not about viewing pornographic material while masturbating. The issue is that destructive and distorted attitudes and beliefs about women and sex within the content of pornography become associated with sexual arousal and can lead ultimately to an increase in violent sexual attitudes and even behavior. The association of masturbation with pornography generally incorporates exposure to attitudes that contradict God's value to love and respect one another.

One who seeks to be holy before God must learn to discern between what one is free to do in Christ, and what is good to do within the context of one's particular life circumstances and relationship with God and others. Only the individual can determine the appropriateness of their fantasy life and its effect on their beliefs and attitudes. Monitoring fantasy is similar to the processes we incorporate to monitor our thoughts concerning world affairs and societal and relationship issues. Persons entertaining romantic fantasy in order to enhance their marital relationship need to consider the impact of fantasy on the marriage. Fantasy can increase responsiveness and receptiveness in the relationship, but can also be used as a substitute for unmet needs in the marriage.

There are also issues that a single person must face in regard to fantasy. Fantasy can create an ideal that sabotages intimacy and the hope of relationship by creating an unrealistic expectation. However, within a healthy context fantasy can perpetuate hope for a relationship with another in a God-centered marital commitment. Regardless of the images associated with one's fantasies, it is important to continually evaluate them and to be willing to change elements of them that are not within God's intention for what it means to be fully human.

Fantasy can evolve into lust, or it can be a way of nurturing an appropriate desire for an intimate relationship. A fantasy about a future mate may keep a young person from becoming sexually active with dating partners. In this case, fantasy reinforces a God-centered value about sexuality.

Not long ago we were at the wedding of a friend's son and noticed the special bond between the groom and his groomsmen. All four had lived together for four years in a dorm at a Christian university, and had become extremely close. They had made a vow to each other to uphold celibacy as a God-given blessing. Dave was the first of the four to marry. The rehearsal dinner was a loving and festive celebration for the young couple. During the dinner, the entire wedding party gathered around them to pray God's blessing on their life. On the wedding day, Dave's friends gave him the "high five" sign after they were pronounced husband and wife. "Do us proud!" was their cheer. Smiling, the entire wedding party understood the meaning of that cheer. It meant, "Take this woman you love and gently love her with all the passion you have. Enjoy the one-flesh union you've patiently waited for, and be richly blessed." This was more than a fantasy, it was real life.

This chapter has focused upon solitary forms of sexuality. Reliance on pornography, and even masturbation, in the extreme can come to have an unhealthy control over an individual. Dependence on pornography and other forms of inauthentic sexuality have increasingly come to be to identified as sexual addiction. In the next chapter we seek an understanding of sexual addiction and what might be done for persons who come to be controlled by inauthentic forms of sexuality.

Suggestions for Further Reading

Hall, L. 1996. *An affair of the mind: One woman's courageous battle to salvage her family from the devastation of pornography.* Colorado Springs: Focus on the Family.

Mielke, A. 1995. *Christians, feminists, and the culture of pornography.* Lanham, Md.: University Press of America.

Russell, D. 1998. *Dangerous relationships: Pornography, misogyny, and rape.* Thousand Oaks, Calif.: Sage Publications.

14

Sexual Addiction

The sexual addict has a "pathological relationship with a mood-altering chemical," according to Patrick Carnes (1983:4). The euphoria that accompanies the "sexual fix" alters the person's mood like an adrenaline high. Carnes likens sexual addiction to athlete's foot of the mind: "It never goes away. It always is asking to be scratched, promising relief. To scratch, however, is to cause pain and intensify the itch" (Carnes 1983:vii).

Unlike an addiction to alcohol or another chemical substance, the sex addict abuses the very core of who he or she is. Familiar with secrets and leading a double life, sex addicts feel like they are the only ones who know what pain is about. "No one could ever understand what I am going through. What's the use in trying to explain it?" they despair.

Definition

Sexual addiction has been defined as a recurrent failure to control sexual behavior despite the significant harmful consequences it has on the person (Goodman 1992). The obsession with sex can have a lifelong hold on a person. There is some controversy about using the term "sexual addict," since labeling may reinforce the notion that they have no control over the acting-out behavior. It may be better to say that they have a sexual preoccupation, sexual dependency or sexual compulsivity, which they can overcome. Some professionals in this field believe the sexual acting out is secondary to the more comprehensive obsessive-compulsive disorder that leads to sexually addictive behaviors (Moser 1993). Although we are sympathetic with these expressed concerns, we use sexual addiction as a concept because it deals with the beliefs, behaviors and attempts to control those behaviors that are part of the repetitive, self-defeating cycle. As with other forms of addiction, surrendering to God (a Higher Power) is an essential key in breaking the cycle and escaping the control/out-of-control double bind (Earl and Earl 1995).

In speculating about why a person gets trapped in compulsive sexual addictions, explanations focus primarily on sociocultural and family factors.

The addictive society. At the sociocultural level, sexual addiction can be understood as the product of living in an addictive society. The twentieth century has been labeled the age of anxiety. Distrust, isolation, abandonment, value confusion, lack of meaning, search for easy solutions, loneliness and a quick-fix mentality are part of modern culture, which make one vulnerable to addictive behaviors.

The fast pace of life within modern technological society tempts one to find relief through anything that can reduce tension or soothe the impact of life stresses. The competitive emphasis on getting ahead, fragmentation of families, impersonal nature of relationships and loss of involved community also make for a climate of exploitation. Needless to say, the commodification of sex proves to be a highly profitable product in an addiction-prone society.

The ever-changing and competing values of modern society, the general lack of meaning, and personal disenfranchisement often lead to value confusion and personal disillusionment. The person searches for meaning or comfort wherever it can be found, whether it's through entertainment, popular culture or media messages. Sex is presented as the ultimate experience that brings personal satisfaction, a commodity that offers release.

Contemporary culture places confidence in technology, where fast, easy solutions are promoted. In our microwave age with its quick-fix mentality, one looks for convenient and instant solutions. Many people use over-the-counter or prescribed drugs to soothe problems of life. The television bombards us with a host of commercials promoting relief for every imaginable irritation—from headaches to hangovers. An advertisement for a well-known brand of aspirin boasts relief "when you haven't got time for the pain!" Our society and culture also promote sex as another quick-fix way to deal with anxiety, distrust, isolation, abandonment, value confusion and meaninglessness.

Family factors. The cumulative research on unstable, fragmented families provides clues about particular types of families that may make an individual prone to various kinds of addictions. Two important characteristics of family interaction are cohesion and adaptability.

Cohesion represents the degree of emotional connectedness or separateness between family members. Effective families are characterized by a sufficient degree of cohesion, in which there is a satisfying emotional connection as well as respect for individual autonomy. In homes where members are not respected, there is often insufficient provision for rules concerning expressions of affection. For example, when sexual behaviors between members cause discomfort, the child does not feel he or she has the right to express objections. Also, the unspoken and sometimes spoken message is to "never to tell anyone outside the family about anything that goes on inside the family," for to do so is an unforgivable act of disloyalty. The no-talk rule keeps others out while covert and overt sexual abuse may be going on inside the home.

At the opposite extreme from overconnection is underconnection, where there is a serious lack of emotional cohesion between family members. In these homes, family members are unable to make a satisfying connection, so everyone learns to fend for themselves. Features of disengaged families include emotional abandonment, inability to talk about sexual feelings and behaviors, tensions around sexual matters, lack of physical or sexual affirmation and isolation that leads to sexual evasion. The emotional distance between family members also makes it difficult for children to learn how to relate in meaningful ways to others outside the home.

Adaptability represents the degree of structure and flexibility in a family. Again, effective families are characterized by appropriate structure as well as the ability to adapt to needed change throughout the family life stages. When a family lacks structure, it can be extremely chaotic in the sense that there are vast discrepancies between values and behavior. The discrepancies often result in inconsistent sexual standards and discipline. Common patterns include sexual unmanageability for both parents and children as well as frequent role reversals in which children take on parental responsibility or even become sexual objects. Children are placed in a double bind, being told one thing about sex but experiencing another reality.

Low adaptability is expressed in rigid values. Parents are uncompromising and extremely strict about moral standards. The features of rigid homes include unreachable expectations about sexuality, black-and-white moral standards, extreme efforts to control a child's sexual behavior and severe punishment of the child's sexual behavior. Children in rigid families find the unrealistic sexual standards frustrating and experience a sense of shame and inadequacy about sexuality. For example, children who are severely reprimanded for touching their genitals tend to reject their sexual self.

Most families fluctuate on the cohesion/adaptability dimensions at different times throughout the various life stages, but families at the extremes are particularly vulnerable to distortions about sexuality. To develop an authentic sexuality, a family must respect individual boundaries as well as establish reasonable and appropriate structures to safeguard a member's sexuality. In order to develop a strong sense of self as a sexual person, a child needs the secure love and connection of family members, as well as a clear affirmation of sexuality and relational strength.

Low self-esteem is a major component in the sexual acting-out patterns of the sex addict. Sex is often used to validate one's femininity or masculinity in a basic, raw manner. Not being affirmed by their family, sex addicts seek a substitute for what's lacking in their personal life.

Understanding the Sexual Addiction Cycle

(Note: *Both men and women struggle with sexually addictive behaviors, but since sexual addicts are predominantly male we will use masculine pronouns when referring to them throughout this section.*)

Our discussion of sexual addiction is greatly influenced by the work of Patrick Carnes (1983, 1989, 1992). In diagramming the addictive cycle, he indicates the importance of sex addicts' mistaken beliefs that bring them into the addictive cycle. Treatment is based on breaking the repetitive, compulsive cycle and changing the underlying belief system of the sexual addict.

Belief system. The core belief of the addict is, "I'm basically a bad, unworthy person and no one wants me as I am. I must find another way to meet my needs, so I focus on sexual pleasure, which helps relieve my self-incriminating thoughts." Carnes (1983) points out that the sexual behaviors engaged in are often quite against the addict's own value system, leaving him with further feelings of shame and regret after engaging in the addictive behavior. The self-condemning behavior after acting out makes him feel even worse about himself than before. He is disgusted with himself for what he has done and promises himself he will never do it again. However, the negative beliefs keep coming back, ringing louder and louder in his mind. So, to drown out the negative noise, he focuses on sexual thoughts and certain sexual behaviors that he believes will make him feel better.

Compulsivity. The compulsion stage involves obsessive, persistent, repetitive thoughts. The addict now becomes preoccupied with these sexual thoughts in such a strong way that it actually interferes with his life and relationships. It is not an occasional fantasy, but one that occupies hours of time and interferes with everything the person does. The tenacious thoughts take control of the addict, and life now revolves around the desire to get the fix (that is, act out the behavior). He will do almost anything to fulfill his goal. With unimaginable denial in full swing, the addict is completely oblivious to any negative consequences of his actions. The compulsive thoughts have taken control, and this moves him into the ritual phase of the cycle.

Ritualized behaviors. Ritualized behaviors include such things as making a phone call to a prostitute, getting in the car to cruise a gay neighborhood or anything else that starts the process of capturing the high. The power themes of conquest, breaking taboos and taking risks can add to the addict's thrill at this point. The addict anticipates the mounting excitement of going through the elaborate routines, which intensify and prolong arousal, eventually leading to the sexual act.

Once the ritual has started, the addict becomes increasingly focused on doing what it takes to get the sexual high. The ritualized actions and trancelike focus on the goal reduce the anxiety felt during the belief and compulsive stages. Sex, the drug of choice, anesthetizes the self-loathing feelings.

Impaired thinking. Once he has his mind on the sexual fix, impaired thinking takes over. Major denial keeps him from dealing forthrightly with his problems. He blames others for his plight and rationalizes his compulsive sexual desires away. He distorts reality, believes his own lies, lives a secret double life that's filled with suspicion and paranoid feelings about being found out. This is particularly true for those who have a moral and religious public life.

His distorted reality leads to risk-taking behaviors. For example, he puts himself and others at lethal risk when, in denial, he fails to take necessary precautions against contracting a sexually transmitted disease. Years can go by before he realizes he has been infected (and may have infected others) with HIV, for example. Impaired thinking gives him a false sense of power that keeps him from considering the actual life-threatening consequences of what he's about to do.

The fix. The unacceptable beliefs about himself and the impaired thinking are now transferred to the unacceptable behavior. He engages in the specific sexual behavior that is the final goal of his obsessions. Although the fix provides temporary relief from his incessant thoughts, the ugly shaming cycle kicks in immediately after he acts out, and profound feelings of remorse become a huge burden. The shaming cycle verifies what he already believes about himself, namely, that he is inherently bad and can never change. And the negative beliefs begin the cycle again.

Control/Out-of-Control Pattern

One clue in identifying an addictive problem is the pattern of trying to control behavior on one hand and being totally out of control on the other hand. This control/out-of-control pattern overarches the entire cycle of negative beliefs, preoccupation with the fix, premeditated rituals, impaired thinking, getting the fix, feelings of remorse and the adamant promises to never to do it again. The in-control periods can last for quite a long time in the beginning, but as time goes by it becomes

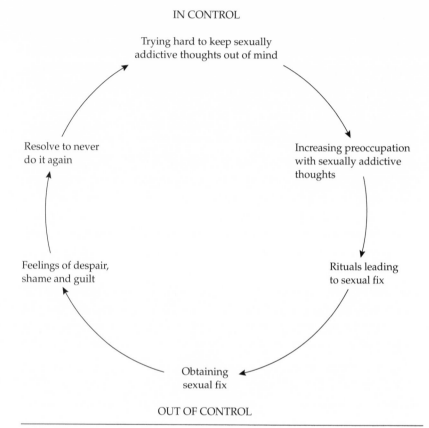

Figure 14.1.   **The cycle of sexual addiction. This figure is based on models developed by Patrick Carnes (1983, 1989) and Fossum and Mason (1989).**

increasingly difficult to maintain long periods of control. The period of time before negative beliefs enter in and trigger the intense out-of-control part of the cycle also becomes shorter and shorter. Figure 14.1 gives a summary depiction of this vicious cycle, which intensifies over time.

The compulsive nature and out-of-control repetitive quality of the sexual action is what drives the sex addict, according to Travin (1995). While the addict is in an acting-out mode, everything else becomes secondary; the job, the wife, the deadlines, even the color of the stoplights seem to take a back seat to the addict's "need" for sex, his need for sexual validation. At times, he feels he is in a trance, driving around for hours looking for sex. Many addicts report that they have been in accidents because they were so completely unaware of their surroundings. All senses seem to be impaired by the person's fixation on finding sex. And once this process begins, it is difficult for sex addicts to pull themselves out of the trance and return to reality. During the act itself, the addict usually feels good because his addiction is being fed and his feelings of inadequacy are numbed for the moment. Unfortunately for the addict, like any addiction, one cannot stay on this high for ever; even though sexual bingeing can sometime last for days, there is a huge letdown after it's over. Then, it isn't long before the entire cycle repeats itself.

Dangerous choices. Because the addict's senses are impaired, the addiction places his life in grave danger. He may find himself in the midst of drug addicts and prostitutes as he attempts to get his sexual fix. His addiction takes him to risky, acting-out locations. Deep in his addiction, unaware of his surroundings, he does not realize that he could be set up for a police sting. All of a sudden, while engaging in anonymous sex at a urinal, he is arrested by an undercover cop for lewd conduct. In fact, most of the men arrested in public restrooms, parks, truck stops or porno shops are married and have families. For men unsure of their sexual orientation, acting out may be the only way they feel validated by other men. Heterosexual, bisexual and homosexual men may engage in both heterosexual and homosexual acting-out behavior. Many addicts do not tell their partners that they have acted out. Even if the partner suspects that there may be a problem, neither of them wants to admit it, for the problem seems too enormous to address. In one afternoon, a secret he has kept for years can be out in the open in a matter of minutes. The out-of-control phase might cost him his job, his marriage and children, his good name and his reputation.

Eventually, the addict returns to reality and is left to deal not only with the pain and consequences of acting out, but the lack of inner peace regarding his self-esteem issues. The void is still present; the negative, self-loathing feelings taunt him once again; and he inevitably returns to the compulsive behavior unless the vicious abuse cycle is broken. While the fix offers some sexual gratification, it only lasts a brief time before the shaming messages hit even harder than before. The addict is now left alone to face himself again. He looks in the mirror and sees someone he knows well, a hopeless wretch of a person who is "bad to the core of his very being." He sees himself as a weak, out-of-control person who is unable to help himself. At this point the addict promises himself he will reform and moves into the control phase. Since he believes he is despicable, he tries harder than ever before to control his desires and sexual behaviors. His negative view of himself continues and he becomes haunted by the idea that sex is the only remedy for his pain. So, once again, sex is set up as the false idol that promises to numb the self-defeating thoughts but gives nothing except pain in return.

Treatment

The ultimate goal of treatment is to help sexual addicts to (1) recognize and understand the false beliefs; (2) commit to relinquishing the compulsive thoughts, ritualized behavior and sexual acts; (3) look to a Higher Power to transform their beliefs and empower them to change; and (4) develop a capacity for emotional intimacy with significant persons in their life. During treatment, denial is a major factor that keeps sexual addicts from taking these steps. The best efforts at breaking the sexual addiction cycle entail a personal commitment to change, combined with support from a group and a personal relationship with God. Twelve-step programs such as Sexaholics Anonymous (SA), Sex Addicts Anonymous (SAA) or Sexual Compulsives Anonymous (SCA) have been especially helpful for many sex addicts. Each group's focus is somewhat different, but the overriding goal is to stop compulsive sexual behaviors.

By the time a sex addict walks into his first twelve-step meeting, he may have two thoughts simultaneously running through his head. "I sure don't want to be here!" and "I really need to be here!" Soon, as he sits with his anxiety and listens to others describe the different characteristics of sexual addiction, he can personally relate to what's being said. As he looks around the room, he sees men and women, all there for the same reason. They all have a problem with using sex to validate unresolved feelings. As the addict hears others share their stories and talk about their recovery, he begins to realize that he too could have a life of recovery.

Sponsors are a wonderful part of the program. A sponsor is a person in the program who has sobriety and becomes a mentor to the addict. As a fellow addict in recovery, a mentor routinely makes contact with the new member to help him develop a plan to stop the vicious cycle of addiction. For example, if compulsive masturbation is the addiction, the sponsor and the addict will decide how to work out a plan of sobriety for this behavior. The first goal may be to masturbate once a week instead of every day. Once that has been accomplished, they reset the goal to twice a month and so on. Sponsors work with the sponsored to discover their cutting edge, making sure the goals are realistic. Each person's moral values and lifestyle help define sexual sobriety. Because sexual addiction is intertwined with the addict's past and the false self he has created to deal with life, therapy will also help an addict understand the underlying issues beneath the addictive behaviors.

The most effective treatment for a sexual addict is a combination of therapy and membership in a sexual addict recovery group. Accountability to the group promotes the idea of integrating sex into his life as a healthy element. The goal is to help him build satisfying relationships with others. Cognitive-behavioral programs include behavior therapy, social skills training, modification of distorted cognition and relapse prevention. Relapse prevention is designed to help the addict anticipate and cope with potential relapses. Effective treatment focuses on the addictive behavior, thought processes and management.

In a comprehensive guidebook *A Gentle Path Through the Twelve Steps*, Patrick Carnes (1991) gives direction and tools to help people reach final success in their recovery. Many sexual addiction intervention programs utilize a combination of strategies for all types of sexual addiction, including programs for an addiction to cybersex (Bingham and Piotrowski 1996).

A core aspect of twelve-step recovery groups is the need to look to a Higher Power to achieve recovery. For so long, the addict has tried to change and control behavior on his own efforts, but he must admit he cannot do it without God's help. This humility keeps a sex addict depending on God each step of the way toward recovery.

Writing in a journal, spending time in meditative prayer, reciting the serenity prayer, making contact with family, establishing close relationships with special friends and belonging to a caring community are ways to share oneself honestly with trusted others. When sex addicts are able to grab hold of the powerful truth that God and others love them unconditionally, when they receive Christ's grace and forgiveness and when they draw on the Holy Spirit for strength and empowerment, they can find their true self. These are the very experiences that turn the negative belief system into a new way of thinking and feeling about oneself. Those with a personal relationship with God through Jesus Christ have a powerful potential for transformation.

Helpful principles might be expressed as follows:

☐ We acknowledge that we can take action to stop being dependent on sex for our self-esteem by trusting in the living God and the Holy Spirit who empowers us.

☐ Our inner healing comes from the source of all healing, Jesus Christ, who is acquainted with our grief and, though tempted in every way, was victorious over sin.

☐ We make a decision to become authentic sexual selves as designed by our Creator God and by trusting in the power of God's word.

☐ We willingly relinquish shame, guilt and any behaviors that prevent God from working in our lives so we can be all that we are intended to be as sons and daughters of Christ.

☐ We admit we have made serious mistakes and engaged in behaviors that are not in accord with God's design for authentic sexuality. We confess to those we have harmed in the process and will take steps to make amends.

☐ We seek to find our inward calling and develop the will to follow in God's way. We look to the Holy Spirit to convict, guide and empower us as we continue our life's journey.

☐ We express gratitude to the people who have come alongside us in our walk, have shown us unconditional love and acceptance and have helped us develop our God-given strengths, talents and gifts.

A Christian Response to Sexual Addiction

Given the destructiveness of sexually addictive behavior, it is good to once again reaffirm sex as a good gift from God. Unfortunately, what God has given for good can be deeply distorted. As we noted in chapter six, 1 Corinthians 6:12-13 says that sex becomes destructive when it has mastery over a person. The basic problem of sexual addiction is that one is enslaved by sexual compulsions. The excesses and repetitive cycles hold the addict captive to ongoing self-destructive beliefs and behaviors.

Since the term *addiction* has become commonplace in modern society, it is necessary to examine whether this merely replaces the concept of *sin*. Christians might understandably be suspicious of using the term addiction too freely because it seems to fly in the face of the biblical emphasis on individual choice and personal accountability. The fear that this may lead to blatant sin, more denial and an unwillingness to take responsibility for one's actions is certainly an important concern.

Romans 1:24-28 offers a perspective on this point. Verse 24 says, "God gave them over in the sinful desires of their hearts to sexual impurity for the degrading of their bodies with one another"; verse 26 reports, "God gave them over to shameful lusts"; and verse 28 states "[God] gave them over to a depraved mind, to do what ought not to be done." In this little phrase, "given over," Richard Mouw (1988) believes we have the basis for a theology of addiction, which he describes as rebellion against God, suppression of the truth and giving in to unrighteousness.

Note that the statement "God gave them over" is preceded by the word *therefore*. Quite clearly, God gave them over only *after* they volitionally rejected and sinned against God. In our thinking about sexual addiction, we must recognize that the addiction begins with a willful act on the part of the addict. Then, after repeating this act over and over, it becomes an addiction. A person must be held accountable, even though the compulsive nature seems to render one incapable of accountability. This is the very reason treatment involves such a strong emphasis on changing the addict's beliefs and breaking that cycle.

We certainly must balance a compassionate understanding along with a clear expectation of intentional choice. Treatment is effective as long as a person continues to be accountable to others and seeks strength from God to overcome. Those who do not believe in an all-powerful, all-loving and forgiving God will find it incredibly difficult to change destructive thinking patterns and recover in their own strength. And, in the more extreme cases, repeat sex offenders often *sear* their conscience to the extent that they feel no guilt or remorse for their crimes. They have "hardened their hearts" and may never seek change or treatment. The only thing that works in this case is the threat of being caught and sent to jail. In order to be released from the prison of addiction and the compulsive bondage of sexual sin, the addict needs to turn to the one who promises wholeness and freedom from the derogatory stigma, pain and shame of the abusive cycle. Philippians 3:10-14 provides promise of hope in Christ.

> I want to know Christ and the power of his resurrection and the fellowship of sharing in his sufferings, becoming like him in his death, and so, somehow, to attain to the resurrection from the dead. Not that I have already obtained this, or have already been made perfect, but I press on to take hold of that for which Christ Jesus took hold of me. Brothers, I do not consider myself yet to have taken hold of it. But one thing I do: Forgetting what is behind and straining toward what is ahead, I press on toward the goal to win the prize for which God has called me heavenward in Christ Jesus.

Suggestions for Further Reading

Carnes, P. 1989. *Contrary to love: Helping the sexual addict.* Center City, Minn.: Hazelden Press.

———. 1992. *Don't call it love: Recovery from sexual addiction.* New York: Bantam Books.

———. 1983. *Out of the shadows: Understanding sexual addiction.* Minneapolis: CompCare Publications.

———. 1994. *A gentle path through the twelve steps.* Minneapolis: CompCare Publications.

Schaumberg, H. 1997. *False intimacy: Understanding the struggle of sexual addiction.* Colorado Springs: NavPress.

Willingham, R. 1999. *Breaking free: Understanding sexual addiction and the healing power of Jesus.* Downers Grove, Ill.: InterVarsity Press.

Part IV
Conclusion

15

The Sexually Authentic Society

Our investigation of human sexuality has been guided by a search for authenticity. Our journey has led to the consideration of a variety of factors that contribute to the formation of an authentic sexuality. Based on an understanding of psychological, sociological, cultural and biological factors affecting the development of one's sexuality, we have sought a deeper meaning through the Holy Scriptures as a way of understanding human sexual authenticity. In the meaning of being created sexual, we make sense of what it is to be an authentic sexual person.

As we come to the end of this discourse on human sexuality, we must stand back and take a broader bird's-eye view of the societal and cultural context within which individuals live out their lives as sexual beings. Clearly the development and nurturing of authentic sexuality does not exist in a vacuum, but is part of a larger social system which can either promote or distort sexuality as God intended it to be.

Individualism and personal autonomy are among the strongest values in modern Western society. Although these values have freed individuals from being dominated and controlled by the collective will of the group, individuals within modern society are in danger of losing two very important correctives that give balance from a wider social system. In order to live consistently sexually authentic lives, individuals need both *support* and *accountability* from social structures. Whereas some forms of inauthentic sexuality are expressed in inauthentic sexual relationships (see chapters ten to twelve), other forms are expressed in more solitary ways, such as pornographic consumption and sexual addiction. Support and accountability from sexually authentic social structures are the two important ingredients lacking in all forms of inauthentic sexuality.

In chapter ten the metaphor of an onion was used to suggest how sexual harassment could be understood in terms of layers of explanation. In a similar way, sexuality is influenced by the fabric of society, which consists of many interwoven layers within which people live, find their identity, seek support and are held accountable. These several layers of social structure can be conceptualized as forming increasingly inclusive concentric circles around an individual's life. Figure 15.1 represents three different layers of social structure, along with a biblically prescribed ideal for each.

For most people the family is the central arena in which sexual norms and behavior are taught and modeled. The *covenant* is the biblically prescribed basis for family relationships that we have discussed throughout this book.

Beyond the family is the local church or fellowship in which Christian believers find their identity, support and accountability. While there is much in Scripture to suggest that a church/fellowship should resemble family relationships, the biblically prescribed ideal is that of

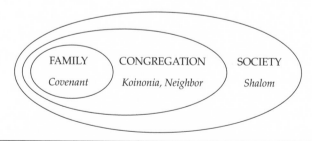

Figure 15.1.   The sexually authentic society: Levels of social structure and biblically prescribed ideals

koinonia. The congregation, as the people of God, are not only called to be a fellowship for each other, but to reach out to the needs of others in their surrounding neighborhood and community. *Neighbor* is the biblically prescribed ideal for believers' relationships with people in their community. Finally, the most inclusive level is society. Here millions of people share identity through common membership in a nation-state that establishes formal laws and informal norms about sexuality. The biblically prescribed ideal here is *shalom.* We shall present a description of what authentic sexuality might be on the familial, local church/fellowship and societal levels.

Authentic Family Sexuality

In chapter two we drew upon the writings of James Maddock to give a picture of family sexual health, which serves as the basis for our discussion. Healthy family sexuality was defined as "the balanced expression of sexuality in the life of the family, in ways that enhance the personal identities and sexual health of individual family members and the organization of the family as a system, functioning effectively within its social and material environment" (Maddock and Larson 1995:52-53).

The basic unit in society, both sociologically and theologically, is the family. Sociologically, the family is the unit into which individuals are born, find their sexual identity and are socialized as male or female sexual beings. Theologically, it is the relationship principles of covenant, grace, empowerment and intimacy that are supremely applicable to family relationships. The family is meant to be an intimate environment where persons can be themselves without fear of violation or rejection. Thus, Adam and Eve were able to stand before one another without shame (Gen 2:25).

Family life is to be a place of security where members experience the faithful, unconditional love of family members through mutual care and regard. For husband and wife this means offering oneself in body, mind and spirit. In becoming "one flesh" the couple grows through a relationship of mutual desire, vulnerability and responsiveness (1 Cor 7:5). For children, the family provides security through an unconditional love that puts their best interest as the priority. When children make mistakes, they are forgiven rather than shamed. Children who are valued know how to value themselves as sexual persons.

Children of empowering parents thrive in an atmosphere of nurture and guidance that builds them up rather than tears them down. Effective parents respect sexual boundaries through nonerotic physical touch, verbal support and affirmation of gender and sexuality. Children learn to freely express their unique personalities rather than be confined by rigidly imposed gender roles. Both parents will have the ability to establish emotional bonds with male and female children.

The intimacy principles of sexually authentic family life ensure that members are able to be emotionally naked and not ashamed (Gen 2:25). It's a place where they can be themselves, free from the demanding requirements of the outside world. In an accepting atmosphere, family members are comfortable with themselves as sexual persons because they are supported and encouraged to be themselves. Home is a place where family members do not hide their feelings because feelings and opinions are honored. It is a place where members listen to and encourage each other to talk openly about sex and gender. There is no distrust in relationships because appropriate boundaries provide safety. Authentic family living affirms sexuality for what it is meant to be.

Unfortunately, not all families are as balanced as this ideal. The family is so often plundered on one side by the demands and intrusions of mass society and on the other by an individualistic emphasis that pulls members away from needed support and accountability of the family group. This is especially true when activities outside the home put such time demands on each member that they have little opportunity for family interaction. As children move through their formative years, they are deprived of strong family connections that contribute to authentic sexual and gender identities.

Family life needs to be reconstructed as a secure emotional holding environment that keeps effective boundaries against the bombardment of negative external influences. The family must protect itself from the intrusion of a multitude of inauthentic sexual messages and forces that sap it of vitality. When family members have a central place where they learn to be accountable to one another, they will know how to be responsible citizens outside the home.

In regard to the idea that a family functions most effectively within a social environment, there is need for a new understanding of biblical family life. In contrast to our individualistic emphasis, Israel held a strong sense of corporate solidarity and identity within the wider community. A recent analysis of families in ancient Israel concludes that they were formed, shaped and sustained by a core of corporate identity and responsibility (Perdue et al. 1997). The family household was not separate from but an essential part of wider society. Israelites learned to look at their "social world and the world of creation as a household or a village of households, in which members took up residence and dwelt, nurtured and protected one another, and provided care for the poor person, who was the 'sibling' or the 'neighbor' to be loved as the self" (p. 254). Although it is not possible to return to these large household units of the past, we believe that the local church can and should be a place where individuals and families find a community of faith that upholds, nurtures, supports, guides, protects and develops people of authentic sexual character.

The Local Church as an Authentic Sexual Community

People in most societies are members of and find a sense of identity and social support from primary groups that exist beyond the family itself. Examples of such groups are churches, clubs, fellowships, and recreational and common interest groups.

Sociologically, a primary group serves as a mediating structure between the isolated, private world of the family and faceless remote societal structures. However, an increasing number of people in modern society are unable to locate supportive primary groups. Along with a decline in significant group accountability comes the loss of effective social control. Our families are more vulnerable today due to moral laxity. A type of impersonal social environment has caused an increasing number of persons to feel like they belong to a "lonely crowd" (Riesman 1950).

Some social scientists believe that networking has become the modern substitute for primary groups. Serving as mediating structures, friendship, occupational and religious networks provide for some needs. However, because these networks are individualized, they are subject to change and lack foundational group-based values like commitment and a sense of secure belonging.

Response to the disintegration of primary-group relationships is varied. There is one trend that promotes an extreme individualism and avoids significant dependence on or commitment to anyone else. Some people try a variety of groups based on interests such as economic sharing, hobbies or religious devotion. Some search for community in institutional contexts like suburban housing developments and take on names that indicate commonality and identity like Homewood, Pleasantville, Community Heights. In our mass society, primary-group identity and relationships are desperately sought out, yet often prove to be exceedingly difficult to achieve.

The local church as "koinonia." The local church serves as a primary group for Christian believers. Sometimes described as a "family of families," the church gives members a source of identity, support and accountability. If the church is to become a "plausibility structure for faith," as Peter Berger (1967) suggests, it must be a place where persons find identity, support and a belief system that is authentic.

The church is to serve as God's transforming agent in the lives of its believers. Peter Selby (1996) points out that "an understanding of the church as a 'family' has its origin in the determination of the New Testament to speak of the human situation in terms of relationship, and of the transformation of that situation by the grace of Christ in terms of transformed relationship." We must "recognize that the language of family and kinship is there in relation to church not for the purpose of encouraging some of the attributes which we have seen to be associated with the concept of family in our time. Rather, it is there to emphasize that character of the transformation which has taken place in the relationships which human beings have to each other and to God in the light of God's grace" (p. 165).

The key to understanding God's ideal with regard to social and sexual relationships within a local church context is found in the New Testament concept of *koinonia*. Scripture used this term in order to refer to a group in which persons were united in identity and purpose by way of a voluntary sharing of all of their possessions. During New Testament times, people associated themselves with two main types of groups: *politeia*, or civic life, and *oikonomia*, or family life. Koinonia came to represent a new type of group situated between the inclusive, impersonal state and the exclusive, blood-based community of the household (Banks 1980).

One of the metaphors that the Apostle Paul uses to describe the church is of the family. Christians are to see themselves as members of a divine family, the head of which is God the Father. Thus Paul, quoting from the Old Testament, writes, "'I will receive you, I will be a father to you, and you will be my sons and daughters'" (2 Cor 6:18 NRSV). We are also told that "God has sent the Spirit of His Son into our hearts, crying Abba! Father!" (Gal 4:6 NRSV), and Ephesians 2:19 states, "You are no longer strangers and aliens, but you are citizens with the saints and also members of the household of God" (NRSV).

God desires that strong family relationships not simply be ends in themselves but exemplary of how we are to care for each other in the local church. Jesus' attitude toward the inclusiveness of the family is clearly shown in Mark 3:31-35. While speaking to a crowd, he is informed that his mother and brothers have arrived. He replies, "'Who are my mother and my brothers?' And looking around at those who sat around him, he said, 'Here are my mother and brothers. Whoever does the will of God is my brother and sister and mother.'" The common membership we have in the body of Christ binds all believers to Christ and to one another as family, and our relationships are to be based upon covenant, grace, empowerment, intimacy and koinonia. The concept of koinonia provides us with a model of the church as a primary support and accountability community.

The decline of primary groups in modern society has more to do with the nature of contemporary mass society with its forces of impersonalization, urbanization, industrialization, rationalization, dehumanization, bureaucratization and secularization than it does with the absence of Christianity. In the face of these societal changes, Christian churches that practice koinonia can be a witness to how God intends persons to relate in primary groups. Sociologically, a primary group other than a Christian fellowship might function as a koinonia-type group. For this to happen, however, this primary group will at the very least need to share common beliefs, values, ideals and goals. Nevertheless, we argue that the New Testament example of koinonia provides us with the best model for how all human beings may live meaningful lives in harmony with themselves, others and their creator.

The local church as neighbor. To this point we have argued that the church needs to be a social unit in which persons and families find support and accountability for their sexual values and behavior. But in addition, the church needs to reach out into society in two important ways if it is to be a sexually authentic community. First, as a community of believers the church needs the courage to play a prophetic role by challenging the sexually unhealthy and inauthentic aspects of society. The church is to faithfully preach the kingdom by exposing the sexual lies, manipulations and illusions perpetuated by elements in society that deny the light of God's redemption in Jesus Christ. Second, the people of God are also called to minister to the sexually wounded and hurting in the community.

In the Parable of the Good Samaritan, Jesus set forth the concept of *neighbor* as the normative model of all community-based relationships. Luke 10:25-37 records this parable as follows:

> On one occasion a lawyer came forward to put his test question to him: "Master, what must I do to inherit eternal life?" Jesus said, "What is written in the Law? What is your reading of it?" He replied, "Love the Lord your God with all your heart, with all your soul, with all your strength, and with all your mind; and your neighbor as yourself." "That is the right answer," said Jesus; "do that and you will live."
>
> But he wanted to vindicate himself, so he said to Jesus, "And who is my neighbor?" Jesus replied, "A man was on his way from Jerusalem down to Jericho when he fell in with robbers, who stripped him, beat him, and went off leaving him half dead. It so happened that a priest was going down by the same road; but when he saw him, he went past on the other side. So too a Levite came to the place, and when he saw him went past on the other side. But a Samaritan who was making the journey came upon him, and when he saw him was moved to pity. He went up and bandaged his wounds, bathing them with oil and wine. Then he lifted him on his own beast, brought him to an inn, and looked after him there. Next day he produced two silver pieces and gave them to the innkeeper, and said, 'Look after him; and if you spend any more, I will repay you on the way back.' Which of these three do you think was neighbor to the man who fell into the hands of the robbers?" He answered, "The one who showed him kindness." Jesus said, "Go and do as he did." (NEB)

How convenient it would have been for Jesus to make a clear distinction between those who are our neighbors and those who are not. Instead, he made the startling assertion that every individual is a potential neighbor. That is to say, neighbor-type relationships are created when one person comes to the aid of another. Moreover, each of us is capable of both being a neighbor and having a neighbor. Thus, when I meet the needs of another, I am being a neighbor to that person. But when someone else serves me, then I have a neighbor.

The Parable of the Good Samaritan is a vivid illustration of Jesus' command to "love your neighbor as yourself" (Mt 19:19). In our own lives this commandment may be observed by our actions in developing ministries for victims of rape and sexual violence, in providing small groups for those troubled by sexual addictions or identity issues, in responding to unwed mothers who need emotional, social and financial support in order to give birth to a child rather than have an abortion. The church can also be instrumental in establishing homeless shelters for runaway children, who are the prime targets for sexual predators, or developing twelve-step groups for persons who struggle with sexual violence or sexual addiction. Church families can open up their homes as places of temporary refuge for sexually abused children. In all these ways we can come to the aid of others just as God in Christ has come to our aid.

When the call to be a neighbor is from God, the resultant action is an empowering one. In this regard Frazier (1986) comments that "a distinction must be made between the kind of aid that takes over and the kind that enables the recipient to continue the task. To take up the cause of another is not to give aid in the first sense. It is not to judge the other incompetent or weak or inadequate, and to set one's own self up as the morally superior deliverer of the sexually wounded. Rather it is to discern that point at which the other must be enabled to carry on a task, and to give that aid regardless of its seeming insignificance or lack of permanent value" (p. 268).

There is no promise that being a neighbor will result in having the other as a neighbor. But regardless of whether or not such neighborliness is reciprocated, God calls us to serve those who are sexually broken.

Authentic Societal Sexuality

At its broadest level, every society has a more or less agreed-upon view of what constitutes acceptable and unacceptable sexual behavior. While there is generally consensus about sexuality in traditional societies, there is considerably less consensus in modern industrialized societies. The very brief historical perspective in chapter one reported that from the landing of the first Puritans up to the present time, there has been an enduring tension between an emphasis on sexual repression and sexual liberation. Note that in the contemporary public debate over sexuality, terms such as "puritanical" and "Victorian" have come to be used as derogatory references to persons holding negative attitudes about sex. Over the past several hundred years the sexual climate has changed from sexual repression to sexual liberation, with modernist and postmodernist thinking influencing changes in attitudes.

Modernist and postmodernist influences. Sexual attitudes and values in society have traditionally been based on the religious beliefs held by a people. In most industrialized and technologically oriented societies, the religious anchors are being ripped from their mooring. The major reason for this is that technology is based on a scientific worldview, which offers an alternative basis for beliefs. This challenges traditional religious systems, which before the scientific revolution had been the main source for foundational values. In this age of modernity, the name given to this era of contemporary cultures reliant upon technologically engendered economic growth (Hunter 1983), modernization begins to challenge the religious sphere "as secularized belief systems begin to replace traditional religions" (Smelser 1973:738).

To further complicate things, it can be argued that modernity itself is now being replaced by postmodernist thought. Rejecting both the moral certainty given by traditional religious systems, and the certainty of scientifically based modernist thinking, this approach embraces the potential good and usefulness of a variety of alternative sexual moralities. Postmodernity represents a radical response to the excessive emphasis on rationalism found in modernity and sees many flavors of truth, depending on one's personal experiences and collective perspective. Postmodernity can be a useful corrective to the certainties of modernity, which promoted human reason as the basis for constructing sexual morality, but it too can be problematic when taken to the extreme that there is no reality except what is constructed by one's experience.

Postmodernists reject the general laws of nature as grounds for accepting or rejecting sexual morality, because reality is viewed as multilayered, with many ways of knowing. While a Christian perspective is acknowledged as one view, there are equally acceptable ways of knowing and therefore it is just one of many plausible realities. In the postmodern view, there is danger in accepting one system of morality over the myriad of other options. To do so is to be restrictive and intolerant. A strict postmodernist view leaves one with little ground upon which to evaluate the moral superiority of one system of sexual morality over another since all reality and alternative forms are acceptable. The problem, of course, is how to respond to the dehumanizing, degrading and abusive forms of sexual behavior that some may defend on the basis of their subjective system of morality. We must stand for a morality that recognizes the potential for evil as well as good in individuals and social systems.

While modernity seeks to construct a sexual ethic and morality on the basis of scientific and naturalistic assumptions, postmodernity is open to any cultural form that can collectively be argued as defensible. In order to avoid the modernist pitfall of idealizing a particular cultural form of sexual morality, postmodernity can go to the opposite extreme by rejecting any criteria for assessing the rightness or wrongness of sexual behavior.

There is a reality that the Christian community must seek to uphold, but to do so effectively demands a good understanding of both the potential benefits and destructiveness of modern and postmodern thinking toward a biblical sexual morality. To embrace modernity and postmodernity uncritically leaves one in the position of merely choosing human perspectives over God's perspective. We believe that Christians must recognize the positive and negative forces of both modernity and postmodernity in order to make a biblically based, proactive response to the current cultural views of sexual morality.

Shalom as a model for a sexually authentic society. Having addressed the reasons why it might be difficult to assess the sexual authenticity of modern society, we suggest that the Old Testament concept of *shalom* is a theologically appropriate way to describe a sexually authentic society. In most modern translations of the Bible, this term *shalom,* which is used 250 times in the Hebrew scriptures, is usually translated as "peace." Peace in Western cultures connotes the absence of conflict.

However, in Scripture and Hebrew culture, shalom is not seen as the mere absence of conflict but rather that which promotes human welfare in both its material and spiritual aspects. It denotes a culture characterized by justice, holiness and righteousness. For shalom to exist there must be justice, holiness and righteousness in the ethical structures of society; there must be fairness and respect in the way human beings treat each other at each social structural level. Such a situation is poignantly described in Isaiah:

> The wolf shall live with the lamb, and the leopard shall lie down with the kid, the calf and the lion and the fatling together; and a little child shall lead them. The cow and the bear shall graze, their young shall lie down together; and the lion shall eat straw like the ox. The nursing child shall play over the hole of the asp, and the weaned child shall put its hand on the adder's den. (Is 11:6-8 NRSV)

Shalom carried with it a holistic connotation of societal well-being. It is "the human being dwelling at peace in all his or her relationships: with God, with self, with fellows, with nature" (Wolterstorff 1983:69). When any one of these relationships is out of focus, disrupted, in tension or hurting, then shalom is not present.

One important sign that shalom is present in a society is evidence that public space is sexual safe space. To the extent to which a person, female or male, feels sexually unsafe while participating in the various arenas of life, to that extent shalom is absent. In the sexually authentic society, social space will be safe from sexual predators of both the less dangerous (sexual harassment) and more dangerous (rapists) variety. In such a society a woman would feel safe walking alone on a neighborhood street and parents would be able to let their children play in a park or leave their child at a daycare center with full trust in the caretakers.

For shalom to be present in society, there must be an affirmation of the goodness of sexuality and a climate of openness and comfort in dealing with sexual content. When authentic sexuality is present, there will be a noticeable absence of inauthentic expressions of sexuality, such as what happens at the extremes when sex is either repressed or excessively expressed. In reality there will probably always be some tension between sexual repression and sexual expression. Although there are subcultural pockets of sexual repression today, we would have to go back nearly one hundred years, when modesty was the order of the day, to find the strongest examples of societal repression of sexuality. At the present time we seem to be struggling much more against the tendencies toward excessive expressions of sexuality.

Excessive expressions of sexuality can most notably be found in the form of the *sexualization* or *eroticization* of nonsexual aspects of life and social relationships. Sexualization can be seen in the present-day use of sex in advertising, the overreliance on sex and sexually suggestive content in the media. Possibly in reaction to former sexual repression, the present mood seems a preoccupation with the sexual.

When relationships are eroticized, it becomes difficult for persons of the opposite sex to develop noneroticized friendships. Although we have not made a point of it, the evidence cited in this book points to profound differences between men and women in the tendency to eroticize relationships. To put it simply, while women are more inclined to seek affection and love in relationships, men are more inclined to seek sex. This observation is supported by the extensive research reported in *The Social Organization of Sexuality* (Laumann et al. 1994). These researchers found that while men report having their first sexual experience because they are curious or because of peer pressure, "love and affection motivate the initiation of sex for women and is the key motivation force that keeps sexual relationships going" (p. 547). The evidence that men more than women eroticize relationships is true of nearly all types of social relationships for which we have data. Men engage in sex with more partners, engage in a greater variety of sexual practices, have more fantasizing and thoughts about sex and are more likely to masturbate than are women. Further, the tendency for men more than women to eroticize relationships is true regardless of sexual orientation.

Perhaps most disturbing are the higher rates of involvement by men than women in the various forms of inauthentic sexual activities. Men more than women have higher rates of premarital sexual involvement, sexual promiscuity, extramarital sex, sexual abuse of children, sexual harassment, consumption of pornography, sexual addiction, rape and other violent sexual offenses. This evidence seems to indicate that men more than women are susceptible to depersonalized forms of sexual activity.

Sociobiologists argue that these differences between men and women are a result of an evolutionary process in which the genetic selection process was different for men than for women. They argue that the goal of human behavior has been to increase the chances that genetic lines will survive. Given the differential contribution of males and females to the reproductive process, members of each gender tried to protect their genetic packages in different ways. Since females have only a few eggs to be fertilized, investment in any conception is great; they therefore sought to save themselves for a strong, dependable male likely to care for their children. Males, on the other hand, had an unlimited number of sperm, so they could diversify their investments. People today, the theory concludes, are descendants of strong, promiscuous males and choosy females.

We believe, however, that much of the difference in sexual behavior between males and females results from unhealthy aspects in the traditional definition of masculinity. To the extent that real manhood is defined in terms of being sexually aggressive, to prove manhood through sexual conquests men will continue to struggle with inauthentic forms of sexual behavior. Based on their research, Laumann et al. (1994) conclude that "it is clear that men's normal socialization and roles in the sexual encounter undermine their ability to recognize limits set by their female partners. Men and women interpret these violations quite differently, as this survey indicates" (p. 547).

We believe that these found differences between men and women have important implications for ministry, especially one that focuses specifically on men and their sexual lives. The current Christian men's movement needs to include male sexuality as part of its emphasis in working with men. Hopefully, men's ministry will take root in the local church, and as it does we pray that male sexuality will be a topic that is directly addressed.

A proactive response to inauthentic societal sexuality. Given the evidence for the increased rates of premarital and extramarital sex, the explicit sanctioning of these behaviors in television and movies, and the multibillion dollar industry in phone sex and cybersex via the Internet, a case can be made that we are now living in the postsexual revolution. That is to say, the sexual revolution has taken place, and these pervasive and invasive forms of sexualized media are becoming normalized and standardized. Being a Christian at this time, perhaps more than at any time in modern history, means one is living out a minority sexual standard. How can a biblical standard of sexual morality be modeled and effectively advocated in the face of alternative and often contradictory standards of sexual morality?

The most noticeable response by the Christian community is reacting to unwholesome expressions of sexuality in society. Much of the activity in the so-called culture wars is symptomatic of this reactionary approach—boycotting products of companies that sponsor sexually offensive television programs or boycotting movies or CDs with objectionable sexual messages. There is a place for this type of response by the Christian community, and we applaud the attempts to combat the corroding effects on public sexual morality of pornography and dishonest treatment of sex.

However, we believe a *reactive* response to sexual immorality needs to be bolstered by a *proactive* response. An effective proactive response allows for the Christian community to set the agenda rather than merely being opposed to an agenda set by another interest group. Making a reactive response to circumstances means one merely responds to the agenda presented in secular society. Picture the movement of a group of balls on a pool table after they have been struck by the cue ball. The force of the cue ball sends all the other balls colliding off each other and against the sides of the pool table. In a reactive model, the persons or things (pool balls) simply make adjustments to pressures (cue ball); while this is good, it is not good enough. Living in the sexual climate of the postsexual revolution, it is easy to feel controlled by damaging forces in society.

While reactivity responds to the actions of an undesirable element in society, proactivity is a form of acting which takes the initiative, and in the process forces the undesirable element to respond. With proactive responses to circumstances, one takes intentional steps toward changing rather than merely reacting to external forces. One seeks a new understanding or a new posture toward a situation. With a proactive response, there is hope that one can be liberated from the sexual pollutant. A proactive response seeks control over the playing field, as it were, over the circumstances that are the source of degrading norms of sexual morality.

An example of a proactive response would be to educate Christians to the subtle and not-so-subtle ways in which popular culture is
dishonest in its depiction of sexual content. We need to train our children to be experts in detecting the dishonest and destructive ways
popular culture treats sex. This would involve teaching persons to
critically analyze the sexual context in popular culture on the basis of
how honestly it treats human sexuality. As a start, such theological
categories as creation, the Fall and redemption could be used in the
analysis. A mark of dishonest treatment of sex in films is the failure to
show the negative consequences of premarital, extramarital or promiscuous sexual behavior. Viewers need to recognize when, for
instance, comedy is used to avoid an honest portrayal of the negative
consequences of promiscuous sexual involvement. The point is to
move Christians beyond automatically rejecting a film, television
program or music video or recording because it includes sexual content toward judging the content in terms of its theological correctness
and honesty.

Although telling youth to "just say no" to sex is a reactive
response, bringing a strong rationale for practicing sexual abstinence
can be a proactive response. The proactive approach involves developing a rationale for abstinence prior to marriage that integrates
social science and biblically based truths. The Christian men's movement, by calling men to be faithful to their wives and to model justice, purity and righteousness to their children and to others, is also a
proactive example since it can set an agenda capable of making a significant difference.

An even more radical proactive response is for Christians to
become involved in the creation of popular art and culture in which
sex is honestly and responsibly handled. Perhaps the Christian community needs to be more open to the good that can be done by an artist such as Amy Grant, who crossed over from singing "Christian"
music to "secular" music. Rather than rejecting the artist for "giving
up her Christian witness," we need to affirm her for treating love and
sex honestly even as it is packaged as a secular product. C. S. Lewis
once said that we don't need more books about Christianity, but
rather more secular books written by Christians. Perhaps the same is
true regarding Christian involvement in the production of popular

culture. We need more Christians in the production of secular popular culture who will treat sex honestly in a way that reflects biblical values.

Developing proactive responses to inauthentic societal expressions of sexuality takes effort. Sometimes the Christian community responds reactively because it is easier. This is not enough. When so much is at stake, the Christian community needs to develop clear rationales that affirm reasons for a biblically based sexuality. The producers of popular culture have often done their homework better than the church in knowing how sex can be used as a means of earning lots of money, especially from youth. The Christian community must be at least as knowledgeable and sophisticated in exposing the dishonest portrayal of sex when it occurs.

Conclusion

We have suggested that sexual authenticity will develop in a social environment that supports and holds members accountable at the *familial, congregational* and *societal* levels. We have used the biblical concepts *covenant love, koinonia* and *neighbor,* and *shalom* as descriptors of ideal social structures that would characterize each of these three levels. When authentic sexuality exists at all levels, each will mutually reinforce the sexual authenticity of the other and of the individuals within them.

We have noted that an authentic expression of sexuality can be confused in what seems to be an enduring tension between a tendency to either *repress* or *excessively express* sexuality. When the authentic expression of sexuality is challenged at any level, the Christian church, as a called-out community, needs to be the *salt* of the earth by responsibly modeling authentic sexuality and be willing to take a prophetic role as the *light* of the world by voicing God's call for authentic expressions of sexuality. This can be a perilous task, sabotaged by either timidity on one hand or self-righteousness on the other. It is our prayer that this book presents a challenge to the community of Christian believers, who are called to sexually authentic living at the beginning of this new millennium through the power of the Holy Spirit and the life of our Lord Jesus Christ, who taught and modeled for us how to be salt and light to the world.

Suggestions for Further Reading

Grenz, S. 1997. *Sexual ethics: An evangelical perspective.* Louisville, Ky.:
    Westminster John Knox.
Laumann, E., et al. 1994. *The social organization of sexuality: Sexual prac-
    tices in the United States.* Chicago: University of Chicago Press.
Thatcher, A., and E. Stuart. 1996. *Christian perspectives on sexuality and
    gender.* Grand Rapids, Mich.: Eerdmans. See section 1, "Sexuality
    and the Christian tradition," pp. 1-51.

References

Allen, M., D. D'Alessio, and K. Brezgel. 1995. A meta-analysis summarizing the effects of pornography: II. Aggression after exposure. *Journal of Human Communication Research* 22 (2):258-83.

Allen, M., et al. 1995. Exposure to pornography and acceptance of rape myths. *Journal of Communication* 45:5-26.

Anderson, R. 1982. *On being human: Essays in theological anthropology.* Grand Rapids, Mich.: Eerdmans.

Atwater, L. 1982. *The extramarital connection: Sex, intimacy and identity.* New York: Irvington.

Axinn, W., and J. Barber. 1997. Living arrangements and family formation attitudes in early adulthood. *Journal of Marriage and the Family* 59:595-611.

Axinn, W., and A. Thornton. 1992. The relationship between cohabitation and divorce: Selectivity or causal influence? *Demography* 29:357-74.

Bailey, J. M., and A. P. Bell. 1993. Familiarity of female and male homosexuality. *Behavior, Genetics* 23 (4):313-20.

Bailey, J., and R. Pillard. 1991. A genetic study of male sexual orientation. *Archives of General Psychiatry* 48:1089-96.

Bailey, J., L. Willerman, and C. Parks. 1991. A test of the maternal stress theory of human male sexuality. *Archives of General Psychiatry* 48:1089-96.

Balswick, J., and J. Balswick. 1990. *The family: A Christian perspective on the contemporary home.* Grand Rapids, Mich.: Baker.

———. 1994. *Raging hormones: What to do when you suspect your teen may be sexually active.* Grand Rapids, Mich.: Zondervan.

———. 1999. *The family: A Christian perspective on the contemporary home.* 2d ed. See chapters 1 and 5. Grand Rapids, Mich.: Baker.

Bandura, A. 1974. Behavior theory and the models of man. *American Psychologist* (December):859-69.

———. 1978. The self system in reciprocal determinism. *American Psychologist* 33 (4):344-58.

———. 1998. Exercise of agency in personal and social change. In *Behavior and cognitive therapy today: Essays in honor of Hans J. Eysenck,* edited by E. Sanavic. Oxford: Anonima Romana.

Banks, A., and N. K. Gartrell. 1995. Hormones and sexual orientation: A questionable link. Special Issue: Sex, cell, and same-sex desire: The biology of sexual preference. *Journal of Homosexuality* 28 (3-4):247-68.

Banks, R. 1980. *Paul's idea of community.* Grand Rapids, Mich.: Eerdmans.

Barbaree, H. E., and W. L. Marshall. 1991. The role of male sexual arousal in rape: Six models. *Journal of Consulting and Clinical Psychology* 20:268-70.

Beeghley, L., and C. Sellers. 1986. Adolescents and sex: A structural theory of premarital sex in the United States. *Deviant Behavior* 7 (4):313-36.

Bell, A., M. Weinbert, and K. Hammersmith. 1981. *Sexual preference: Its development in men and women.* Bloomington: Indiana University Press.

Bell, S. T., P. J. Kuriloff, and I. Lottes. 1994. Understanding attributions of blame in stranger rape and date rape situations: An examination of gender, race, identification, and students' social perceptions of rape victims. *Journal of Applied Social Psychology* 24 (19):1719-34.

Bem, D. 1996. Exotic becomes erotic: A developmental theory of sexual orientation. *Psychological Review* 103 (2):320-35.

Bender, R. 1982. *Christians in families.* Scottdale, Penn.: Herald Press.

Bennett, G. 1987. *Crimewarps: The future of crime in America.* Garden City, N.Y.: Anchor Books.

Bennett, N. G., A. K. Blanc, and D. E. Bloom. 1988. Commitment and the modern union: Assessing the link between premarital cohabitation and subsequent marital stability. *American Sociological Review* 53 (1):127-38.

Bentler, P., and M. Newcomb. 1978. Longitudinal study of marital success and failure. *Journal of Consulting and Clinical Psychology* 46 (5):1053-70.

Berdahl, J. L., V. J. Magley, and C. R. Waldo. 1996. The sexual harassment of men? Exploring the concept with theory and data. *Psychology of Women Quarterly* 20 (4):527-47.

Berger, P. 1967. *The sacred canopy.* Garden City, N.Y.: Doubleday.

Bermant, G. 1995. To speak in chords about sexuality: Hormonal and neural modulation of physiological and behavioral function. *Neuroscience and Bio-behavioral Reviews* 19 (2): 343-48.

Bieber, I. 1962. *Homosexuality.* New York: Basic Books.

————. 1976. Psychodynamics and sexual object choices: A reply to Dr. Richard C. Friedman's paper. *Contemporay Psychoanalysis* 12:366-69.

Bigner, J., and F. Bozett. 1989. Parenting by gay fathers. *Marriage and Family Review* 14:155-75.

Bill, J., K. Tanfer, W. Grady, and D. Klepenger. 1993. The sexual behavior of men in the United States. *Family Planning Perspectives* 25:52-60.

Bingham, J., and C. Piotrowski. 1996. Online sexual addition: A contemporary enigma. *Psychological Reports* 79:257-58.

Blader, J., and W. Marshall. 1989. Is assessment of sexual arousal in males worthwhile? *Clinical Psychology Review* 9:569-87.

Booth, A., and J. M. Dabbs Jr. 1993. Testosterone and men's marriages. *Social Forces* 72 (2):463-77.

Booth, A., and D. Johnson. 1988. Premarital cohabitation and marital success. *Journal of Family Issues* 9:255-72.

Boswell, J. 1980. *Christianity, social tolerance, and homosexuality.* Chicago: University of Chicago Press.

Bowen, M. 1978. *Family therapy in clinical practice.* New York: Aronson.

Briere, J., and D. Elliott. 1994. Immediate and long-term impacts of child sexual abuse. *Future of Children* 4:54-69.

Brookings, J., A. McEvoy, and M. Reed. 1994. Sexual assault recovery and male significant others. *Families in Society: The Journal of Contemporary Human Services* 75:295-99.

Brown, W., N. Murphy, and N. Maloney. 1998. *Whatever happened to the soul? Scientific and theological portraits of human nature.* Philadelphia: Fortress.

Brownmiller, D. 1975. *Against our will.* New York, Random House.

Bruderl, J., A. Dickman, and H. Engelhardt. 1997. Premarital cohabitation and marital stability? An empirical study with the family survey. *Kolner Zeitschrift fur Soziologie und Sozialpsychologie* 49 (2):205-22.

Buechner, F. 1992. *Listen to your life: Daily meditations with Frederick Buechner.* HarperSanFrancisco.

Buhrich, N., M. Bailey, and N. G. Martin. 1991. Sexual orientation, sexual identity, and sex-dimorphic behaviors in male twins. *Behavior Genetics* 21 (1):75-97.

Bumpass, L., T. Martin, and J. Sweet. 1991. The impact of family background and early marital factors on marital disruption. *Journal of Family Issues* 12 (1):22-24.

Bumpass, L., and J. Sweet. 1989. National estimates of cohabitation. *Demography* 26:615-25.

———. 1991. The role of cohabitation in declining rates of marriage. *Journal of Marriage and the Family* 53:913-27.

Bumpass, L., J. Sweet, and A. Cherlin. 1989. The role of cohabitation in declining rates of marriage. Working paper no. 5, National Survey of Families and Households, University of Wisconsin Center for Demography and Ecology, Madison, Wis.

Burns, J. 1992. *Radical respect: A Christian approach to love, sex and dating.* Eugene, Ore.: Harvest House.

Byer, C., L. Shainberg, and G. Galliano. 1998. *Dimensions of human sexuality.* 5th ed. New York: McGraw-Hill.

Byne, W. 1994. The biological evidence challenged. *Scientific American,* May, pp. 50-55.

Byne, W., and B. Parsons. 1993. Human sexual orientation: The biological theories reappraised. *Archives of General Psychiatry* 50:228-39.

Cadwallader, M. 1966. Marriage as a wretched institution. *Atlantic Monthly* 218:62-66.

Cameron, P., and K. Cameron. 1996. Homosexual parents. *Adolescence* 31:757-76.

Carnes, P. 1989. *Contrary to love: Helping the sexual addict.* Minneapolis: CompCare.

———. 1983. *Out of the shadows: Understanding sexual addiction.* Minneapolis: CompCare.

———. 1991. *A gentle path through the twelve steps.* Minneapolis: CompCare.

———. 1992. *Don't call it love: Recovery from sexual addiction.* New York: Bantam Books.

Cassidy, L., and R. M. Hurrell. 1995. The influence of victim's attire on adolescents' judgments of date rape. *Journal of Adolescence* 30 (118):319-23.

Chatworthy, N. M., and S. Scheid. 1977. A comparison of married couples: Premarital cohabitant with non-premarital cohabitant. Unpublished manuscript, Ohio State University, Columbus.

Chicago Statistics. 1994. Contemporary sexuality. *American Association of Sex Educators, Counselors and Therapists Newsletter* 28 (11):1.

Clarkberg, M., R. M. Stolzenberg, and L. J. Waite. 1995. Attitudes, values, and entrance into cohabitational versus marital unions. *Social Forces* 74 (2):609-32.

Clayton, R., and H. Voss. 1977. Shacking up: Cohabitation in the 1970s. *Journal of Marriage and the Family* 39:273-83.

Comiskey, A. 1989. *Pursuing sexual wholeness: How Jesus heals the homosexual.* Lake Mary, Fla.: Creation House.

Cook, J., A. Boxer, and G. Herdt. 1989. First homosexual and heterosexual experiences reported by gay and lesbian youth in an urban community. Paper presented at the American Sociological Association.

Court, J., and N. Whitehead. 1994. The ten per cent solution: Homosexuality then and now. Paper presented at the 23rd International Congress of Applied Psychology.

Dannecker, M. 1983. Towards a theory of homosexuality: Socio-historical perspective. *Journal of Homosexuality* 9 (4):7.

Danzinger, C. 1976. *Unmarried heterosexual cohabitation.* New Brunswick, N. J.: Rutgers. Cited in Newcomb and Bentler 1980.

Dawn, M. J. 1993. *Sexual character: Beyond technique to intimacy.* Grand Rapids, Mich.: Eerdmans.

Deblinger, A., and A. Heflin. 1996. *Treating sexually abused children and their nonoffending parents.* Thousand Oaks, Calif.: Sage.

DeGaston, J. F., L. Jensen, and S. Weed. 1995. A closer look at adolescent sexual activity. *Journal of Youth and Adolescence* 24 (4):465-79.

DeGaston, J. F., S. Weed, and L. Jensen. 1996. Understanding gender differences in adolescent sexuality. *Adolescence* 31 (121):217-31.

DeMaris, A., and G. Leslie. 1984. Cohabitation with the future spouse: Its influence upon marital satisfaction and communication. *Journal of Marriage and the Family* 46:77-84.

DeMaris, A., and W. MacDonald. 1993. Premarital cohabitation and marital instability: A test of the unconventionality hypothesis. *Journal of Marriage and the Family* 55:399-407.

DeMaris, A., and K. Rao. 1992. Premarital cohabitation and subsequent marital stability in the United States: A reassessment. *Journal of Marriage and the Family* 55:178-90.

Diamond, M. 1997. Sexual identity and sexual orientation in children with traumatized or ambiguous genitalia. *Journal of Sex Research* 32:199-211.

Doell, R. G. 1995. Sexuality in the brain. Special issue: Sex, cell and same-sex desire. Part 2: The biology of sexual preference. *Journal of Homosexuality* 28 (3-4):345-54.

Donnelly, D. A. 1993. Sexually inactive marriages. *Journal of Sex Research* 30 (2):171-79.

Donovan, C. 1996. Young people, alcohol and sex: Taking advantage. *Youth and Policy* 52 (spring):30-37.

Dorner, G. 1976. *Hormones and brain differentiation.* Amsterdam: Elsevier.

Dorner, G., et al. 1983. Stressful events in prenatal life of bi- and homosexual men. *Experimental and Clinical Endocrinology* 81:83-87.

Draucker, C. B. 1996. Family-of-origin variables and adult female survivors of childhood sexual abuse: A review of the research. *Journal of Child Sexual Abuse* 5 (4):35-63.

Duncombe, J. A., and D. Marsden. 1994. *Whose orgasm is this anyway? "Sex work" and "emotion work" in long-term couple relationships.* Los Angeles: American Sociological Association.

Durfield, R., and R. Durfield. 1991. *Raising them chaste.* Minneapolis: Bethany.

Equal Employment Opportunity Commission. 1980, April. Guidelines on discrimination because of sex under title VII of the civil rights act, as amended adoption of interim interpretive guideline. Title 29-labor, chapter 14, part 1604. Washington, D.C.: Government Printing Office.

Ehrensaft, D. l992. *Parenting together: Men and women sharing the care of children*. Chicago: University of Illinois Press.

Ellen, J. M., S. Cahn, S. L. Eyre, and C. B. Boyer. 1996. Types of adolescent sexual relationships and associated perceptions about condom use. *Journal of Adolescent Health* 18 (6):417-21.

Ellis, H. 1936. *Studies in the psychology of sex*. New York: Random House.

Ellis, L. 1991. A synthesized (biosocial) theory of rape. *Journal of Consulting and Clinical Psychology* 59:631-42.

Ellis, L., and M. Ames. 1987. Neuro-hormonal functioning and sexual orientation: A theory of homosexuality-heterosexuality. *Psychological Bulletin* 101:233-58.

Ellis, L., M. Ames, W. Peckham, and D. Burke. 1988. Sexual orientation of human offspring may be altered by severe maternal stress during pregnancy. *Journal of Sex Research* 25:152-57.

Erikson, E. 1968. *Childhood and society*. New York: W. W. Norton.

Eyre, S. L., N. W. Read, and S. G. Millstein. 1997. Adolescent sexual strategies. *Journal of Adolescent Health* 20 (4):286-93.

Faust, J., M. K. Runyon, and M. C. Kenny. 1995. Family variables associated with the onset and impact of intrafamilial childhood sexual abuse. Special issue: The impact of the family on child adjustment and psycho-pathology. *Clinical Psychology Review* 15 (5):443-56.

Federal Bureau of Investigation. 1984. *Uniform crime reports for the United States*. Washington, D. C.: Department of Justice.

———. 1990. *Uniform crime reports for the United States*. Washington, D.C.: Department of Justice.

Fergusson, D. 1999. *Childhood sexual abuse: An evidence-based perspective*. Thousand Oaks, Calif.: Sage.

Finkelhor, D. 1994. Current information on the scope and nature of child abuse. *The Future of Children* 4:31-53.

———. 1980. Sex among siblings: A survey on prevalence, variety, and effects. *Archives of Sexual Behavior* 9:171-94.

———. 1986. *A sourcebook on child sexual abuse*. Newbury Park, Calif.: Sage.

Finkelson, L., and R. Oswalt. 1995. College date rape: Incidence and reporting. *Psychological Reports* 77 (2):526.

Firth, M. T. 1997. Male partner of female victims of child sexual abuse: Treatment issues and approaches. *Journal of Sexual and Marital Therapy* 12 (2):159-71.

Fischer, G. 1996. Deceptive, verbally cohesive college males: Attitudinal predictors and lies told. *Archives of Sexual Behavior* 25:527-33.

Fitzgerald, L., and S. Shullman. 1993. Sexual harassment: A research analysis agenda for the 1990s. Special issue: Sexual harassment in the workplace. *Journal of Vocational Behavior* 42:5-27.

Ford, C. A., and F. J. Donis. 1996. The relationship between age and gender in workers' attitudes toward harassment. *Journal of Psychology* 130 (6):627-33.

Forman, D., and C. Chilvers. 1989. Sexual behavior of young and middle aged men in England and Wales. *British Medical Journal* 298:138-48.

Forste, R., and T. Heaton. 1988. Initiation of sexual activity among female adolescents. *Youth and Society* 19:250-68.

Forste, R., and K. Tanfer. 1996. Sexual exclusivity among dating, cohabitating, and married. *Journal of Marriage and the Family* 58:33-47.

Fortune, M. 1983. *Sexual violence: The unmentionable sin.* New York: Pilgrim.

———. 1996. *Sexual abuse prevention: A study for teenagers.* New York: United Church Press.

Frazier, E. 1986. *Barth and an evangelical feminist theology.* Ph.D. diss., Vanderbilt University.

Friesen, L. 1989. *Sexuality: A biblical model in historical perspective.* D.Min. diss., Fuller Theological Seminary.

Freud, S. 1905. Three essays on the theory of sexuality. In *The Standard Edition* 7 (London: Hogarth Press, 1953), p. 182.

Fromm, E. 1956. *The art of loving.* New York: Bantam Books.

Gallagher, B. J., J. A. McFalls, and C. N. Vreeland. 1993. Preliminary results from a national survey of psychiatrists concerning the etiology of male homosexuality. *Journal of Psychology: A Journal of Human Behavior* 30 (3-4):1-3.

Gelles, R., and G. Wolfner. 1994. Sexual deviance and victimization: A life course and life span perspective. In *Sexuality Across the Life Course*, edited by A. Rossi. Chicago: University of Chicago Press.

Glick, P., and G. Spanier. 1980. Married and unmarried cohabitation in the United States. *Journal of Marriage and the Family* 42 (1):19-30.

Goleman, D. 1985. Study lists ways to deter rapists. (Study by R. Prentky and A. Burgess.) *New York Times*, May 5, 1985, p. 35.

Goodman, A.. 1992. Sexual addiction: Designation and treatment. *Journal of Sex and Marital Therapy* 18 (4):303-14.

Goodman, P. 1960. *Growing up absurd*. New York: Vintage.

Grant, J. M., W. A. Folger, and J. J. Hornak. 1995. College students' perception of victim responsibility in an acquaintance rape situation. *College Student Journal* 29 (4):532-35.

Green, R. 1987. *The "sissy-boy syndrome" and the development of homosexuality*. New Haven, Conn.: Yale University Press.

Greil, A. L., K. L. Porter, and T. A. Leitko. 1987. So near and yet so far: Sex and intimacy among infertile couples. *Society for the Study of Social Problems* 2 (2):117-38.

Grenz, S. 1997. *Sexual ethics: An evangelical perspective*. Louisville, Ky.: Westminster John Knox.

Gunther, A. C. 1995. Overrating the X-rating: The third-person perception and support for censorship of pornography. *Journal of Communication* 45:138.

Gwartney-Gibbs, P. 1986. The institutionalization of premarital cohabitation: Estimates from marriage license applications, 1970 and 1980. *Journal of Marriage and the Family* 48:423-34.

Hall, D., and J. Zhao. 1995. Cohabitation and divorce in Canada testing the selectivity hypothesis. *Journal of Marriage and the Family* 57:421-27.

Hall, D. R. 1996. Marriage as a pure relationship: Exploring the link between premarital cohabitation and divorce in Canada. *Journal of Comparative Family Studies* 27 (1):1-12.

Hamer, D. H. 1993. A linkage between DNA markers on the X chromosome and male sexual orientation. *Science* 261 (5119):321-27.

Harry, J. 1988. Parental physical abuse and sexual orientation in males. Paper presented to the American Sociological Association in Atlanta.

Hart, A. 1995. *The sexual male*. Waco, Tex.: Word.

Hart, A., C. Weber, and D. Taylor. 1998. *Secrets of Eve*. Waco, Tex.: Word.

Hatfield, E., G. W. Walster, and E. Berscheid. 1978. *Equity theory and research.* Boston: Allyn & Bacon.

Haynes, J. D. 1995. A critique of the possibility of genetic inheritance of homosexual orientation. Special issue: Sex, cells, and same-sex desire: The biology of sexual preference. *Journal of Homosexuality* 28 (1-2):91-113.

Hays, K., and S. Stanley. 1996. The impact of childhood sexual abuse on women's dental experience. *Journal of Child Sexual Abuse* 5:65-74.

Hays, R. 1996. *The moral vision of the New Testament.* San Francisco: Harper Collins. See chapter 16, "Homosexuality," pp. 379-406.

Henderson-King, D. H., and J. Veroff. 1994. Sexual satisfaction and marital well-being in the first years of marriage. *Journal of Social and Personal Relationships* 11 (4):509-34.

Herrn, R. 1995. On the history of biological theories of homosexuality used to justify homosexuality. Special issue: Sex, cells, and same-sex desire: The biology of sexual preference. *Journal of Homosexuality* 28 (1-2):31-56.

Heston, L., and J. Shields. 1968. Homosexuality in twins: A family study and a registry study. *Archives of General Psychiatry* 18:149-60.

Hirshfield, M. 1935. *Sex in human relationships,* translated by J. Rodker. London: John Lane.

Hite, S. 1976. *The Hite report.* New York: Macmillan.

Holcomb, D. R., P. D. Sarvela, K. A. Sondag, and L. H. Holcomb. 1993. An evaluation of a mixed-gender date rape prevention workshop. *Journal of American College Health* 41 (4):159-64.

Holzman, C. 1994. Multicultural perspectives on counseling survivors of rape. *Journal of Social Distress and the Homeless* 3:81-97.

Horwitz, A., and H. White. 1998. The relationship of cohabitation and mental health: A study of a young adult cohort. *Journal of Marriage and the Family* 60:505-14.

Houston, S., and N. Hwang. 1996. Correlates of the objective and subjective experiences of sexual harassment in high school. *Sex Roles* 34 (3-4):189-204.

Hudson, J. 1996. Characteristics of the incestuous family. In *Women, Abuse, and the Bible,* edited by C. Kroeger and J. Beck. Grand Rapids, Mich.: Baker.

Hughes, P. 1993. *Christian ethics in secular society.* Grand Rapids, Mich.: Baker.

Humphreys, T. P., and E. Herold. 1996. Date rape: A comparative analysis and integration of theory. *Canadian Journal of Human Sexuality* 5 (2):69-82.

Hunt, M. 1959. *The natural history of love.* New York: Grove Press.

Hunter, J. 1983. *American evangelism: Conservative religion and the quandary of modernity.* New Brunswick, N.J.: Rutgers University Press.

Hunter, J. 1990. Violence against lesbian and gay male youths, *Journal of Interpersonal Violence* 5:295-300.

Hunter, J. and M. Rosario. 1994. Suicidal behavior and gay-related stress among gay and bisexual male adolescents, *Journal of Adolescent Research* 9:498-508.

Hyde, J. S. 1994. *Understanding human sexuality.* New York: McGraw-Hill.

Jacques, M., and K. Chason. 1979. Cohabitation: Its impact on marital success. *Family Coordinator* 28:35-39.

Janssen, E. 1995. Understanding the rapist's mind. *Perspectives in Psychiatric Care* 31:9-13.

Javaid, G. 1993. The children of homosexual and heterosexual single mothers. *Child Psychiatry and Human Development* 23:235-48.

Jehu, D. 1992. Adult survivors of sexual abuse. In *Assessment of family violence: A clinical and legal sourcebook.* New York: John Wiley.

Jewett, P. K. 1976. *Man as male and female.* Grand Rapids, Mich.: Eerdmans.

Johnson, J. D., L. A. Jackson, L. Gatto, and A. Nowak. 1995. Differential male and female responses to inadmissible sexual history information regarding a rape victim. *Journal of Basic and Applied Social Psychology* 16 (4):503-13.

Johnson, R., A. Nahmins, and L. Madger. 1989. *Sexual behavior in the human male.* Philadelphia: Saunders.

Jones, S., and B. Jones. 1993. *How and when to tell your kids about sex.* Colorado Springs: NavPress.

Joy, D. M. 1986. *Re-Bonding: Preventing and restoring damaged relationships,* Waco, Tex.: Word.

Kahn, J. R., and K. A. London. 1991. Premarital sex and the risk of divorce. *Journal of Marriage and the Family* 53 (4):845-55.

Kaiser, W. 1983. *Toward Old Testament Ethics.* Grand Rapids, Mich.: Zondervan.

Kanin, E. 1985. Date rapists: Differential sexual socialization and relative deprivation. *Archives of Sexual Behavior* 14:219-31.

Kallmann, F. 1952. Comparative twin study on the genetic aspects of male homosexuality. *Journal of Nervous and Mental Disease* 115:283-98.

Kaplan, M. S., and A. Green. 1995. Incarcerated female sexual offender: A comparison of sexual histories with eleven female non-sexual offenders. *Sexual Abuse Journal of Research and Treatment* 7 (4):287-300.

Kendall-Tackett, K., A. Williams, and D. Finkelhor. 1993. Impact of sexual abuse on children: A review and synthesis of recent empirical studies. *Psychological Bulletin* 113:164-80.

Kerr, M. and M. Bowen, M. 1988. *Family evaluation.* New York: W. W. Norton.

King, B., and J. Lorusso. 1997. Discussions in the home about sex: Different recollections by parents and children. *Journal of Sex and Marital Therapy* 23 (1):52-60.

Kinsey, A., W. Pomeroy, and C. Martin. 1948. *Sexual behavior in the human male.* Philadelphia: Saunders.

———. 1952. *Sexual behavior in the human female.* Philadelphia: Saunders.

Kliever, D. Managing sexual feeling in the Christian community. *Journal of Pastoral Counseling* 5 (4):51.

Laumann, E., J. Gagnon, R. Michael, and S. Michaels. 1994. *The social organization of sexuality: Sexual practices in the United States.* Chicago: University of Chicago Press.

Lebowitz, L., and S. Roth. 1994. "I felt like a slut": The cultural context and women's response to being raped. *Journal of Traumatic Stress* 7:363-89.

Lee, V., R. Croninger, E. Linn, and X. Chen. 1996. The culture of sexual harassment in American secondary schools. *American Educational Research Journal* 33:383-417.

LeVay, S. 1991. A difference in hypothalamic structure between heterosexual and homosexual men. *Science* 253:1034-36.

Lewis, C. S. 1960. *Mere Christianity.* New York: Macmillan.

———. 1963. *Four loves.* London: Collins/Fontana.

Lindsey, B., and W. Evans. 1927. *Compassionate marriage*. New York: Boni & Liveright.

Lisak, D., and C. Ivan. 1995. Deficits in intimacy and empathy in sexually aggressive men. *Journal of Interpersonal Violence* 10:296-308.

Loe, M. 1996. Working for men: At the intersection of power, gender, and sexuality. *Sociological Inquiry* 66 (4):399-421.

Loftus, E. 1993. False memory syndrome. *Family Therapy Networker*, September/November, p. 27.

Long, E., R. Cate, D. Fehsenfelt, and K. Williams. 1996. A longitudinal assessment of a measure of premarital conflict. *Family Relations* 45:302-8.

Lottes, I. L. 1997. Sexual coercion among university students: A comparison of the United States and Sweden. *Journal of Sex Research* 34 (1):67-76.

Luo, T. Y. 1996. Sexual harassment in the Chinese workplace: Attitudes toward and experiences of sexual harassment among workers in Taiwan. *Violence Against Women* 2 (3):284-301.

MacKay, P. 1974. *The clockwork image*. Downers Grove, Ill.: InterVarsity Press.

Macklin, E. D. 1972. Heterosexual cohabitation among unmarried college students. *Family Coordinator* 21:463-72.

———. 1974. Cohabitation in college: Going very steady. *Psychology Today* 8 (6):53-59.

———. 1978. Review of research on non-marital cohabitation in the United States. In *Exploring intimate life styles*, edited by B. I. Murstein. New York: Springer.

———. 1983. Non-marital heterosexual cohabitation: An overview. In *Contemporary families and alternative lifestyles: Handbook on research and theory*, edited by E. D. Macklin and R. H. Rubin. Beverly Hills: Sage Publications.

Madanes, C. 1990. *Sex, love and violence: Strategies for transformation*. New York: W. W. Norton.

———. 1995. *The violence of men: New techniques for working with abusive families: A therapy of social action*. San Francisco: Jossey Bass.

Maddock, J. 1975. Sexual health and health care. *Postgraduate Medicine* 58:52-58.

Maddock, J., and N. Larson. 1995. *Incestuous families: An ecological approach to understanding and treatment.* New York: W. W. Norton.

Malamuth, N. M. 1981. Rape proclivity in males. *Journal of Social Issues* 37 (4):138-57.

———. 1984. Aggression against women: Cultural and individual causes. In *Pornography and sexual aggression,* edited by N. Malamuth and E. Donnerstein. New York: Academic.

———. 1996. Sexually explicit media, gender differences, and evolutionary theory. *Journal of Communication* 46 (3):8-31.

Malamuth, N. M., M. Heim, and S. Feshback. 1980. Sexual responsiveness of college students to rape depictions: Inhibitory and disinhibitory effects. *Journal of Personality and Social Psychology* 38:399-408.

Malamuth, N. M., R. J. Sockloskie, M. P. Koss, and J. S. Tanaka. 1991. Characteristics of aggressors against women: Testing a model using a national sample of college students. *Journal of Consulting and Clinical Psychology* 59:670-781.

Markowski, E. M., and M. J. Johnston. 1980. Behavior, temperament and idealization of cohabiting couples who married. *International Journal of Sociology of the Family* 10:115-25.

Masters, W. H., and V. E. Johnson. 1979. *Homosexuality in perspective.* New York: Bantam.

McCann, J. T., and M. K. Biaggio. 1989. Sexual satisfaction in marriage as a function of life meaning. *Archives of Sexual Behavior* 18 (1):59-72.

McLanahan, S., and L. Bumpass. 1988. Intergenerational consequences of family disruption. *American Journal of Sociology* 94:130-52.

McLean, S. 1984. The language of covenant and a theology of the family. Paper presented at seminar, Consultation on a Theology of the Family. Fuller Theological Seminary, November 19-20.

McRae, S. 1997. Cohabitation: A trial run for marriage? *Journal of Sexual and Marital Therapy* 12 (3):259-73.

Mead, M. l966. Marriage in two steps. *Redbook* 127:48-49.

Miller, B., and K. Moore. l990. Adolescent sexual behavior, pregnancy, and parenting: Research through the 1980s. *Journal of Marriage and the Family* 51:1025-44.

Miller, B., and T. Olson. l988. Sexual attitudes and behavior of high school students in relation to background and contextual factors. *Journal of Sex Research* 24:194-200.

Miller, B. C., and T. B. Heaton. 1991. Age at first sexual intercourse and the timing of marriage and childbirth. *Journal of Marriage and the Family* 53 (3):719-32.

Miller, L. L. 1997. Not just weapons of the weak: Gender harassment as a form of protest for army men. *Social Psychology Quarterly* 60 (1):32-51.

Moberley, E. 1983. *Psychogenesis*. London: Routledge.

———. 1993. *Homosexuality: A new Christian ethic*. Greenwood, S.C.: Attic Press.

Moeller, I., and J. Sherlock. 1981. Making it legal: A comparison of previously cohabiting and engaged newlyweds. *Journal of Sociology and Social Welfare* 8:97-110.

Money, J. 1987. Sin, sickness, or status? *American Psychologist* 42 (4):384-99.

Monti, J. 1995. *Arguing about sex: The rhetoric of Christian sexual morality*. Albany, N.Y.: SUNY Press.

Moser, C. 1993. A response to Aviel Goodman's "Sexual addiction": Designation and treatment. *Journal of Sex and Marital Therapy* 19 (3):220-24.

Mott, S. 1982. *Biblical ethics and social change*. New York: Oxford University Press.

Mouw, R. 1988. Toward a theology of social change. Paper presented at the second IFACS Sociology Conference at Wheaton College, Wheaton, Ill.

Muehlenhard, C. L., P. A. Harney, and J. M. Jones. 1992. From "victim-precipitated rape" to "date rape": How far have we come? *Annual Review of Sex Research* 3:219-53.

Nathanson, S. 1987. *Ultimate penalties: capital punishment, life imprisonment, physical torture*. Columbus: Ohio State University Press.

Neal, C. J., and M. W. Mangis. 1995. Unwanted sexual experiences among Christian college women: Saying no on the inside. *Journal of Psychology and Theology* 23 (3):171-79.

Nelson, J., and S. Longfellow. 1994. *Sexuality and the sacred: Sources for theological reflection*. Louisville, Ky.: Westminster John Knox.

Newcomb, M. 1986. Cohabitation, marriage and divorce among adolescents and young adults. *Journal of Social and Personal Relationships* 3:473-94.

Newcomb, M. D., and P. M. Bentler. 1980. Assessment of personality and demographic aspects of cohabitation and marital success. *Journal of Personality Assessment* 4:11-24.

Nicolosi, J. 1991. *Reparative therapy of male homosexuality.* Northvale, N.J.: Jason Aronson.

Nock, S. L. 1994. A comparison of marriages and cohabiting relationships: Commitment relationship quality, intergenerational integration and ideal fertility. *Journal of Family Issues* 16 (1):53-76.

Olthuis, J. 1975. *I pledge you my troth: A Christian view of marriage, family, friendship.* New York: Harper & Row.

Orten, J. 1990. Coming up short: The physical, cognitive, and social effects of Turner's Syndrome. *Health and Social Work* 15 (2):100-106.

Pallard, P. 1995. Pornography and sexual aggression. *Current Psychology* 14:200-221.

Paul, J. P. 1993. Childhood cross-gender behavior and adult homosexuality: The resurgence of biological models of sexuality. Special issue: If you seduce a straight person, can you make them gay? Issues in biological essentialism versus social constructionism in gay and lesbian identities. *Journal of Homosexuality* 24 (3-4):41-54.

Payne, L. 1984. *The healing of the homosexual.* Westchester, Ill.: Crossway.

Penner, C., and J. Penner. 1981. *A gift of sex: A guide to sexual fulfillment.* Waco, Tex.: Word.

————. 1994. *Getting your sex life off to a great start.* Waco, Tex.: Word.

Perdue, L., J. Blenkinsopp, J. Collins, and C. Meyers. 1997. *Families in ancient Israel.* Louisville, Ky.: Westminster John Knox.

Peterman, D. J. 1975. Does living together before marriage make for a better marriage? *Medical Aspects of Human Sexuality* 9:39-41.

Peters, D., and L. Range. 1995. Childhood sexual abuse and current suicidality in college women and men. *Journal of Child Abuse and Neglect* 19:335-41.

Petersen, J., A. Kretchmer, B. Nellis, K. Lever., and R. Hertz. 1983. *The Playboy readers' sex survey,* parts 1 and 2. *Playboy,* January, 108; March, 90.

Pillard, R. C., and J. D. Weinrich. 1986. Evidence of the familial nature of male homosexuality. *Archives of General Psychiatry* 43 (8):808-12.

Pittman, F. 1987. *Turning points: Treating families in transition and crisis.*

New York: W. W. Norton.

———. 1989. *Private lies: Infidelity and the betrayal of intimacy.* New York: W. W. Norton.

Pittman, F., and T. Wagers. 1995. Crises of infidelity. In *Clinical handbook of couple therapy,* edited by N. Jacobson and A. Gurman. New York: Guilford Press.

Popenoe, D., and B. Whitehead. 1999. Should we live together? What young adults need to know about cohabitation before marriage. <http://marriage.rutgers.edu:80/shouldwe.htm>.

Posner, R. 1992. *Sex and reason.* Cambridge, Mass.: Harvard University Press.

Prins, K. S., B. P. Buunk, and N. W. Van Yperen. 1993. Equity, normative disapproval and extramarital relationships. *Journal of Social and Personal Relationships* 10 (1):39-53.

Quinsey, V., and T. Chaplin. 1984. Stimulus control of rapists and non-sex offender's sexual arousal. *Behavioral Assessment* 6:169-76.

Raviv, M. 1993. Personality characteristics of sexual addicts and pathological gamblers. *Journal of Gambling Studies* 9 (1):17-30.

Recker, G. 1986. The family and gender identity disorders. *Journal of Family and Culture* 2-3:28-31.

Regan, P. C., and E. Berscheid. 1997. Gender differences in characteristics desired in a potential sexual and marriage partner. *Journal of Psychology and Human Sexuality* 9 (1):25-37.

Reid, K., and M. Fortune. 1994. *Preventing child sexual abuse: A curriculum for children ages five through eight.* New York: United Church Press.

Reid, K. S., R. Wampler, and D. K. Taylor. 1996. The "alienated" partner: Responses to traditional therapies for adult sex abuse survivors. *Journal of Marital and Family Therapy* 22 (4):443-53.

Reisman, J., E. Eichel, J. Court, and J. Muir. 1990. *Kinsey, sex, and fraud: The indoctrination of a people.* Lafayette, Ind.: Huntington House.

Reiss, I. 1986. *Journey into sexuality.* Englewood Cliff, N.J.: Prentice Hall.

Reiss, I,. R. Anderson, and G. Sponaugle. 1980. A multivariate model of the determinants of extramarital sexual permissiveness. *Journal of Marriage and the Family* 42:395-411.

Renshaw, K. L. 1994. Child molesters: Do those molested as children report larger numbers of victims than those who deny childhood sexual abuse? *Journal of Addictions and Offender Counseling* 15 (1):24-32.

Resick, P. 1993. The psychological impact of rape. *Journal of Interpersonal Violence* 8:223-55.

Rich, A. 1986. *Of woman born.* New York: W. W. Norton. See p. 225.

Ricoeur, P. 1967. *The symbolism of evil,* translated by E. Buchanan. New York: Harper & Row.

Ridley, C., D. Peterman, and A. Avery. 1978. Cohabitation: Does it make for a better marriage? *Family Coordinator* 27:130-44.

Riesman, D. 1950. *The lonely crowd.* New Haven, Conn.: Yale University Press.

Risman, B., C. Hill, R. Zick, and L. Peplau. 1981. Living together in college. *Journal of Marriage and the Family* 43:77-83.

Rogers, J. K., and K. D. Henson. 1997. "Hey, why don't you wear a shorter skirt?" Structural vulnerability and the organization of sexual harassment in temporary clerical employment. *Gender and Society* 11 (2):215-37.

Rogers, S., and C. Turner. 1991. Male-male sexual contact in the U.S.A.: Findings from five sample surveys, 1970-1990. *Journal of Sex Research* 28:491-519.

Romano, E., and R. V. DeLuca. 1996. Characteristics of perpetrators with histories of sexual abuse. *International Journal of Offender Therapy and Comparative Criminology* 40 (2):147-56.

Romans, S., J. Martin, and P. Mullen. 1996. Women's self-esteem: A community study of women who report and do not report childhood sexual abuse. *British Journal of Psychiatry* 169:696-704.

Romans, S. E., J. L. Martin, J. C. Anderson, and M. L. O'Shea, et al. 1995. Factors that mediate between child sexual abuse and adult psychological outcome. *Psychological Medicine* 25 (1):127-42.

Roosa, M., J. Tein, C. Reinholt, and P. Angelini. 1997. The relationship of childhood sexual abuse to teenage pregnancy. *Journal of Marriage and the Family* 59:131-42.

Rosenbaum, E., and D. B. Kandel. 1990. Early onset of adolescent sexual behavior and drug involvement. *Journal of Marriage and the Family* 52 (3):783-98.

Ross, L. F. 1996. Adolescent sexuality and public policy: A liberal response. *Politics and the Life Sciences* 15 (1):13-21.

Rossi, A. 1994. *Sexuality across the life course.* Chicago: University of Chicago Press.

Rousenau, D. 1994. *A celebration of sex: A Christian couple's manual.* Nashville: Thomas Nelson.

Rousseau, M., and C. Gallagher. 1986. *Sex is holy.* Amity, N.Y.: Amity House.

Russell, D. E. H. 1986. The incest legacy: Why today's abused children become tomorrow's victims of rape. *The Sciences* 26 (2):28-32.

Sanday, P. 1981. The socio-cultural context of rape: A cross-cultural study. *Journal of Social Issues* 37:5-27.

Sandefur, G., S. McLanahan, and R. Wojtkiewicz. 1992. The effects of parental marital status during adolescence on high-school graduation. *Social Forces* 71:103-21.

Saunders, R. M., and P. J. Naus. 1993. The impact of social content and audience factors on responses to sexually explicit videos. *Journal of Sex Education and Therapy* 19 (2):117-30.

Scanzoni, L., and V. R. Mollenkott. 1978. *Is the homosexual my neighbor?* New York: Harper & Row.

Schaumberg, H., and H. Schaumberg. 1997. *False intimacy: Understanding the struggle of sexual addiction.* Colorado Springs: NavPress.

Schewe, P. A., and W. O'Donohue. 1996. Rape prevention with high-risk males: Short-term outcome of two interventions. *Journal of Archives of Sexual Behavior* 25 (5):455-71.

Schillebeeckx, E. 1965. *Marriage: Secular reality and saving mystery.* Vol. 2, *Marriage in the history of the church.* London: Sheed and Ward.

Schnarch, D. 1991. *Constructing the sexual crucible.* New York: W. W. Norton.

———. 1993. Treating affairs in the sexual crucible. *American Association of Sex Educators, Counselors and Therapists Newsletter* 27 (9):1-4.

———. 1997. *The passionate marriage.* New York: W. W. Norton.

Schneider, H. J. 1996. Violence in the mass media. *Journal on Studies of Crime and Crime Prevention* 5 (1):59-71.

Schoen, R., and D. Owens. 1992. A further look at first unions and first marriages. In *The changing American family,* edited by S. South and S. Tolnay. Boulder, Colo.: Westview.

Schoen, R., and R. Weinick. 1993. Partner choice in marriages and cohabitations. *Journal of Marriage and the Family* 55:408-14.

Schuklenk, U., and M. Ristow. 1996. The ethics of research into the causes of homosexuality. *Journal of Homosexuality* 31 (3):5-30.

Schultz, Q., R. Anker, J. Bratt, W. Romanowski, J. Worst, and L. Zuidervaart. 1991. *Dancing in the dark: Youth, popular culture and the electronic media.* Grand Rapids, Mich.: Eerdmans.

Scriven, M. l968. Putting the sex back into sex education. *Phi Delta* 49.

Selby, P. 1996. Is the church a family? In *The family in theological perspective*, edited by S. Barton. Edinburgh: T & T Clark.

Sex Addicts Anonymous. *Sex as an addiction.* Northbrook, Ill.: Sex Addicts Anonymous.

Sheldon-Keller, A., E. Lloyd–McGarvey, M. West, and R. Canterbury. 1994. Attachment and assessment of blame in date rape scenarios. *Social Behavior and Personality* 22:313-18.

Smedes, L. 1993. *Forgive and forget.* San Francisco: Harper.

Smedes, L. B. 1976. *Sex for Christians.* Grand Rapids, Mich.: Eerdmans.

Smedes, L. B. F. 1994. *Sex for Christians.* Rev. ed. Grand Rapids, Mich.: Eerdmans.

Smelser, N. 1973. Processes of social change. In *Sociology: An introduction*, edited by N. Smelser. New York: Wiley.

Smith, A., and J. Minson. 1997. Discipline. *Economy and Society* 26 (2):191-210.

Song, J. A., M. B. Bergen, and W. R. Schumm. Sexual satisfaction among Korean-American couples in the midwestern United States. *Journal of Sex and Marital Therapy* 21 (3):147-58.

Spanier, G. 1983. Married and unmarried cohabitation in the United States: 1980. *Journal of Marriage and the Family* 45:277-88.

Spong, J. S. l988. *Living in sin? A bishop rethinks human sexuality.* San Francisco: Harper & Row.

Steele, T. 1992. Lesbian identity and childhood abuse: Facts and fallacies. Paper presented at the American Sociological Association in Pittsburgh.

Sternberg, R. 1987. A triangular theory of love. *Psychological Review* 93:119-35.

Stets, J. E. 1993. The link between past and present intimate relationships. *Journal of Family Issues* 14 (2):236-60.

Stets, J. E., and M. A. Straus. 1989. The marriage license as a hitting license: A comparison of assaults in dating, cohabiting, and married couples. *Journal of Family Violence* 4 (2):161-80.

Storaska, F. 1975. *How to say "no" to a rapist and survive.* New York: Random House.

Storms, M. 1981. A theory of erotic orientation development. *Psycholog-ical Review* 88:340-53.

Stott, J. 1998. *Same-sex partnerships: A Christian perspective.* Grand Rap-ids, Mich.: Baker.

Strong, B., and R. Reynolds. 1982. *Understanding our sexuality.* St. Paul, Minn.: West.

Strouse, J., M. Goodwin, and B. Roscoe. 1994. Correlates of attitudes toward sexual harassment among early adolescents. *Sex Roles* 31:559-77.

Surra, C. 1990. Research and theory on mate selection and premarital relationships in the 1980s. *Journal of Marriage and the Family* 52:844-65.

Sweet, J., L. Bumpass, and V. Call. 1988. The design and context of the national survey of families and households. Working paper no. 1, National Survey of Families and Households, University of Wis-consin Center for Demography and Ecology, Madison, Wis.

Tan, A. 1993. *The joy luck club.* New York: Vintage.

Tanfer, K. 1987. Patterns of premarital cohabitation among never-married women in the United States. *Journal of Marriage and the Family* 49:483-95.

Tangri, S., M. Burt, and L. Johnson. 1982. Sexual harassment at work: Three explanatory models. *Journal of Social Issues* 384:33-54.

Tangri, S., and S. Hayes. 1997. Theories of sexual harassment. In *Sexual harassment: Theory, research, and treatment,* edited by W. O'Donohue. Boston: Allyn & Bacon.

Tannahill, R. 1980. *Sex in history.* New York: Stein & Day.

Tasker, F., and S. Golombok. 1995. Adults raised as children in lesbian families. *American Journal of Orthopsychiatry* 65:203-15.

Thacker, R. A. 1996. A descriptive study of situational and individual influences upon individuals' responses to sexual harassment. *Human Relations* 49 (8):1105-22.

Thatcher, A. 1993. *Liberating sex: A Christian theology.* London: SPCK.

Thatcher, A., and E. Stuart. 1996. *Christian perspectives on sexuality and gender.* Grand Rapids, Mich.: Eerdmans. See section 5, Sexuality and spirituality.

Thomson, E., and U. Colella. 1992. Cohabitation and marital stability: Quality or commitment? *Journal of Marriage and the Family* 54:259-67.

Thornton, A., W. Axinn, and J. Teachman. 1995. The influence of school enrollment and accumulation on cohabitation and marriage in early adulthood. *American Sociological Review* 24:323-40.

Thornton, A., and D. Camburn. 1987. The influence of the family on premarital sexual attitudes and behavior. *Demography* 24:323-40.

———. 1989. Religious participation and adolescent sexual behavior. *Journal of Marriage and the Family* 51:641-53.

Timmerman, G., and C. Bajema. 1996. Limited policy: Management policy against sexual harassment in secondary schools. *Comenius* 16 (3):306-19.

Tomasson, R. 1998. Modern Sweden: The declining importance of marriage. *Scandinavian Review* (August):83-89.

Travin, S. 1995. Compulsive sexual behaviors. *Clinical Sexuality* 18 (special issue):155-69.

Trepper, T., and M. Barrett. 1989. *Systemic treatment of incest: A therapeutic handbook.* New York: Brunner/Mazel.

Trible, P. 1987. *God and the rhetoric of sexuality.* Philadelphia: Fortress.

Trobisch, W. 1968. *Essays on love: A His reader.* Downers Grove, Ill.: InterVarsity Press.

Trost, J. 1975. Married and unmarried cohabitation: The case of Sweden, with some comparison. *Journal of Marriage and the Family* 37:677-82.

Truman, D. M., D. M. Tokar, and A. R. Fischer. 1996. Dimensions of masculinity: Relations to date rape supportive attitudes and sexual aggression in dating situations. *Journal of Counseling and Development* 74 (6):555-62.

Tubman, J. G., M. Windle, and R. C. Windle. 1996. Cumulative sexual intercourse patterns among middle adolescents: Problem behavior precursors and concurrent health risk behaviors. *Journal of Adolescent Health* 18 (3):182-91.

Udry. J. R. 1988. Biological predispositions and social control in adolescent sexual behavior. *American Sociological Review* 53:709-22.

U.S. Bureau of the Census. 1988. *Households, families, marital status, and living arrangements: March 1988 advance report.* Current Population Reports, series P-20, no. 432. Washington, D.C.

U.S. Public Health Service. 1992. *Latest facts about AIDS, American Red Cross, U.S. Public Health Service.* Washington, D.C.

Ussher, J., and C. Dewberry. 1995. The nature and long-term effects of childhood sexual abuse: A survey of adult women survivors in Britain. *British Journal of Clinical Psychology* 34 (2):177-92.

Van Leeuwen, M., A. Knoppers, M. Koch, D. Schuurman, and H. Sterk, 1993. *After Eden: Facing the challenge of gender reconciliation.* Grand Rapids, Mich.: Eerdmans.

Van Leeuwen, M. S. 1984. Sexual values in a secular age. *Radix Magazine,* November/December, pp. 4-11.

Vicary, J. R., L. R. Klingaman, and W. L. Harkness. 1995. Risk factors associated with date rape and sexual assault of adolescent girls. *Journal of Adolescence* 18 (3):289-306.

Vukovich, M. C. 1996. The prevalence of sexual harassment among female family practice residents in the United States. *Violence and Victims* 11 (2):175-80.

Walker, A. 1982. *The color purple.* New York: Washington Square Press.

Ward, I. 1974. Sexual behavior differentiation: Prenatal hormonal and environmental control. In *Sex differences in behavior,* edited by R. Friedman et al. New York: Wiley.

Warren, R. C., and M. T. Green. 1995. Challenging the current paradigm amidst a culture of denial: Transformative treatment of sex offenders. *Canadian Journal of Human Sexuality* 4 (4):299-309.

Watson, R. 1983. Premarital cohabitation vs. traditional courtship: Their effects on subsequent marital adjustment. *Family Relations* 32:139-47.

Watson, R., and P. DeMeo. 1987. Premarital cohabitation vs. traditional courtship and subsequent marital adjustment: A replication and followup. *Family Relations* 36:193-97.

Whitam, F., C. Daskalos, and C. T. Mathy. 1995. A cross-cultural assessment of familial factors in the development of female homosexuality, *Journal of Psychology and Human Sexuality* 7:59-76.

White, J. 1993. *Eros redeemed: Breaking the stranglehold of sexual sin.* Downers Grove, Ill.: InterVarsity Press.

White, M. 1994. *Stranger at the gate.* New York: Simon & Schuster.

Whitehead, N. E. 1996. What can sociological surveys contribute to the understanding of the causation of homosexuality? *Journal of Psychology and Christianity* 15 (4):322-35.

Wiederman, M. W., and E. R. Allgeier. 1996. Expectations and attributions regarding extramarital sex among young married individuals. *Journal of Psychology and Human Sexuality* 8 (3):21-35.

Willingham, R. 1999. *Breaking free: Understanding sexual addiction and the healing power of Jesus.* Downers Grove, Ill.: InterVarsity Press.

Wistow, F. 1988. The facts of life. *Family Therapy Networker,* March/April, pp. 20-31.

Wolfe, L. 1981. *The Cosmo report.* New York: Arbor House.

Wolff, C. 1971. *Love between women.* New York: St. Martin's Press.

Wolterstorff, N. 1983. *Until justice and peace embrace.* Grand Rapids, Mich.: Eerdmans.

Workman, J. E., and R. L. Orr. 1996. Clothing, sex of subject, and rape myth acceptance as factors affecting attributions about an incident of acquaintance rape. *Clothing and Textiles Research Journal* 14 (4):276-84.

Worthen, A., and B. Davies. 1996. *Someone I love is gay: How family and friends can respond.* Downers Grove, Ill.: InterVarsity Press.

Wu, Z. 1995. Premarital cohabitation and postmarital cohabiting union formation. *Journal of Family Issues* 16 (2):212-32.

Wu, Z., and T. Balakrishnan. 1992. Attitudes towards cohabitation and marriage in Canada. *Journal of Comparative Family Studies* 23 (1): 1-12.

Wylie, M. S. 1993. The shadow of a doubt. *Family Therapy Networker* 17 (5):18-29, 70-73.

Yamaguchi, K., and D. Kandel. 1985. Dynamic relationships between premarital cohabitation and illicit drug use: An event-history analysis of role selection and role socialization. *American Sociological Review* 50:530-46.

Yapko, M. 1993 The seductions of memory. *Family Therapy Networker* 17:31-37.

Yoder, J. D. 1996. When pranks become harassment: The case of African American women firefighters. *Sex Roles* 35 (5-6):253-70.

Young, E. B. 1996. A psychoanalytic approach to addiction: The formation and use of a precocious paranoid schizoid depressive organization. *Melanie Klein and Object Relations* 14 (2):177-95.

Zillmann, D., and J. Bryant. 1988. Effects of prolonged consumption of pornography on family values. *Journal of Family Issues* 9 (4):518-44.

Zuger, B. 1988. Is homosexuality familial? A review, some data, and a suggestion. *Comprehensive Psychiatry* 29 (5): 509-19.